Beyond Virtue

Educating students for emotional wellbeing is a ⎯⎯⎯⎯. However, educating emotions is not straightforward. Emotional processes can be challenging to identify and control. How emotions are valued varies across societies, while individuals within societies face different emotional expectations. For example, girls face pressure to be happy and caring, while boys are often encouraged to be brave. This text analyses the best practices of educating emotions. The focus is not just on the psychological benefits of emotional regulation, but also on how calls for educating emotions connect to the aims of society. The book explores psychology's understanding of emotions, 'the politics of emotions', and philosophy. It also discusses education for happiness, compassion, gratitude, resilience, mindfulness, courage, vulnerability, anger, sadness, and fear.

LIZ JACKSON is Professor at the Education University of Hong Kong, China. She is also President of the Philosophy of Education Society of Australasia.

STUDIES IN EMOTION AND SOCIAL INTERACTION

Second Series

Series Editors

Brian Parkinson
University of Oxford

Maya Tamir
The Hebrew University of Jerusalem

Titles published in the Second Series

(Continued after the index)

Beyond Virtue

The Politics of Educating Emotions

Liz Jackson

The Education University of Hong Kong

CAMBRIDGE
UNIVERSITY PRESS

Shaftesbury Road, Cambridge CB2 8EA, United Kingdom

One Liberty Plaza, 20th Floor, New York, NY 10006, USA

477 Williamstown Road, Port Melbourne, VIC 3207, Australia

314–321, 3rd Floor, Plot 3, Splendor Forum, Jasola District Centre, New Delhi – 110025, India

103 Penang Road, #05–06/07, Visioncrest Commercial, Singapore 238467

Cambridge University Press is part of Cambridge University Press & Assessment, a department of the University of Cambridge.

We share the University's mission to contribute to society through the pursuit of education, learning and research at the highest international levels of excellence.

www.cambridge.org
Information on this title: www.cambridge.org/9781108711609

DOI: 10.1017/9781108699747

First published 2021
First paperback edition 2022

A catalogue record for this publication is available from the British Library

ISBN   978-1-108-48213-4   Hardback
ISBN   978-1-108-71160-9   Paperback

Cambridge University Press & Assessment has no responsibility for the persistence or accuracy of URLs for external or third-party internet websites referred to in this publication and does not guarantee that any content on such websites is, or will remain, accurate or appropriate.

Contents

Foreword

In our everyday language, moral and emotional terms are intertwined in ways we barely notice. We are exhorted to 'just be kind', urged to control our anger, and offered practical tips for raising a resilient child. The moral significance accorded to certain emotional concepts, and assumptions about the emotional component of moral qualities, form an invisible backdrop to such discussions. Much of our contemporary discourse surrounding the emotions reflects the resonance, in everyday practices, of the philosophical notion of 'the moral emotions' and the language of virtues. It is the language of virtues, too, that suffuses contemporary talk of the moral dimension of education. Whether reflected in school policy statements and curricular documents or popular parenting literature, it seems uncontroversial to regard the development of moral qualities as a goal, if not *the* goal, of children's education and upbringing. As David Bakhurst reflects, articulating a desire that he suggests is shared by most parents for their children:

> I want [them] to develop virtues of kindness, generosity, courage, sensitivity, honesty, compassion, and loyalty, among others. ... I want them to be kind ... to be resolute, but not dogmatic; to be bold but not impetuous; to listen but not be gullible; to collaborate but to know when to assert themselves; to be tolerant, but uncompromising about serious wrong doing; to be conscientious, but not obsessive, and so on. (2005, pp. 270–271)

Yet it is one thing for people to believe that it would be good if children – their own and others' – grew up exhibiting these qualities, and quite another to suggest that schools can and should ensure this, not to mention to make claims about how they should do so and what this would achieve. Such claims and proposals, however, abound in policy documents, popular literature, and academic research. Again, the language of the emotions is intertwined, in such proposals, with the language of virtues, as evident in the recent announcement by UK Secretary of State for Education that, as part of a new compulsory subject of health education, 'young people will learn how to discuss their emotions accurately and sensitively' (DfE, 2019). Current mainstream educational discourse is underpinned by the conviction that the emotions – particularly the moral ones – are an integral part of the aspiration to shape children's character in desirable ways.

It is as part of a recent emphasis on children's well-being that this new focus on educating the emotions has emerged in educational policy and practice. As Kathryn Ecclestone notes, emotional and psychological well-being has become an umbrella term that

> draws in an extensive set of 'constructs' seen as amenable to development. These include resilience, stoicism, an optimistic outlook, an ability to be in the moment (or 'in flow'), feelings of satisfaction, being supported, loved, respected, skills of emotional regulation, emotional literacy (or emotional intelligence) as well as empathy, equanimity, compassion, caring for others and not comparing yourself to others. (2012, p. 464)

As the previous list indicates, this contemporary enthusiasm for educating the emotions embraces not just the concepts traditionally regarded as 'moral emotions' – defined by Haidt (2003, p. 853) as 'those emotions that are linked to the interests or welfare either of society as a whole or at least of persons other than the judge or agent' – but also more explicitly individual, psychological traits or abilities. The perhaps intentionally vague phrasing of Haidt's definition hints at an ambiguity which runs through a great deal of work intended to defend the educational value of putting the emotions on the curriculum: is the alleged link between emotions and the good of society a result of the fact that emotional responses – or in Hume's term 'passions' – are the basis of our moral norms and actions; or is it the case that cultivating moral values and dispositions will give rise to particular emotional responses? Nowhere, perhaps, is this ambiguity more evident – centuries of philosophical literature on these questions notwithstanding – than in contemporary policy statements about character education. For the above emphasis on well-being and the associated proposals for a form of moral education that assigns the emotions central place are part of the broad project of character education. It is indeed under the rubric of this widespread talk of virtues, the moral emotions, and their importance for individual and social well-being that the notion of character education, once a deeply unpopular idea, has become mainstream in educational policy and practice in many state education systems around the world. Talk of character in mainstream educational discourse is infused with references to the emotions and their moral significance, as in the following definition from the UK-based Association for Character Education – a definition that reflects the ambiguity noted earlier: 'Character is a set of personal traits that produce specific emotions, inform motivation and guide conduct.' A similar conflation between emotions, moral values, and personal traits is evident in the UK Government guidance on character in schools, which states the intention to help 'young people to explore and express their character and build the skills they need for resilience, empathy and employability' (DfE, 2019b).

The implementation and promotion of these goals, whether in formal education or parenting support, is often underpinned by references to empirical evidence from the field of psychology. It is easy, in the face of this array of claims and evidence, for parents and teachers to be seduced by the promise of interventions that will help children to flourish in a bewildering and stressful world. Underpinning these contemporary trends is the age-old hope that society will be less cruel, less unfair, if only we can raise a generation of kind and happy children. But equally one can be tempted, in the face of such an onslaught, to retreat into a familiar cynicism, driven by a conviction that political and social ills cannot be addressed and may indeed be masked by a focus on personal virtues. Schools, the cynics and critics may argue, should just get on with the job of teaching children how to read and write and basic knowledge about the world, and not be tasked with solving what are essentially political problems.

Liz Jackson manages to tread a fine balance between cynicism and hope. Ever conscious of the political context of our educational debates – as revealed by the book's title – she nevertheless does not allow her trenchant criticism of some prominent approaches to educating the emotions to get in the way of a rigorous and sensible appraisal of the value of such programmes in different educational contexts.

There is a significant body of critical academic literature on the politics of the emotions. Given the wealth of philosophical work on the emotions and their role in education, and the growing body of psychological research in this field, it is no mean feat to draw both the critical insights and the empirical findings of this broad intellectual landscape together in a clear and accessible way.

As Jackson notes herself in her Introduction, while the book is called 'beyond virtue', it should not be read as a total rejection of the tradition of virtue ethics nor of the substantial body of recent educational research and scholarship that draws on this tradition. Her project, rather, is to show both sceptics and fans of this project of moral education that 'there is more to educating emotions than people tend to realise'.

This admirable balance runs through the entire text. It is reflected in Jackson's acknowledgement of her indebtedness to the work of theorists such as Megan Boler, who have questioned the way in which some emotions are conceptualised and valued in classrooms and analysed how political questions of power and agency interact with these practices, and to philosophers such as Kristjan Kristjánsson who have charted the conceptual underpinnings of virtue ethics and related programmes of social and emotional learning.

Jackson is also clear about the modest scope and limitations of her discussion, explaining that her goal is not to defend a particular theoretical orientation towards emotions, but rather to 'shed light on theoretical insights related to educating emotional virtues, primarily in schooling contexts'.

Jackson is a well-established philosopher of education and her philosophical background and orientation is evident throughout the book. Nevertheless, she manages to avoid the trap that Morwenna Griffiths warns of in her discussion of educational philosophy, namely of philosophers becoming like a 'raiding party', 'using education as one more example where their laws and insights can be applied' (Griffiths, 1999, p. 152). Griffiths' preferred model of engagement is one of 'mutual enrichment' (Griffiths, 1999), and this model is reflected in Jackson's careful and respectful engagement with the theoretical and practical resources developed by proponents of virtue ethics in education, such as those produced by researchers at the UK-based Jubilee Centre for Character and Virtues. Much of this work, she acknowledges, can play a valuable role in schools. A similar approach is evident in Jackson's insistence on balancing external philosophical critique of the conceptual and normative underpinnings of work in psychology and other fields with a rigorous engagement with critical literature from within the disciplines, whether critical psychology, sociological critique, or methodological questions.

Similarly, throughout the book Jackson reflects, at key moments in the discussion, on concrete examples from educational practice. This includes a refreshing discussion of teachers' own emotional responses, a positive use of examples of classroom pedagogy, and some practical suggestions for teachers, not least concrete proposals for giving them greater professional agency.

This book is helpfully divided into a first section that develops a broad theoretical framework for understanding the way in which discussions of emotional virtues in education has been informed by different philosophical traditions and empirical approaches, followed by seven chapters, each addressing a particular emotion. These chapters aim to offer a broad overview of the diversity of perspectives on emotions in society and their implications for educating emotional virtues, with a focus on the goals of moral and civic education.

The theoretical section offers a useful overview of different philosophical traditions, indicating connections with work in the social sciences. While covering standard Western philosophical approaches, namely deontology, consequentialism, virtue ethics, care ethics and other relational views, and existentialism, this section is engaging and accessible to non-philosophers. It includes a valuable discussion of non-Western philosophical approaches, specifically Confucianism, Daoism, and Buddhism, and helpfully alerts readers to the connections between these traditions and some Western ideas when it comes to philosophical reflection on the moral and social significance of the emotions. This discussion also serves as a helpful reminder to Western scholars that Western views of educating emotional virtues are not universal. Here as elsewhere, Jackson's practical observations as an educator are always clearly in view, as she acknowledges her frustration with observing Western educators in diverse classrooms who 'often take up educating emotional virtues among diverse students with little appreciation for differences in view, due to culturally particular assumptions they bring into these tasks'. Likewise, Jackson does not lose sight of empirical, social factors in discussing philosophical ideas, thus illustrating, rather than just arguing for, the value of an interdisciplinary approach when it comes to thinking about emotions in education.

This section would make an excellent introduction to the topic of educating the emotions for people wishing to navigate the frequently bewildering contemporary debates, to unpack the philosophical assumptions involved, and to map out the often contrasting educational implications and tensions.

The book has both a descriptive, analytical strand and a critical strand. An important part of the critical strand involves indicating the weaknesses of many empirical studies on educating the emotions, whether through discussing specific methodological flaws such as the limitations of self-reporting, or making the important point that, as is the case with a great deal of education policy and research, studies developed in one area are often hastily applied to educational settings without an appropriate sensitivity to context. This is perhaps particularly true for psychological research, where theoretical positions are developed in therapeutic rather than educational contexts. Yet while critical of some of the methodological flaws of the theories she surveys, Jackson does not dismiss their significance for educational practitioners. Nor does she reject the possibility that empirical work in this field could usefully inform the work of committed educators.

A further element of this critical strand is conceptual, and here Jackson draws on philosophical work that conceptualises education as a moral practice (see Hogan, 2011; Pring, 2001), and on the broader tradition of philosophy of education that reminds us of the need for attention to the meaning and significance of our educational concepts. She also draws attention to the need to adopt an interdisciplinary perspective in discussions of the emotions, drawing on the conceptual frameworks offered not just by philosophers but by social theorists and psychologists. Such work has done much to articulate and explore 'the situational and social nature of psychological phenomena like emotions', yet has 'hovered at the edges of psychological research [and] have never become central' (Turner & Trucano, 2014, p. 645, in Jackson, p. 17). Jackson's interdisciplinary approach produces a highly readable excursion through a range of complex ideas, where psychological and sociological perspectives are often juxtaposed so as to draw out the different normative and conceptual assumptions that they suggest. This approach is reflected most clearly in her discussion of the way psychologists and sociologists theorise and reflect on 'feeling rules'.

However, the main thrust of the critical strand of this book is a political one. As the title indicates, the political perspective is central to the book; yet this perspective, while evident throughout, is not hammered home or laboured. Although Jackson's concern with questions of social justice runs through this work, this is a nuanced account which recognises the pitfalls of overlooking the important role of individual agency and emphasises that education is not just about creating better societies but about supporting the individual children encountered in classrooms.

Thus while the social–political context of education is always in view, Jackson's own political perspective is not presented explicitly as a normative overarching framework at the outset. This could perhaps be seen as a weakness of the work, but I found it refreshing. Jackson's aim, which I think the book admirably achieves, is not to convince the reader of a substantive moral or political view, but to alert them to the ways in which 'moral and justice considerations are bypassed' in certain prominent ways of thinking and talking about education. This is reflected not just in her analysis of research and academic literature, but in the examples she provides from everyday lives of teachers in schools.

In emphasising the political aspect of education, what Jackson is intent on doing is reminding readers – and teachers – that students have lives beyond the school gates, and urging them not to lose sight of the complexity of this social context and the challenges it raises for justice and equality.

As mentioned earlier, Jackson is clearly sympathetic to the strand of philosophy of education that has developed accounts of education as a moral practice. While many philosophers working within this tradition conflate education with schooling, this account leaves room, one must assume, for forms of educational practice outside the institutional structures of contemporary schools – forms like, for example, the radical deschooling experiments and therapeutic communities of the 1960s and 1970s, as well as contemporary democratic schools. Indeed,

Jackson hints at the importance of extending her analysis and critique to informal and non-traditional educational settings when she notes that 'a politics of educating emotions approach considers how different groups are expected or encouraged (or not expected or encouraged) to feel and express particular emotions. Such expectations are educational, whether found inside or outside schools.'

Again echoing the concerns of many philosophers of education, and reflecting her own political commitments, Jackson notes that 'social scientists do not have a particularly strong arsenal to justify educational practices based on their *moral* status, or their relation to social justice concerns', tending rather to focus on 'what practices and organisational patterns are functional or dysfunctional for individuals, groups, or systems'. There is nothing new in pointing out that, in the absence of a robust moral or political argument, what is considered functional or adaptive may not necessarily lead to normative educational conclusions. Yet this point bears repeating in a context where, as Jackson reminds us, the pitfalls of translating psychological insights from therapeutic and experimental contexts into normative recommendations for educational policy and practice have serious consequences. One of the perhaps inevitable consequences of this tendency for educational policymakers to enthusiastically embrace and translate findings from other fields is to suggest that there is a consensus or common-sense view on things like the role of happiness in education or the teachability or desirability of cultivating certain emotions and avoiding others. In demonstrating the conceptual and political problems with this tendency, this book serves as an important antidote to what has become, in many Western educational systems, something of an orthodoxy.

It is important to recall that, as Thomas Dixon notes (2012, p. 481), 'The surge of interest in emotional intelligence and emotional literacy since the 1990s has given this topic new currency but, on all sides of the debate, it is mistakenly assumed that the idea of educating the emotions is something new.' It is, however, certainly true that particular emotions have received renewed prominence and attention from policymakers in recent years, and have attracted a growing body of critical literature. Among these are the notions of resilience and grit. Thus it is not surprising to see these ideas, and some critical contemporary discussions of the political context within which they have emerged, given extensive treatment here. Yet there are more surprising inclusions, such as the discussion of vulnerability, which at first glance seems counter-intuitive, but which demonstrates the same careful balance between critical sociological analysis of contemporary discourses, insights from philosophy and psychology, and political reflection. The analysis of the different ways in which vulnerability is conceived also makes some insightful comments on the interaction between different emotions and virtues in their social–political context. Another refreshing surprise is the inclusion of theorists not usually encountered in contemporary philosophical scholarship on the emotions, such as the eighteenth-century French philosopher Sophie de Grouchy.

It is notable that the list of chapter titles includes only one term – courage – that appears on Aristotle's classic list of the twelve moral virtues. Jackson's list of headings has more in common, in fact, with the list of 'character strengths and virtues' developed by Peterson and Seligman (2004) and with the similar approach of the Jubilee Centre for Character and Virtues, who state: 'We believe that character is constituted by the virtues, such as courage, justice, honesty, compassion, self-discipline, gratitude, generosity and humility.' While some of these concepts have a more obviously emotional component, and can in fact be appropriately classified as 'moral emotions', using Haidt's (2003) definition, others do not. Similarly, some of the concepts on this list have a more explicitly political connotation.

The omission of justice, the most political virtue of all, and on some views the central political value, from Jackson's list is, I think, telling. It draws attention to the point that, although justice is, at least partly, 'the first virtue of social institutions' (Rawls, 1971), that is, a quality of societies and systems and not (or not just) of individuals, its political meaning is downplayed if not obscured altogether by its usual inclusion on such lists of the kinds of character traits that schools should be nurturing in young people. By clearly excluding this 'virtue' from the list of other character traits into which it is often smuggled, Jackson arguably highlights its distinctiveness. To the extent that the notion of justice features in her account, which it does at several points, it does so not in the context of discussions of individual qualities, but in the context of analyses of the background social and political conditions in which these qualities are valued and make sense. This is in marked contrast to the discussion of 'The Virtue of Justice' in the pedagogical resources developed by the Jubilee Centre, where it is conceptualised as a character strength: 'We need to practise the virtue of justice in any situation where we feel unfairness is at work' (Jubilee Centre, n.d.). If discussions of justice in the classroom avoid addressing ideas about a just society, notions of distributive justice, or just institutions, emphasising instead the idea of justice as a personal quality, then such educational interventions are not, as Jackson would no doubt agree, politically neutral.

As one of those who instinctively sides with the sceptics and the cynics regarding the recent enthusiasm for programmes of character education, it is such political suspicions that have driven my concerns. As I have expressed elsewhere (Suissa, 2015), I find it troubling that an educational focus on questions about what a good or just society would look like and how it can be brought about seem to be pushed aside by a focus on cultivating a list of desirable character strengths in individuals. In attempting to chart a middle ground between the enthusiastic proponents of positive psychology and virtue ethics in education, and the critics of such projects, Jackson hasn't exactly cured me of my cynicism. What she has done, though, is offer a thoughtful and rigorous articulation of the difficult balancing act that all educators concerned with social justice have to manage: a refusal to accept a status quo that undermines human freedom, justice, and equality, and a commitment to challenging and changing it, alongside a pragmatic concern for the individual children they encounter, who are experiencing this political reality.

In responding to the criticism that character education is individualistic, prioritising an inward gaze over collective political action for change, Kristjan Kristjansson (2013) notes that proponents of character education, while ultimately desirous of 'the creation of positive institution', generally hold that 'the question of individual versus societal reform is a chicken-and-egg one – we need to start somewhere and, for developmental and pragmatic reasons, it is more feasible to start with the individual child, student or classroom than the whole school system of society at large'.

Yet Jackson's approach suggests powerfully that this is not, in fact, 'a chicken and egg problem'. As she puts it, 'Adopting an approach cognisant about the politics of emotion does not focus on promoting the cultivation of personal contribution well-being regardless of [social] conditions, but questions whether people should be asked or expected to adapt (or blamed for not adapting) to such systems … .' Such an approach can 'scrutinise the system, as much as individuals within it'. Her worry is that, in the current climate, for many educational practitioners, researchers, and policymakers, 'changing feelings has become the exclusive goal, dismissing the value of possibly changing situations'.

This is not a rejection of virtue ethics, a rich philosophical tradition with much to say about social and political engagement. But it is a warning against the enthusiastic adoption of seductively simple programmes of social and emotional learning and character education, where the message is that 'one's feelings […] are the main locus of one's moral responsibility'. Grappling with political questions in the classroom when the world students experience is frequently an unjust and scary place is a risky and uncomfortable challenge for teachers. But as Jackson reminds us, this is what teaching students to understand the real world demands, and it is what is demanded of us if we are to be effective political agents as well as effective educators.

Judith Suissa

References

Bakhurst, D. (2005). Particularism and moral education. *Philosophical Explorations*, 8(3), 265–279.

DfE (2019a). Press Release www.gov.uk/government/news/all-pupils-will-be-taught-about-mental-and-physical-wellbeing

DfE (2019b). Character Education Framework Guidance https://assets.publish ing.service.gov.uk/government/uploads/system/uploads/attachment_data/file/849654/Character_Education_Framework_Guidance.pdf

Dixon, T. (2012). Educating the emotions from Gradgrind to Goleman. *Research Papers in Education*, 27(4), 481–495, DOI:10.1080/02671522.2012.690240

Ecclestone, K. (2012). From emotional and psychological well-being to character education: challenging policy discourses of behavioural science and 'vulnerability'. *Research Papers in Education*, 27(4).

Griffiths, M. (1999). Aiming for a fair education: what use is philosophy? In Roger Marples, ed., *The Aims of Education*. London: Routledge.

Haidt, J. (2003). The moral emotions (PDF). In Richard Davidson, Klaus Scherer & H. Goldsmith, eds., *Handbook of Affective Sciences*. Oxford University Press.

Hogan, P. (2011). The ethical orientations of education as a practice in its own right. *Ethics and Education*, 6(1), 27–40.

Jubilee Centre, www.jubileecentre.ac.uk/355/about-the-centre

Jubilee Centre, Secondary Programme of Study www.jubileecentre.ac.uk/1636/character-education/resources/secondary-programme-of-study

Kristjánsson, K. (2013). Ten myths about character, virtue and virtue education – plus three well-founded misgivings. *British Journal of Educational Studies*, 61 (3), 269–287, DOI:10.1080/00071005.2013.778386

Peterson, C. & Seligman, M. E. P. (2004). *Character Strengths and Virtues: A Handbook and Classification*. Oxford: Oxford University Press.

Pring, R. (2001). Education as a moral practice. *Journal of Moral Education*, 30(2), 101–112, DOI:10.1080/03057240120061360

Rawls, J. (1971). *A Theory of Justice*. Cambridge, MA: Harvard University Press.

Suissa, J. (2015). Character education and the disappearance of the political. *Ethics and Education*, 10(1), 105–117.

Acknowledgements

This book represents the culmination of many years of thought about particular emotions and their uses and abuses in society and education. This book may seem gloomy in comparison with the many joyous and optimistic books previously published on the topic of educating emotions (particularly those on happiness and other virtuous emotions). Yet I have had many delightful experiences in writing it, and in discovering insights from philosophical and social science traditions along the way. This book thus intends to express my deeply held gratitude, my concerns about gratitude notwithstanding, to those who have educated me about feeling and thinking, across fields and around the world, and to many others who have otherwise contributed to this work.

I gave my first seminars on altruism and gratitude in education at the Philosophy of Education Society of Australasia annual conferences in 2013 and 2014, respectively. At these events, many colleagues were supportive of my critical approach, which led to further examinations of these and other emotional virtues at other events over time. I gave many invited talks about the risks of gratitude in society and education in the coming years, including one in the Philosophy Department at the University of Hong Kong, and another at the University College London Institute of Education, chaired by Judith Suissa. Another valuable experience for me in theorising gratitude occurred in 2019, when I was invited to a conference on 'The Shadow Side of Gratitude', organised by Liz Gulliford, Blaire Morgan, Kathi Beier, and Martin Hähnel, at the University of Erfurt, Germany. On this occasion I was pleased to share and learn from leading philosophers and psychologists of gratitude, including those mentioned earlier, as well as Terrance McConnell, Philip Watkins, and Henning Freund. At this conference I was pleasantly surprised to find less resistance to my ideas about gratitude than I sometimes find among educational researchers, who may have more faith in the philosophy and psychology of gratitude than those in philosophy and psychology!

I was also fortunate in 2019 to share my work on educating emotions with Megan Boler and Lauren Bialystok, at an invited seminar at the University of Toronto Ontario Institute for Studies in Education, as well as at the American Educational Research Association Annual Conference in Toronto, where I joined a panel on the emotions of teaching organised by Barbara Stengel, with Megan Boler, Doris Santoro, Polina Kukar, and Grace Chen. Another special opportunity for me in 2019 was speaking at the inaugural seminar of the Center for East-West Studies in Education at Hangzhou Normal University, organised by Leonard Waks, where I enjoyed meeting and exchanging ideas about emotions and diversity in education with On-cho Ng, Roger Ames, and Jessica Chingsze Wang. Additionally, I want to thank Kristján Kristjánsson for sharing his work and ideas with me, when I visited the Jubilee Centre for Character and Virtues at the University of Birmingham.

I am incredibly grateful for the reading of a draft of this text and many helpful comments made by Judith Suissa. My doctoral students Cong Lin (Jason) and Victor Ali also provided thoughtful assistance, by reading and giving comments on a draft of this text. The anonymous peer reviewer and series editors from Cambridge University Press also provided a valuable service to me, inspiring some small, but hopefully highly meaningful, late additions and changes to this text.

I am also thankful for my colleagues and friends in Hong Kong, especially Emily Matchar, Jamin Asay, Michael Johnson, Jennifer Nado, and Amit Chaturvedi, for engaging in brainstorming and endless arguments with me, and providing other forms of moral support. Discussions with Peter Roberts have also been significant for me in writing this work. Last but not least, thanks to Paul Trudgian for encouraging me, in life and in writing, and accompanying me on my path of learning about emotions over these years.

CHAPTER 1

Introduction

Emotions fundamentally shape our experiences and interactions. Yet the role of emotions in moral and social life is contested, from an interdisciplinary view. In relation, how emotions are involved in education has been a subject of scrutiny and debate, in the history of education, and across diverse cultural and social contexts. This book explores the intersection of emotions, social life, and education from a fresh perspective. It emphasises education of emotions as a moral process with significant interpersonal, social, and political implications. And it fleshes out a relational approach, through considering the value of various feelings and dispositions in social life and in education, such as happiness, gratitude, resilience, and anger.

In this introductory chapter, I provide a preliminary discussion of the role of emotions in education. I focus on some common assumptions that readers may have about this topic. These assumptions are examples of contrasting perspectives about emotions and education, which highlight divergent approaches to educating (or not educating) about and for particular emotions and related dispositions in school settings. These are also views which, if held by readers, might make a book such as this one seem unnecessary. Critically analysing them here thus helps underscore the value of this present work. These are the views that (1) education does not particularly involve emotions, and (2) emotions are a part of education, but this is non-controversial, with a consensus on the topic established. I examine each of these assumptions and challenge them. Next, the chapter lays out the goals of this book and gives an overview of the main contents of the chapters that follow. Finally, I make some preliminary remarks about the nature of emotions in relation to moral epistemology and virtue as I understand it, which may be helpful for philosophically oriented readers to note at the outset.

1.1 The Role of Emotions in Education

While emotions play a vital role in human life and society, understanding emotions, as experiences and processes, is not straightforward. On the one hand, emotions are often felt as internal sensations and changes. In this way, emotions are said to occur or to be located 'inside' of people. This seems the case when one 'hides' their emotions, for example. One is said to be able to bury their feelings inside themselves, rather than let them 'out', into their relationships or interactions with others. On the other hand, emotions are typically related to what happens in a person's life. That is, they are related to what happens *outside* an individual's body or mind. Generally speaking, one is not normally expected to become mad, angry, or happy without an external cause. It is usually regarded as functional and normal to be happy after one wins an award or other recognition from others, for example. One is normally expected to be sad at the death of a loved one. Yet people also experience and express emotions in diverse and, sometimes, unpredictable ways, for personal and social reasons. Not everyone feels happy when they win an award. Circumstances can make a difference.

How emotions are personal and individual, versus social and relational, has interested people throughout history. Philosophers have explored at length whether good living requires impartial, passive Stoicism, or steady, determined exercise of personal rationality. They have questioned whether the key to ethics in social life is to increase overall human happiness, or for each person to work to cultivate particular personal habits and emotional dispositions. In modern times, psychologists and anthropologists have focused on what is and is not normal and functional emotional experience and expression, within and across societies. Other social scientists and theorists, from backgrounds such as sociology, economics, political science, and education, have also dwelled upon the question of what is functional and good when it comes to emotional experiences and expressions. They have also explored how personal experiences and perspectives can bias psychologists and anthropologists (among others) towards viewing certain traits as normal or deviant. For example, they may privilege common emotional experiences and expressions of men as normal over those of women, or describe emotional expressions of non-Europeans as backward, irrational, and in need of control.

Different people hold contrasting perspectives and assumptions about the place of emotions in human social life. One might assume that this is not a bad thing. There are contrasting views about all sorts of things around the world. However, contrasting visions about emotions in social life entail different possibilities and directions for education, for what young people do and learn in schools.

This matters because education is a moral practice. Schooling aims to enhance people as individuals and society as a whole. This may not always be obvious, since schools also are oriented towards economic productivity and developing young people as human capital. But a glimpse at any society's educational policies, or a visit to any school, will reveal that education indeed touches on the moral development of young people, even if it is not the principal objective in any given teacher's lesson plan. At the same time, education impacts people differently. In this context, that there are contrasting views about emotions in society makes a difference for education. It makes a difference for young people's lives and potential, and for society at large. Contrasting orientations to emotions unfold into different approaches to educating the emotions of young people, and for how teachers should treat students, in relation to their emotional experiences and expressions, at schools and in classrooms. These visions also unfold into clashing positions on how young people can and should engage with others around them in society, as citizens and residents of local and national contexts, in the broader world.

1.2 Does Education Really Involve Emotions?

Some people assume that education does not particularly involve emotions or has nothing important to provide when it comes to youth emotional development. When people hold this view, they tend to see emotions and schooling as separate topics. There are three understandings of emotions that support this perspective. These are the views of emotions as (1) mostly personal, (2) not moral (i.e. they are not part of the moral domain), and (3) not teachable.

The first view, which is prevalent in some Western societies, is that emotions should be seen as *personal* rather than as part of the social, public, or civic sphere. As mentioned earlier, emotions are often thought to be 'inside' people. Furthermore, because emotions are often regarded as part of the personal domain rather than the social or public domain, there is a sense that schools have no good reason to interfere with, or interact with, students' ordinary emotional development.

John Rawls argues that emotional feelings should have no place in public deliberation, where impartial, neutral reason should prevail (1993). He thus describes a sense of separation between the personal and private, and the public and political. In relation, he encourages teaching of political principles in education, and teaching about a sense of separation between one's strongly held feelings and their participation in society.

This sense that feelings are personal and private, while civic participation should be impartial and reasoned, reflects the philosophical heritage of the United States. Early political leaders there were worried about a population divided by religious values and related interpersonal community attachments, who could be unwilling to put the personal aside for the public good. In relation, education in 'common schools' was to be neutral, accessible, and palatable to people with different (western European) traditions and (Christian) beliefs.

Many people in the United States today still feel that schools should not teach students about or for cultivating (or not cultivating) strong beliefs, or any related intense feelings or sense of attachment to anything, except perhaps the nation-state (Noddings, 1993). According to this view, the ethical principles of society should be taught. However, teachers and schools should strive to be as neutral as possible about deep, potentially divisive issues. In relation, teaching that supports or invites strong emotional feelings is often viewed as indoctrinatory, and therefore as morally wrong, in public (government) schools in that country, and many others today, as it could impact who children 'become' (Maxwell & Reichenbach, 2005; see also Noddings, 1993; Hand, 2011).

Yet Rawls' divide of the personal versus the public is not easy to pinpoint, when it comes to emotions and feelings. Rawls promotes as part of a public cultural heritage 'the virtues of tolerance and mutual trust ... the forms of thought and feeling that sustain fair cooperation' (1993, p. 195). In the public sphere, he tries to separate these virtues, these 'forms of thought and feeling', from 'comprehensive views'. 'Political' feelings are *minimal* then, in Rawls' view. Rawls promotes the teaching of a kind of thin layer of emotional virtues and related feelings. So feelings, about oneself and others in society, are not altogether absent here.

In contrast to Rawls' recommendations, in the domain of education emotions have not historically been regarded as separable from the social world, even if they are often seen as part of a person's 'internal' experience. Contrary to the assumption that emotions are mostly personal, and therefore not properly involved in schooling, Megan Boler highlights how educators have regarded emotions as a significant part of the public sphere historically (1999). As she shows, the role of emotions in education was discussed at the turn of the twentieth century, in terms of the need for cultivating student discipline and moral training. At that time, teacher handbooks stressed how emotional experiences, for example, of curiosity and activeness, enabled behavioural tendencies towards learning. Anger and cowardice were labelled as deviant and abnormal emotional states, which would disturb the exercise, or functionality, of mental capacity (Boler, 1999), historically (and today). As men and women were seen as playing different roles in society, different emotions were encouraged from boys and girls on different subjects, such as on 'Domestic Economics' classes for girls. As Boler points out, in the medieval ages and beyond, cultivating 'good' emotions and discouraging 'bad' emotions in schooling was also not uncommon, and was normally connected with developing a good society, as a whole. Boler additionally shows how emotional education has remained common more recently, despite the hesitation by many thinkers to acknowledge it as such.

A second, related view that may underpin the notion that education does not involve, or should not involve, emotions is the assumption that emotions are not part of the moral domain. Some people may think that emotions are not moral, because they are (or can be) 'irrational', separate from and possibly disruptive to capacities for systematic, reflective reasoning, and autonomous personal choice. Kant's 'An Answer to the Question: "What is Enlightenment?"' (1784) contrasts methodical thought, which he casts as 'autonomous', with the influences on thought that can arise from internal 'fear of phantoms', or external pressures. More recent scholars similarly contend that emotions 'get in the way' of 'clear' thought, 'clouding' judgement (Hand, 2011; see also Nagel, 1970). Relatedly, as Kristján Kristjánsson notes (2007, p. 50), 'contemporary popular and academic literature on emotion regulation routinely berates the so-called negative emotions', framing a subset of emotions (e.g. sadness, anger) as entirely harmful, and therefore, expendable. On the other hand, some may assume that emotions are not subject to external moral evaluation or education because of their view of the ideal person as *authentic*, with an 'inner voice', marked by personal feelings that should not be judged or manipulated by external forces (Maxwell & Reichenbach, 2005; Kristjánsson, 2018).

Yet if we continue on these lines of thought, the solution advocated by most political and educational theorists, psychologists, and others writing in this area is not that one 'do nothing' about their emotions, in relation to their possibly 'non-moral' status. Few suggest that one should just ignore their risky emotions, or 'let them be'. Given these possibly 'irrational' feelings, what is commonly recommended is some kind of action or reaction by the individual towards their 'natural instincts' or tendencies, at least so that they do not obstruct the capacity to learn, think and evaluate, and behave well, in accordance with their aims and conditions. School textbooks and teachers have taught students, historically and today, to adjust and control their emotions, to make them more manageable and 'better'. Martha Nussbaum (2001, 2016) argues that it is a moral endeavour to control and cultivate one's emotions. Positive psychologists also assume that positive emotions are important to good life, to be educated accordingly. Thus, emotions are normally related across various fields and perspectives to moral thought and action, even if the relationship is not always particularly straightforward.

The third view of emotions, which can intersect with thinking of them as personal and as not moral, is that they are *not teachable* and are therefore not in the realm of schooling. This view can stem from the assumption that emotions are not controllable. If emotions are not controllable, then it does not make sense to try to educate them. On the one hand, it is true that emotions are not entirely controllable and that (at least) some people are not adept at controlling their emotions. On the other hand, emotions are, to some extent, often controllable, for most people. Most people can learn, with personal effort and guidance, to recognise, reflect upon, and regulate how they feel in everyday life, as part of becoming a good person in society. This assumption undergirds common parenting and schooling practices, for example, of encouraging children not to cry, be selfish, or fight others out of rage.

Yet there are three related, more nuanced positions, worth further considering in relation to this view. The first is that emotions should not be taught even if they are teachable, since they may introduce irrational rather than rational processes and behaviour. Thus, they can only be taught in an indoctrinatory way. This position has already been considered in part. Even for those who are against education for indoctrination and propaganda, and who argue for clear-headed, autonomous thinking, such as Michael Hand (2011), Rawls (1993), and Kant (1784), the answer is not to ignore or 'leave alone' the way that emotions enter into decision making. On the contrary, these thinkers advocate for education to enhance thinking and behaviour, in part through discouraging reliance upon irrational impulses or overly emotional dispositions and inclinations. Teaching students passionate, irrational feelings can be indoctrinatory. But teaching about and for self-regulation of emotions and related processes is distinct from this, and commonly held as beneficial.

A second relevant view is that because emotions are not entirely the products of autonomous personal choices, it is not moral and/or realistic to expect people to (learn or be able to) control them. As previously mentioned, emotions are not entirely controllable. People's emotional experiences are impacted by many things outside of their control (Appiah, 2008). These feelings are also influenced by physical, biological, and cognitive processes, which are also difficult to understand, let alone to control (Doris, 2005). There are also puzzles surrounding 'moral luck', and when one is or is not blameworthy for 'bad emotions' or a lack of virtuous emotions, given that emotional processes related to thought and behaviour are not absolutely controllable (McConnell, 1993). Thus, how much we can expect emotional control among others and regard it as praiseworthy (and deficiency in this area as blameworthy) are questions of longstanding debate.

Here, the question of *how* to regulate and control emotions can also be related to the question of *should*. When and how to intervene, or exercise tolerance or acceptance, in relation to one's problematic emotions or those of others is a practical question and a moral one. Emotions and emotional control are not just internal processes, but complicated interpersonal and institutional ones. In some Western societies, there are debates over how to view and manage children's (especially boys') hyperactivity. Some hold that youth hyperactivity is partly a 'natural instinct', that should not be controlled and that has benefits. Others see it as a barrier to discipline and social and intellectual development. The value of anxiety and sadness (more prevalent in girls) is also controversial. Again, debate relates to how these states impact people's lives in society. Anxiety and sadness can be seen as natural responses to external stimuli. It can be functional to feel anxiety before a test or grief after the loss of a friend or family member. Yet these feelings can also reflect dispositions than can be destructive and anti-social over time. They may therefore be regarded as undesirable and avoidable with tools like medication, therapy, and behavioural treatment. Those who question whether it is moral to intervene in others' emotions in relation to these topics may be more precisely concerned with the morality of emotional manipulation for instrumental ends, particularly in cases where the benefits of treatments are not obvious in the first place for those receiving them.

Additionally, it is important to note that generalisations and expectations about normal capacities for emotional control and regulation do not reflect the experiences of all people, or all the experiences of many people. Across societies, over ten percent of people experience *alexithymia*, a trait characterised by the inability to identify, name, or describe one's emotions (Panaite & Bylsma, 2012). Normally distributed in a population, alexithymia is often related by psychologists to emotional developmental challenges (Goerlich, 2018). People with alexithymia can be 'highly reflective, self-aware, and conscientious' (Kennett, 2017, pp. 372–373). Yet common forms of guidance for developing emotional identification and control may not particularly benefit them, given their different emotional processing capacities. Alexithymia is not psychopathy, and it need not prevent people from living good, more or less ordinary lives. Yet if it is assumed that people can and should learn to identify and control their emotions, people with alexithymia may be held as deviants and moral failures.

Such diversity requires careful consideration, in relation to the moral and practical implications of teaching emotional regulation in schools. More generally, sceptics of education for emotional control are right in identifying and questioning how some taken-for-granted techniques in schooling use emotional manipulation for non-moral, convenient purposes, such as to attain particular behavioural outcomes, apart from other considerations (Maxwell & Reichenbach, 2007).

There is one final viewpoint worth identifying here that challenges people in thinking about emotions as teachable, and as part of education.

This is the view that because emotions are internal in a sense, and cannot be seen or known by another with full transparency, they cannot be effectively educated in schools, compared to things that can be learned more visibly. Schooling involves measuring of student learning and demonstration of skills in increasingly standardised tests. In relation, there is a sense that education should primarily provide certain kinds of visible changes in young people (Hattie, 2008; Biesta, 2017). Given that significant human and material resources go into schooling, some question here the value of 'soft skills' education, when it is difficult to evaluate its effectiveness through empirical means. Opening a window on subjective internal states and how they change is more difficult than testing student retention of content knowledge. This is therefore considered an obstacle to enhancing education for emotional cultivation, when contrasted with learning in content areas. One way that some work to resolve this issue of visibility is by taking into account student expressions – verbal and nonverbal – as indicative of emotional states. A researcher or educator may ask students about their emotional states, or about their experiences and perspectives about their capacities to regulate their emotions. Such methods have value, but also limitations. The challenge of identifying emotional processes should be recognised in approaches to educating emotions.

In sum, emotions clearly play a role in moral life and society, and there is value in teaching young people about emotions in schools. Yet it remains the case that understanding and educating emotions is not easy or straightforward, from a moral or practical perspective. Emotional processes can be challenging to identify, learn about, and control in the best of cases, and they are complexly related to other important practical and moral purposes of schools in society. The question this work centrally tackles is how to educate emotions in a society and on what empirical and moral grounds.

1.3   Is There a Consensus View on Educating Emotions?

Some may recognise that education involves emotions, and assume that the research literature has developed a clear consensus on the topic: on what emotions are, their value, and how to educate about them. That all of this has been established and is easily applied is suggested in texts such as *Authentic Happiness: Using the New Positive Psychology to Realize Your Potential for Lasting Fulfilment* (Seligman, 2002), *Exploring Well-Being in Schools: A Guide to Making Children's Lives More Fulfilling* (White, 2011), and *Positivity: Discover the Upward Spiral that Will Change Your Life* (Fredrickson, 2009), and in scores of articles in academic and popular presses reporting on the benefits of educational and other kinds of inventions for emotional development.

One prevalent view that frames educating emotions as straightforward comes from psychology, particularly positive psychology. Psychology deals primarily with individual functioning (and dysfunction). Positive psychology can be distinguished from other forms of psychology for its focus on positive rather than deviant or problematic emotional states, and how positive experiences promote health and well-being (Seligman, 2002). In this case, psychologists aim to benefit people with knowledge about how to function better with regard to their emotional processes. Positive psychologists view the task of people learning to manage their emotions as personally and socially beneficial, and therefore as valuable and worthwhile. A related trend is the promotion of 'emotional intelligence' or 'emotional quotient'. Similarly, associating emotional regulation with personal and social value and benefits, 'EQ' and 'EI' have become common-sense notions about educating emotions in some Western societies (Goleman, 1995).

Psychologists base their views on therapeutic rather than educational contexts. Scholarship in education and philosophy often echoes psychological views, however, framing educating emotions as fairly straightforward work, and worthwhile. Scholars with the Jubilee Centre for Character and Virtues at the University of Birmingham argue that teaching emotion-related virtues enhances students' experiences and behaviours, for good living. The Jubilee community has included academics influenced by psychology and educational psychology, as well as by philosophy, particularly virtue ethics (Arthur et al., 2014; Arthur, 2019). Nel Noddings also emphasises that young people can and should learn to regulate their emotions for flourishing, and that schools should particularly cultivate caring and happiness among students (2003). Nussbaum (2013, 2016) examines emotional regulation and emotional cultivation as part of character development.

The next chapters will analyse the extent to which there is consensus across these and related disciplines and views, regarding educating emotions. Across this text, I expose divergences in research orientations and findings, which debunk the notion that there is a substantive consensus view on this topic. I provide a look beneath the surface of apparent consensus, to reveal conceptual, empirical, and perspectival differences. Conceptually, how emotions are understood, within and across fields, is not uniform. This means that processes involved in identifying, developing, and regulating emotions are not understood in the same way by diverse scholars. Empirically, what is sought and how it can be observed and studied is also messier when one dives into the research literature, than it appears in commonplace calls to follow 'what works'. Thinking about methods brings us to differences of perspective. How and why a particular kind of educational intervention is regarded as effective, moral, or socially just is also understood differently across thinkers. What is called for in educating for emotional virtues, and on what moral or other justificatory grounds, is a matter of debate, not consensus.

Take one emotion: anger. Many people, including laypeople and academics across the social sciences and arts, regard anger as generally negative. Anger is the kind of state educators, psychologists, and philosophers typically encourage young people to 'work through', eradicate, or 'move beyond' (Noddings, 2003; Seligman, 2007; Nussbaum, 2016). It is said to inspire 'payback', negative outward behaviour displays of harm, or intention to harm others (most commonly, those seen as causing a wound to the angry person). If anger leads to negative outcomes and harms to others (and possibly to oneself), then it makes sense to encourage people to recognise and work against their anger in schools, alongside other settings. This may be described in terms of 'anger management', or 'conflict resolution'.

However, people have different definitions of anger. Some would include an instinctive rage not directed towards any other person as part of their definition, while others would focus on a cognitive-based desire or plan for retaliation (Nussbaum, 2016). How one understands what anger is makes a difference in what they think should be done about it. For those who view anger as an instinctive feeling, the plan to eradicate anger entails understanding it as such and finding ways to induce oneself emotionally to avoid or evade it (e.g. APA, 2019). For those who view anger as more cognitively based, related to a sense of reactive self-interest and self-preservation or self-maintenance, its resolution will involve a different tactic, such as acting on the capacity to see the difference between reasonable and unreasonable experiences of and reactions to anger (Nussbaum, 2016).

On the other hand, some do not think that anger is altogether negative. Again, this may depend on how anger is defined as an emotion. When one thinks about emotions as 'inside' people, then it perhaps makes sense to think of anger as basically negative: as an unpleasant experience, compared to others. However, emotions are also part of social interactions and communal experiences. In such cases, anger can lead to harm, but it can also serve to prevent harm. The situation and context of anger make a difference (Srinivasan, 2018). Boler (1999), Patricia White (2012), and Cris Mayo (2016) explore the potential for a positive place for anger in education. Kristjánsson (2007) also emphasises anger not as expendable, but as possibly justified. Sara Ahmed defends anger (2004a, 2010) as valuable in understanding injustice. A notion of 'righteous anger' is seen as good in relation to horrible situations of oppression, and is invoked in texts across religious traditions (Kristjánsson, 2007). Raymond Novaco (2016) notes anger's personal and communal functions from a psychological view. He argues that anger 'serves as a guardian to self-esteem, operates as a means of communicating negative sentiment, potentiates the ability to redress grievances, and boosts determination to overcome obstacles to our happiness and aspirations' (p. 286).

While anger can be useful or harmful, it is also noteworthy that different people's expressions of anger are often variously assessed in communities. That is, some are regarded as entitled to anger more than others (Spelman, 1989; Manne, 2017). In US politics (for example), some expressions of anger by men (particularly white men) are regarded as dignified and righteous (Kimmel, 2017). Yet angry women (and particularly women of colour) are more often seen as hysterical, oversensitive, crazy, or irrational, with their anger dismissed out of hand (Ahmed, 2010). In schools, gender roles are also expected of boys and girls, when it comes to emotions like anger. Teachers may treat anger as generally bad; but they may also regard it as deviant for girls and normal for boys.

How a person is treated is part of the world around them, spiralling back to shape and reshape their emotions. Women share how it is difficult to respond to someone encouraging them to 'calm down', when they did not feel 'un-calm' in the first place, particularly when making a complaint or expressing something negative. The plea to 'calm down' received by a person feeling calm can make them feel less calm (Ahmed, 2010). On the other hand, a man seen to have a righteous, passionate sense of indignation and anger about injustice may be effectively encouraged to 'keep it coming', and 'fight the good fight'. Little boys may notice their teachers enjoying their fighting spirit, on or off the sports field. Little girls may notice their anger disturbing their teachers, obstructing their ability to please their teachers as they might hope to do.

There is a risk of stunting emotional development by taking an approach that is intolerant of any expression or indication of anger. Anger repression can be harmful. Yet some people might 'hide' or 'repress' their anger 'inside' in an unhealthy way, particularly if their expressions of anger are treated with intolerance. Susceptibility or vulnerability to this kind of harm would appear to be unequal in contexts where some people's anger is tolerated more than that of others. Primal therapy, a once-popular psychological approach, supports expressing anger and frustration as a method of coping with the harms of anger repression in a safe environment (Janov, 1991). Although this approach is no longer popular, the notion that one should sublimate angry energy into a healthy outlet, such as sports or musical pursuits, continues to be popular. Thus, some people recommend a systematic, useful transformation of anger, rather than its avoidance or eradication.

That all people's emotions are not treated as equal is also important to consider in seeing education of emotions as a moral act in schools.

Unequal expectations make particular kinds of impacts on diverse people's development. So how do we know which anger is good, which is bad, and how to understand it, see it, and evaluate it, and what to do with it, in education? There is no compelling, comprehensive, consensus view when it comes to the ins and outs of educating about anger across psychology, philosophy, political science, and sociology (among other fields). Likewise, the extent of consensus about whether and how to educate for 'positive' emotional virtues, such as happiness, compassion, and gratitude, is also sometimes overstated, as the chapters that follow will explore.

There are also lingering questions about what works in educating emotions *for what purpose*. That it is good, morally and politically, to intervene in and educate young people's emotions in schools also should be explored from a social view that examines how emotions operate both *within* individuals and *across* them: inside a person, in relationships where emotions are educated, as well as in larger social settings. Examining this field more holistically, and developing a clearer understanding of the politics of educating emotions, is the goal of this volume.

1.4   Aims and Overview of the Text

This text gives a big-picture analysis of educating emotions, with special recognition of the politics of educating emotions. By 'politics' here, I mean to signal the way that educating emotions or emotion-related virtues is considered socially good and desirable. Psychologists would describe this goodness or desirability in terms of 'pro-social benefits' and behaviours, while educators and philosophers may be more focused on how emotional education leads to good character development, effective socialisation, and civic-mindedness. So here, my focus is not just on individual psychological benefits of emotional regulation, but also on how calls for emotional regulation connect to aims of enhancing society. In relation, *how* emotional regulation and development of young people lead to *what kind* of good society is an important question underpinning this work. This text thus explores moral philosophy and education for social justice, alongside psychology.

My political account is indebted in part to Boler's (1999) analysis of educating emotions as a socio-political issue, rather than as a simple matter of developing universal character and 'academic emotions'. Yet common understandings of the role of emotions in education, and particularly character education, have transformed radically in the past decades (Boler & Zembylas, 2016). There has been a significant rise in interest in this topic, with thinkers coming from many different academic fields contributing to extending understanding. Yet often, it seems that 'too many people are paddling their own little canoes, without much interest in what their fellow-travellers are doing' (Kristjánsson, 2018, p. 181). Research in this area should become more interdisciplinary and cross-disciplinary, to better and more holistically understand the roles and processes of emotions in personal and social life. Here, I aim to provide an account that is sensitive to significant findings and insights across varying disciplinary perspectives, including recently emerging views.

In this text I use the term 'emotional virtues' to emphasise emotions as moral. In everyday practice, many emotions are regarded as moral (or immoral), and are treated as such in schools. So by using the term 'emotional virtue' I mean to signal that these emotions are held, by me and many others, as morally relevant. Among 'emotional virtues', I also consider here some dispositions and traits which might not normally be described as emotions (or as virtues), but are 'tinged' with, or associated with, one or more emotional states: for example, resilience, vulnerability, grit, and mindfulness. Some may identify these as attitudes, dispositions, or tendencies, rather than as emotions. However, I include them here, because they are among major traits promoted in education across societies that interrelate in substantive ways with more traditional emotional virtues (like happiness and gratitude), and are thought to have emotional components or associated emotional states. They intersect with more traditional emotional virtues and are important reference points in contemporary discussions of teaching for or about emotions. As Kristjánsson (2018, p. 169) notes, social and emotional learning discourses in schools 'uphold a very capacious conception of what an "emotion" is'. This warrants that researchers interested in the matter of educating emotions similarly broaden their scope, as I do here.

My use of the term 'emotional virtue' does not imply that my position in this text is a virtue ethics view. Considering 'educating emotions' as 'educating emotional virtues' serves simply to place emphasis on emotions and education of emotions as matters of moral import. Relatedly, I normally use the terms 'feelings' and 'emotions' in this book interchangeably, in line with this umbrella approach to considering emotions-related phenomena from educational, political, and other perspectives. On the other hand, this book is called 'beyond virtue'. This is not meant to frame virtue ethics as a faulty orientation. I mean rather to signal here that there is more to educating emotions (as 'emotional virtues') than people tend to realise. The important insights that virtue ethics, among other approaches, bring to moral and civic education, as well as their limitations, are discussed here.

This chapter aims to give a broad overview of debates and issues related to educating emotions. In the next two chapters, I depict more systematically major approaches to understanding emotions, social and moral life, and education. This exploration indicates how people frame emotions in personal and social life in very different ways, based on their chief aims and interests (Roberts, 2003). The next chapter focuses on what I broadly describe as social science-based views. I trace the highly influential views on emotions, morality, and social life in psychology and educational psychology in the first section, and then turn to more sociologically and politically influenced accounts, which I describe in terms of the 'politics of emotions', in the second. How the thinkers discussed here understand emotions in relation to individuals in society, and their implications for a moral and socially just education (education that is good at individual and social levels) will be analysed across the two sections. One of the key arguments of this chapter is that despite the benefits of psychological approaches to identifying, managing, and interacting with emotions in schools (and elsewhere), many popular approaches are not without significant limitations, related to how psychologists (particularly positive psychologists) frame emotions in their work, and the way their work is applied in education. This chapter does not aim to argue that established psychological orientations are therefore invalid or unhelpful, but it aims to complicate and encourage greater caution in applying some kinds of psychological orientations to educating emotions, as the politics of emotions perspective elucidates different insights about emotions in educational and other settings.

The third chapter continues the theoretical overview. This chapter examines the role of emotions in moral philosophy and other related philosophies that reflect significantly on good living. In the course, it also considers how insights from these views intertwine in some cases with the aforementioned social science views. The views explored here are deontology, consequentialism, virtue ethics, care ethics and other relational views, and existentialism. How their treatments of emotion in moral and social life overlap with those found in some Eastern traditions, Confucianism, Daoism, and Buddhism, will also be reflected upon. This chapter does not aim to give a full and systematic treatment of each of these philosophies, and all that has been theorised about emotions from such views. That project would take several books, at least. Instead, it aims to highlight the diversity of orientations on emotions, morality, and ethics, and their contrasting implications when it comes to learning to become a 'good' person in society, and educating emotional virtues.

One strand of research I do not focus on in this text is affect studies. Researchers of affect consider common views of emotion as socially constructed, and recognise 'precognitive sensory experience, relations to surroundings, and generally the body's capacity to act, to engage, to resist, and to connect', prior to a 'domestication' or 'assimilation' of such experiences under the category of emotion (Zembylas, 2014, p. 397).

Affect studies provide valuable insights about understanding, socially constructing, and processing affective and emotional experiences. However, while the 'affective turn has done us the major service of popularizing the study of emotion', its separation of affective feeling from consciousness leads most theorists in this area to gloss over political and educational issues in their work (Boler & Zembylas, 2016, p. 23). Furthermore, while I will discuss more about my philosophical view of emotion in the next section of this chapter, my ultimate goal in this text is not primarily to elucidate in full and argue for the best theoretical orientation towards emotions. It is rather to shed light on theoretical insights related to educating emotional virtues, primarily in schooling contexts, that can guide informed future action. Key findings and theories from affect studies do not immediately lend themselves to such discussions.

I make one other choice here people may query, in discussing some Eastern and particularly Chinese philosophical and cultural views in this text. Related to this choice, some may ask what the purpose is in introducing such views, when there are other orientations, from Asia, Africa, South America, and indigenous communities, that I hardly (if ever) mention. My reason for introducing these views here and considering them across chapters is to highlight that Western philosophical and cultural conceptions underlying common perceptions and practices are just that; they are not universally held, and they may not be the most widely held. Western and Asian views need not be seen as incommensurable or mutually incomprehensible (Ng, 2018). They are comparable, and in significant senses, they may be seen as intersecting (Hall & Ames, 1995). However, there is too often a tendency to assimilate other cultures' views to Western ones among Western scholars (Ng, 2018). This is normally done with good intentions, to relate and compare views to one another, to enhance mutual understanding, and to broaden discussions. Sometimes, it can also be an outcome of translation. Nonetheless, such practices sometimes result in the whitewashing of distinctive views. For example, as I discuss in Chapter 3, some feel that framing Confucian philosophy as similar to Western virtue ethics is oversimplifying to an unhelpful extent.

Western thinkers (among others) can better appreciate how their views are particular, not universally held, by developing more substantive understanding of other traditions, on the terms of those traditions. There is no firm boundary separating 'East' and 'West': 'Easterners' and 'Westerners' can be found in every society. Yet often people fail to recognise or appreciate that people around them hold different views deeply, while functioning well in the same society. One inspiration for this text is my observation that Western educators and scholars often take up educating emotional virtues among diverse students with little appreciation for differences in view, due to culturally particular assumptions they bring into these tasks. This means that their well-intentioned (and otherwise possibly well-justified) work is not necessarily effective, or equitable in diverse classrooms, as it is based on questionable assumptions.

Given these observations, I cannot portray the world, and societies and classrooms, as culturally homogeneous, Western-oriented spaces, to construct a neatly scoped book. By exploring Eastern and especially Chinese philosophical and cultural views of emotions in education in part, I thus aim to signal profound diversity when it comes to understanding emotions in society and educating emotional virtues. The aim of this book is not to review views of emotions held around the world. But bringing Eastern views into the discussion demonstrates how Western views of educating emotional virtues are culturally particular, not universal. This is one elaboration (among others) of the politics of educating emotions.

Returning to the overall content of this book, the second and third chapters develop a framework for understanding the moral and ethical and empirical approaches that broadly influence thought about emotional virtues education. These chapters aim to illustrate some of the diversity of perspectives on emotions in society, and their divergent implications for educating emotional virtues, from a broad view. They are the least practical chapters. Readers less interested in theoretical perspectives and methodological considerations may prefer to skip ahead to the chapters on specific emotional virtues, which they may find easier to relate to, and which comprise the bulk of this text. These chapters survey major emotional virtues that have been an increasing focus of education. Each considers what is known and thought, from a broad view across fields, about a particular emotional virtue: what it is, and why it is valuable and useful, or threatening and challenging. Then, it interrogates these foundations, in relation to common practices and other possibilities for teaching and learning about these emotional virtues within the context of moral and civic education.

Chapter 4 focuses on education for *happiness*. Happiness has been promoted particularly as a significant aim of education by Noddings (2003) and as a personal and social good in positive psychology. Happiness, as well as well-being, has been linked to various other good dispositions, states of mind, and pro-social behaviour (Seligman, 2002). Distinct yet related forms of contentment and *eudemonia* are encouraged from other philosophical and religious traditions (such as Confucianism and Aristotelian virtue ethics), which seek to promote positive and (perhaps moderately) pleasurable feelings, in relation to oneself and/or others. This chapter explores different philosophies related to happiness as an emotional virtue for their educational implications and associated educational discourses, classroom curricula, and pedagogical strategies for teaching about and for happiness. It contrasts perspectives which are individualistic and agent-based, with relational and critical political views. It examines the pitfalls of encouraging happiness as an individual attribute across diverse contexts, particularly considering the case of Hong Kong, where the role of educational circumstances in enabling or challenging youth well-being has been dismissed by government leaders. The chapter thus emphasises the value of developing a balanced, critical approach to happiness in education.

Chapter 5 turns to *caring, compassion,* and *altruism*. It is framed very broadly by the 'empathy-altruism' thesis. Initially articulated in psychology, this view asserts that empathy and compassion lead to altruism (Batson, 1991; see also Cialdini et al., 1997). Now this view tends to be assumed across fields. Even more so than is the case with happiness, schools are places where caring, compassion, and empathy are embraced and taught. Noddings' approach to care ethics (1984) shifted the landscape of Western ethics, by suggesting that caring relations are at the heart of good moral action, and thus should be at the centre of moral education. Similarly, Nussbaum (2001) argues that compassion is key to a flourishing civic life. The major distinctions made among compassion, empathy, and pity as they relate to education are examined in this chapter, which also considers views of caring, compassion, and empathy in psychology, Aristotelian virtue ethics, Confucianism, and Buddhism. This chapter contrasts approaches which assume that care and compassion lead to altruism and other-oriented beneficence, with more critical relational and political orientations. For instance, some argue that compassion for 'like' others is much easier to attain than compassion for 'distant' and dissimilar others. This can hinder the value of cultivating compassion and empathy in education for social justice. The value of caring and compassion is also queried in this chapter from a feminist orientation and in relation to initiatives for service learning and international exchange. How education for caring, compassion, and altruism can better align with social justice and civic aims of education is explored here.

Chapter 6 focuses on educating for *gratitude*. Gratitude is widely seen as another major pro-social emotional virtue, which corresponds with and mutually reinforces the emotional virtues highlighted in the previous chapters. Gratitude has become popular in psychology and in education, as it is seen to connect to happiness and well-being, and to larger social and individual benefits. Literature on educating gratitude encourages people to think about things they are grateful for as a means of cultivating gratitude as a disposition. In this case, there is a tendency to focus on individual development of gratitude, apart from broader considerations.

Yet a relational, more culturally and politically oriented approach to gratitude reveals that some recommended behaviours and other expectations for gratitude can lead to negative feelings, of shame and guilt, in some contexts (Morgan, Gulliford, & Kristjánsson, 2014). Furthermore, educating individuals to cultivate gratitude in the worst of times can risk promoting servility, harm, and other forms of injustice, as expectations of generalised gratitude can imply disregard for problematic social and personal issues (Jackson, 2016). This chapter thus contrasts individualistic versus relational and political orientations to gratitude and their educational implications.

Chapters 7 and 8 consider some emotional virtues that are prominent in character education today, although they are not typically seen as basic or primary emotions, in contrast to those focused on in the last three chapters. Chapter 7 explores *resilience* and *mindfulness*. While these traits are not normally described as emotions, they invoke emotional states. As a broad orientation towards adaptability, the focus in resilience scholarship has been on psychological interventions to make challenging circumstances manageable. With resilience, strong emotional reactions to challenges are evaded through changing oneself to stay calm and rational. Mindfulness involves developing a similarly peaceful and calm state, more closely associated with Buddhist and related traditions of meditative practice. In education and society, resilience and mindfulness are valued for functioning, and practices such as meditation and yoga may be encouraged to cultivate mindfulness, in particular. Yet there can be problematic aspects of promoting and cultivating these dispositions in schools and society. As with other emotional virtues explored here, popular promotions of resilience and mindfulness may be useful for some kinds of student emotional development, but at the same time may be limited in value in relation to education for social justice.

Chapter 8 discusses *vulnerability*, *courage*, and *grit*. These emotions, or emotion-related traits, may not initially appear to have much in common, but they intersect in interesting ways in educational discourse. In contrast with the emotional virtues discussed thus far, vulnerability and courage are not frequently prized in education. Vulnerability is often seen as negative. Promotions of resilience and mindfulness in education are often in part responses to perceived vulnerability. Yet there is also a bright side to vulnerability, and there can be a positive role for some kinds of vulnerability in communities. Courage is encouraged in virtue ethics, but it must be tempered, so that it is not reckless, careless, or brash. Thus, courage, like vulnerability, can be of value within situations, but it should not be seen as beneficial regardless of context. It is also possible to think of vulnerability and courage as similar emotional and cognitive dispositions. On the other hand, courage can be considered as a value underlying grit. Grit is a relatively new concept, seen to enable emotional perseverance, similar to resilience and mindfulness. Grit has gained a great deal of attention in recent years, yet it can also be used in moral and non-moral ways. This chapter thus explores vulnerability, courage, and grit, and their relationship to one another and to educating emotional virtues for social justice.

Chapters 9 and 10 explore common emotional states often regarded as negative. Chapter 9 explores *anger* in moral and civic education. Discussions of the benefits of gratitude and grit often compare these emotional virtues favourably with anger and resentment. Anger is very negatively viewed by many philosophers and psychologists. It is typically regarded as always to be avoided, and as never good, useful, or beneficial. Often theorists focus on ideal examples here, of Martin Luther King, Jr., Gandhi, Nelson Mandela, and the Dalai Lama (e.g. Nussbaum, 2016). These heroes, and the heroism of their (apparent) lack of anger, are also represented in schooling contexts, as something young people might aspire to. More generally, schools normally work to decrease student anger, for the sake of happiness and well-being, and to prevent and resolve conflicts. This chapter analyses philosophical and psychological arguments against (and for) anger and their analogues in educational theory and practice. Whether there can be political or moral value to anger is also explored, as well as possibilities for the toleration of anger, and even positive recognition of it, in educational settings.

Chapter 10 explores *sadness, fear,* and *anxiety*. Sadness and fear are usually considered as basic 'negative' emotions. Like anger, these experiences are often framed as to be avoided, worked through, or 'gotten over' in educational places, among other contexts in the public sphere. Sadness is sometimes cast as the opposite of happiness, while fear can be said to oppose or prevent courage. Fear is also said to be the basic emotion which underlies anxiety. Anxiety is widely seen as distracting and disruptive to educational achievement. Yet unhappiness and particular sorts of sadness, fear, and anxiety may be moral and functional, not simply feelings to avoid at all costs. Despite calls to diminish such negative and mixed feelings, they can be regarded as socially and personally valuable, and psychologically functional in some contexts. This chapter thus argues that sadness and fear should not be diminished as simply negative feelings devoid of value or function. Feelings of sadness, fear, and anxiety can be righteous, functional, and normal, and interrelated with critical understanding, while they can also be problematic and pathological in other cases.

Chapter 11 concludes this text. It draws from the in-depth exploration of educating emotions given in the preceding chapters, to reflect more on the nature of emotions and educating emotions, also considering the point of view of teachers and others who are interested in cultivating and developing young people's emotional states. This chapter gives a more holistic view of how emotional virtues relate to moral and political aims.

1.5   Are Emotions Virtuous?

Before moving on, some readers may find it useful for me to briefly indicate how I understand the nature of emotions in relation to moral epistemology and virtue. In philosophy, there has been a tendency to examine emotional virtues within moral theory generally, rather than systematically considering particular emotional virtues in their own standing (Roberts, 2003; Kristjánsson, 2018; Sreenivasan, 2020). Robert Roberts particularly comments on this as a challenge; he himself 'promised', and by his own terms has (thus far) 'failed' to deliver a text (2013, p. 211) that would 'treat a number of main virtues both individually and organically, going into sufficient depth to map the deep structure of virtues in the various kinds of diversity ... to show their structural relations within the moral personality'. In relation, he notes how philosophers tend to rely upon their preferred virtues as exemplars to illustrate general rules, without duly considering the potentially large number of counter cases.

This kind of concern, with thinking about the morality of emotions in an overly abstract way, and my own related observation of a gap in research literature, between philosophical and applied insights, motivated my choice in this text to focus to a large extent on particular emotional virtues, which are seen as significant within education. So I have little ambition to provide and defend a singular, comprehensive theory of emotional virtues as such here. Nonetheless, as Kristjánsson (2018) observes, one can hardly outline a practical philosophy on emotional education without an undergirding moral epistemology (presumed, if not made explicit).

Systematic conceptual explorations of emotions, such as those provided by Roberts (2003, 2013), demonstrate how complex emotions are in lived experience. While I generally use 'emotion' and 'feeling' interchangeably in this text, emotions can be felt or experienced without feeling, in a less conscious way. They generally relate to concrete experiences in the external world, but not always. They may be seen as justified or unjustified by those experiencing them. They may motivate action, or not. Observing them, and expressing them outwardly, may lead to an intensity or lessening of the experience. Emotions can cohere with cognitive-based belief and understanding, of what is good or right, or be incoherent with it, or simply be experienced more randomly. They can be related to other people strongly, or only be experienced and directed in relation to oneself.

Relatedly, I follow moral philosophers such as Kristjánsson (2018) and Gopal Sreenivasan (2020) in regarding a virtue as ideally constituted by component parts, of cognitive and emotional qualities, reflective (in part) of capacities to recognise and consider complexity within particular situations. I further tend to agree with Kristjánsson (2018), that a kind of soft rationalist stance undergirds any positive view of educating emotional virtues. To rephrase comments from earlier in this chapter, I reject the view that emotions are basically distracting from moral development (hard rationalism), while I also am not compelled by sentimentalist views, that suggest that emotions are morally authoritative, and entirely distinguishable from cognitive and other forms of knowing. There would be no use in educating emotions, if they are simply distracting, or if they are ineducable, or cannot be educated as better or worse, or as less or more morally appropriate.

On the other hand, another concern inspiring this text is that emotional identification and emotional self-regulation are too quickly valued and framed in mainstream discourse on educating emotions, as commonly used, always applicable capabilities, for all or most people. In relation, some psychologists (and some philosophers) are at risk of attributing as 'normal' capabilities they themselves have and cherish, and enjoy cultivating, which may not be so broadly experienced, or of universal value.

Here, one does not need to go as far as defending moral relativism (e.g. Prinz, 2007), to argue that tolerance and acceptance of some forms of well-observed and reasonable diversity in emotional life are worth encouraging, over an unnecessarily narrow view. Reasonable and tolerable diversity of emotional experiences and expressions can be harmfully dismissed and misrecognised within highly prescriptive (and often paternalistic) strategies of emotional education that rely upon narrow-minded assumptions about the normal trajectory of emotional and moral development. People have very different views of the norms of emotional and moral development. In this case, the practice of framing a particular variant of such development as universal is problematic, and can lead to stigmatising and exclusion of those who do not fit the given norms and expectations. The chapters that follow detail this.

Given my focus on the diversity of emotional experience in real-world contexts, I am not satisfied by some particular kinds of Aristotelian accounts that grant educators moral authority and superior understanding of something like 'moral truth' as a matter of course, to simply work to change young people's emotions in the 'right' ways, as if the 'right' ways are easy to identify and enact. Such a view is too prescriptive and reductive, in light of the great quantity and quality of scholarship that has explored various ins and outs of educating emotional virtues, much of which provides helpful further guidance on the matter. Overall, I thus advocate for more caution in educating emotional virtues, to apply what is known critically and reflectively. I will return to these points in more detail in the conclusion to this text.

CHAPTER 2

Psychology and the Politics of Educating Emotions

Emotions are involved in education. Schooling practices impact students' and teachers' emotional states. Teachers can, and generally do, work to influence students' emotional states and dispositions, inside and outside classrooms, recognising this work as aligned with broader educational aims to cultivate good, flourishing individuals and members of society. This might be thought about in terms of classroom behavioural management, as teachers want to prepare students to be focused and ready to learn. Or, it might be thought about in terms of teaching students 'right and wrong': to feel sorry when they hurt others, good when they have studied hard, or thankful when others are generous towards them.

As discussed in Chapter 1, many people think how this unfolds is common sense and is basically agreed upon. However, from different traditions and disciplinary orientations, and based on different sorts of findings and analyses, people have contrasting views of the significance of emotions in social life. These different approaches to what emotions are, and how they operate, lead to a variety of paths for education. It is worth examining these varied foundations to educating emotional virtues, as we (as educators, researchers, school leaders, etc.) aim to benefit young people with education, as individuals, and as members of society.

In this chapter, I examine social science approaches to understanding emotions and their educational implications. By social science approaches, I refer to fields that study human personal and social life empirically, drawing out patterns and relationships that can inform policy and practice, in education and other fields. This chapter does not aim to consider all the findings in the social sciences about emotions. That would be too much to do in a book, let alone a chapter. Here, I simply flesh out what I take as major relevant theoretical orientations to emotions that can inform education of emotional virtues. Inevitably, I must leave some potentially interesting topics out (such as anthropological views, for example). My main task is to introduce, and juxtapose with the mainstream, alternative perspectives on educating emotional virtues which have thus far been left off the table, to highlight the insights of the politics of emotions for emotional virtues education.

The first and longest section of this chapter examines psychological views of emotions as applied in education. The methodology and orientation towards emotions in these approaches are explored at length, given their prominence in relation to emotional virtues education. Findings in psychology have positively influenced education about emotional well-being in significant ways. However, it is important to consider what is and is not captured in influential psychological approaches to understand their limitations. Any distinctive perspective on the social world has some limitations: some processes and experiences it does not focus in on, or enable understanding about, compared to others. As Boler notes, 'emotion, affect, or consciousness cannot possibly be grasped by any one disciplinary approach except as a highly partial narrative' (in Boler & Zembylas, 2016, p. 24). Psychologists of emotions in education also emphasise their need to learn from cross-disciplinary studies to further develop their work (Pekrun & Linnenbrink-Garcia, 2014). The second section of this chapter thus introduces approaches and views related to the politics of educating emotions, which includes insights about emotions developed in social psychology, sociology, feminist theory, cultural studies, and related areas.

Educators should be informed by a holistic view of primary discipline findings (such as those in psychology, sociology, and philosophy), and by other knowledge that is specific to schooling contexts, in their work. However, primary discipline findings can be complex, and require further thought to apply in education. Educational applications must be reflective, but also critical, as most psychologists are not normally thinking about educational settings when they are studying or making recommendations regarding emotions. Indeed, I have observed some psychologists express surprise about how some psychological research gets taken up in education, given that psychologists primarily direct their work to other psychologists, not educators or educational researchers (e.g. Pekrun & Linnenbrink-Garcia, 2014; Gulliford & Morgan, 2019). Collie Conoley and colleagues (2014, p. 497) note in this context that 'a chasm exists between effective positive psychology research findings and successful school-based implementation – a chasm caused not only by ignorance of new programs but also by the lack of attention to program implementation challenges'. I have also found some philosophers express surprise at how philosophical work can be applied in education, given (again) that the target audience is not educators.

Relatedly, it is not uncommon that debates and the plurality of views on issues within primary disciplines are neglected by educators aiming to quickly apply primary field findings to their work. The search for easy fixes may be encouraged by the growth of grant-based research, which often insists that findings be practically applicable with an immediate positive impact, making it less of a priority for researchers to critically nuance and complicate their discussions of the implications of their work. In this context, by articulating the politics of educating emotions, I hope to enhance the picture of educating emotional virtues, and expose some aspects of practice that have not been previously explored in a systematic way.

As I observe, social scientists do not have a particularly strong arsenal to justify educational practices based on their *moral* status, or their relation to social justice concerns. Taken as a whole, the orientations discussed across this chapter tend to focus on what practices and organisational patterns are functional or dysfunctional for individuals, groups, or systems, rather than their moral status (Pekrun & Linnenbrink-Garcia, 2014). The missing component here is an understanding of morality and ethics, as education has moral implications, not just implications for functioning. I explore views related to the morality of educating emotions in Chapter 3.

2.1 Psychological Views of Emotions

In psychology, 'deciding what emotions are is still a controversial issue' (Shuman & Scherer, 2014, p. 19). There are some commonly held understandings across the field, however, to take as a starting point. According to psychological views, emotions are episodes experienced by persons evoked by external or internal stimuli, which consist of subjective feelings, physiological and/or motor changes, action or behavioural tendencies, and some kind of judgement or appraisal (Shuman & Scherer, 2014). This is not far off from the observations of other scholars focused on understanding emotions conceptually (i.e. Roberts, 2003, 2013). What makes a psychological view of emotions distinctive from others is that emotions are framed as having *functions* for individuals in their environments. Such functions include monitoring a situation or making meaning out of it, motivating action, communicating with others, and supporting physiological functioning. Psychologists understand emotions to have biological and evolutionary functions, as well as social and cultural value.

A student is about to give a presentation. They feel a sense of anxiety. They want to do a good job and gain positive recognition from their teacher and peers. But they also feel a heightened sense of being inexperienced and insufficiently prepared. These feelings may be partly triggered by memories (or nightmares) of presentation experiences which were accompanied by stress and hectic conditions, where they were not able to achieve their goals satisfactorily. The student experiences a sensation of their heart beating rapidly, shortness of breath, and sweating. They may experience a heightened sense of alertness and feel as if they are moving more quickly and abruptly. They may feel more sensitive to noises, activities, and other people around them.

These feelings and appraisals have functions from a psychological view: to alert a person to a stressor, challenge, or risk; to focus their attention; and to enable them to react, respond, and communicate in an effective way to others. When properly understood and managed, student anxiety can enhance a presentation. It can help a student keep their voice loud, their movements clear, and their demeanour active, engaged, and responsive to others. But the anxiety could also be less functional and could go wrong. The student could become frozen with panic. They may stutter and stammer. The anxiety could decrease the performance, just as feared (Zeidner, 2014).

Psychologists generally aim to decrease dysfunctional emotional states and dispositions, and other subjective experiences, and reshape them to be functional and useful for individuals and groups. They study the operations and processes of emotions and related experiences to develop theories they can apply to practice in their work. Psychologists and educational psychologists may also focus on school settings, or consider the best ways for educators to apply their findings and interventions in schools (among other contexts). To understand and work with emotions, in schooling among other settings, psychologists – and educators and educational psychologists following psychological orientations – gather and analyse data from people.

2.1.1   *Understanding Emotional Processes*

Psychological understanding of emotions is typically based on analyses of empirical data which may come from direct observation, experiments, interviews, psychoanalysis, or other forms of participant reports (such as surveys or other texts). That psychology is evidence-based provides a strong justification for relying on psychological findings in education (for less traditional approaches to emotion in psychology, see Zembylas & Schutz, 2016). Such findings are more valued than other perspectives less tied to empirical, directly observed data. As education has a moral purpose, most feel that school practices should not be based on theories disconnected from reality, but should focus on what is known, verifiable and verified, and generalised about the effects of behaviour and action. Verification and generalisability are prized qualities of scientific research which psychologists usually aspire to in their work (Morris, 2012). With references to observable, measurable data, psychological claims about the effects of behaviour and action are often persuasive, despite methodological challenges in bringing to light and studying emotions.

Direct observation is one approach to understanding psychological processes. This may seem straightforward. However, it is not fail-proof when used in research on emotions. One person's emotional experience – such as what I described in the preceding paragraphs, about the anxious student – is not necessarily apparent to another person. A psychologist interested in understanding the emotions of a student about to give a presentation may not observe the clammy hands and heaving chest, the flushed face, or vocal changes. The symptoms may come and go. The student might try to hide them. The observer may or may not be fully attentive. Cues may not be seen due to differences in cultural expressions, or the personal biases or blind spots of the researcher (Williams & Wyatt, 2015). Some emotions may be more easily observed than others. Psychophysiological methods can be used here, particularly to access aspects of emotional responses (e.g. heart rate or eye blink) which are difficult to observe directly (Fox et al., 2007). However, incorporating various methods of observation can be labour-intensive in terms of data gathering, particularly if generalised understanding is sought (Linnenbrink-Garcia, Wormington, & Ranellucci, 2016).

Furthermore, psychological analysis of emotions may not be effectively based on single events or situations. A diagnosis of anxiety (among other psychological states) may be characterised as manifesting a majority of a set of possible traits in contexts where they are dysfunctional, or with dysfunctional frequency or intensity. Yet some traits associated with emotion-related disorders may be more visible than others. Some patients may claim to experience anxiety more than it is apparent. Others may present obvious visual symptoms, of sweating and appearing excitable, but not consciously or cognitively experience anxiety in a problematic way. Additionally, emotions can exist in an unstable, dynamic state within situations. Emotions fluctuate in an event and may not be the same across multiple events. Emotions are dynamic and multidimensional. Yet 'the situational and social nature of psychological phenomena like emotions has hovered at the edges of psychological research [and] have never become central' (Turner & Trucano, 2014, p. 645).

Taking a situational approach to understanding emotions is thus warranted. This presents limitations to psychologists, in relation to developing predictive power and capacity to derive causal conclusions from their research (Pekrun & Linnenbrink-Garcia, 2014). One can experiment to create situations, or observe in normal settings over time, to recognise how emotions are situated in time and place and develop causal conclusions. However, experiments to understand such processes are not necessarily ecologically valid. Knowing they are in an experiment, not ordinary life, can impact people's feelings. Observations in an authentic setting, for example a classroom, can cause interruptions and divert attention. Thus, situational observations can augment situations (Biesta, 2007; Turner & Trucano, 2014). Deception can be used to hide the experimental nature of the experience, but this raises ethical complications. For understanding and studying problematic emotional states, which may bring serious risks, experimenting is rarely used.

Given these challenges to observation, psychologists may rely entirely or in part on people's verbal descriptions of their experiences, which can be given through an oral or a written report. For studying people as groups or for general understanding, psychologists have developed ways for people to measure their emotional states, such as surveys, interviews, structured journaling, and more (Pekrun, 2016). There are many benefits to self-report: More people can be studied, and their emotions can be compared and correlated across a population (Pekrun, 2016; Linnenbrink-Garcia et al., 2016). However, there are also challenges. People can bias their self-presentations in terms of what they think is desirable to others. For example, a participant may express experiencing happiness, because they think it is socially good (Pekrun & Buhner, 2014). Priming may influence this. If a researcher says they are focused on the relationship between happiness and achievement, a participant is more likely to express that they experience happiness. These are particularly pertinent issues in educational contexts, where people have roles in relation to one another, and may see it as a responsibility to strive for or cultivate particular emotions, as a result (Frenzel, 2014; Pekrun, 2016). Thus, teachers and students may be more susceptible than other groups to biased self-reporting.

Furthermore, people do not necessarily give accurate self-reports even when they intend to, due to such factors as different beliefs about emotionality, memory limitations, and differences in implicit theories about emotions (Frenzel, 2014). This is particularly the case when it comes to dynamic rather than stable emotional experiences, which are often of significance to, if not the main focus of, psychological investigations. People may use the words and concepts in self-reporting tools in different ways, making correlations across populations less convincing (Pekrun, 2016; Linnenbrink-Garcia et al., 2016). Relatedly, such research is quite limited in terms of the scope of people systematically studied. Only the emotional experiences of particular groups of Western, white, socioeconomically advantaged subjects, like university students, have been comprehensively explored with such methods, due to factors such as the desire for consistent data (DeCuir-Gunby & Williams-Johnson, 2014). In relation, how various emotions are understood, described, and expressed differs across cultural and language groups. This means that claims of universality that may lead some educators towards a 'one-size-fits-all' educational approach require scrutiny, when thinking about diverse schools and groups (DeCuir-Gunby & Williams-Johnson, 2014; Boler & Zembylas, 2016).

A related challenge for self-report is that not all people articulate their subjective feelings well, effectively sense them, or sense them in scientifically useful ways. As mentioned in Chapter 1, alexithymia impacts at least 10 per cent of people in a society, as an inability to identify and voice emotions. Given that not all people across a society seek out psychological services, the implied assumption here of many psychologists, that it is normal to be able to identify and articulate one's feelings and abnormal to not be able to do so, is worth further questioning. Learning at a young age other people's views about appropriate and inappropriate emotional expressions is also relevant, in relation to cultural and social norms about understanding, identifying, and communicating emotional experiences to others. Additionally, different norms may apply in this context when it comes to particular emotions, in relation to people's identities, social roles, and other characteristics. For instance, boys often learn (informally if not formally) to ignore and overlook feelings of sadness and vulnerability. Meanwhile, girls learn to sidestep anger, or see it and articulate it as something else.

More generally, as memory and consciousness are subjective, memory retrieval and unconscious emotional processes may not be captured adequately through self-report (Pekrun, 2016). This makes self-report particularly challenging to use with children. Psychologists see early childhood experience as vital to emotional development, but, at the same time, they recognise young children as less capable of understanding and expressing their emotional experiences (Turner & Trucano, 2014).

Given the challenges of observing, experimenting with, and self-reporting about emotional phenomena, psychologists aiming to help people with problematic or disordered emotional experiences, as individuals, couples, or small groups, favour a more isolated, longitudinal approach – counselling or psychotherapy. To try to systematically make sense of emotions across individuals, despite diverse forms of self-understanding and the limitations of different methods, researchers can also triangulate data from different sources, such as self-report, observation, and working theories (Schutz, DeCuir-Gunby, & Williams-Johnson, 2016). When working with children and young people, psychologists consider reports from teachers and parents, and different kinds of observations, not just experiments or self-report.

Some hope that beyond participant reports and observations, neuroscience can play a role in the future (Reisenzein et al., 2014). As previously mentioned, psychophysiology can often be used to shore up these various approaches in relatively non-invasive ways, by studying physiological responses of the brain and body as they intersect with other

observations and reports on experience. Over time, technological innovations have clearly increased their usefulness to this field, by bringing to
light phenomena that were previously intangible, and by revealing significant correlates and effects between physiological and psychological
processes (Cacioppo, Tassinary, & Berntson, 2007; Jennings & Gianaros,
2007). For instance, brain imaging can be useful when it comes to understanding various abnormalities, and how psychological interventions
(such as behavioural and pharmaceutical approaches) function in different ways as neural processes (Posner, Rueda, & Kanske, 2007). As a result
of such possibilities, neuroscience is often heralded as the next big thing
in education, in light of the many emotional and behavioural challenges
observed in this context.

Yet at a more general level, it remains unclear how neuroscience findings can be usefully worked into theoretical models of educating emotions (Immordino-Yang & Christodoulou, 2014; Azevedo et al., 2016).
Mapping psychological events onto physiological ones can be
a complicated process in the best of conditions, while the relationship
between the two can never 'be assumed to hold across situations or
individuals' (Cacioppo et al., 2007, p. 10). Cultural, gender, and other
differences are still found in such research, as both the psychological and
physiological domains are also shaped by personal experiences. Thus, as
Boler indicates (in Boler & Zembylas, 2016, p. 25):

> Contemporary scientific investigations and research on the brain and
> in the areas of neuroscience has potentially radical significance for
> studies of emotion. However, no matter how advanced these new
> forms of measurement and data visualization become, there will
> remain variables, idiosyncratic differences, cultural differences, and
> differences in social mores and rules that govern emotional behaviour,
> conduct, expression, and reflective practices with regards to human
> experience of emotions. So while some may anticipate that emotions
> will be entirely described and predicted by neuro- and brain science in
> years to come, it would be easy to overstate how and what such
> measurements and visualizations will contribute.

Furthermore, such studies cannot shed light on questions of moral significance and the morality of educational practice, which are (indeed) not
the focus of neuroscientists or psycho-physiologists. This is an important
limitation to bear in mind for those interested in enhancing education as
a moral practice, oriented towards good living and social justice (see also
Roberts, 2003).

Reinhard Pekrun and Lisa Linnenbrink-Garcia (2014, p. 659) summar-
ise the state of psychological research on emotions: 'research on emotions
in education is still at an early stage. Theories, research strategies, and

measures for analysing emotions in education are not fully developed . . . much more work is needed if educational research on emotions is to evolve in ways benefiting education and society.' Nonetheless, some understandings from psychology strongly influence approaches to educating emotional virtues.

2.1.2 Understanding the Role of Emotions in School and Society

From a psychological viewpoint, emotions have always had a major role in education, its challenges, and its enhancement. Psychological discourse treats emotions as factors enhancing or obstructing student or educator efficacy. Given that emotions have functions within educational settings, too much student anger is seen to distract from learning, while more motivated feelings like curiosity are encouraged and promoted. In the twentieth century educational psychologists considered attention deficit, lack of anger management, and depression and anxiety as major challenges to achievement. Self-report and observation have been essential for understanding such issues, among psychologists and schoolteachers (Shuman & Scherer, 2014).

Boler analyses the history of educating emotions, showing the role of psychological thought over time. As she notes, emotional virtues were taught in terms of 'mental hygiene' in the United States (Boler, 1999). The 1909 National Committee on Mental-Hygiene considered 'mental illness' and 'poorly developed personalities of children' as 'the most serious evil of the time' (Cohen, cited in Boler, 1999, p. 49). Child emotional functioning was the focus of various educational techniques, which regarded mental hygiene as the answer to social conflicts and challenges.

One particular concern was how schools might set up youth expectations that could not be met in a society marked by massive inequalities. As one 1938 text notes, 'Either the attitudes must be replaced, or social changes must come about, or the individual must compartmentalize his thinking and submit to permanent dissociation due to the lack of harmony between his beliefs and his actions' (Prescott, cited in Boler, 1999, p. 51). Seen here, emotions can be functional and dysfunctional, in different ways at the same time. Emotions that 'help the individual assert his or her interests can conflict with functions that help maintain the larger social context', while those that 'respond in harmony with the world as it exists can conflict with functions that kick against the world . . . in order to defend valued ideas or bring the self closer to a desired goal' (Giner-Sorolla, 2012, p. 21).

A student may express a 'bad attitude' if they have expectations and desires that they feel cannot be met through schooling (such as to substantially enhance their socio-economic standing over time). They may rebel in this case with distracting classroom behaviour, or they may otherwise refuse to respond to educators in an emotionally pleasing way, for instance by sulking, working on tasks slowly, or expressing indifference or apathy. Such actions and emotional expressions may be seen as dysfunctional to overall educational efficacy from the teacher's view, but may be functional from the view of the student, if they do not regard classroom tasks as personally beneficial, but see them instead as distracting or unnecessary 'busy work'. On the other hand, a student may interact in the classroom in a motivated and emotionally positive way, helping and pleasing the teacher in their work, while potentially neglecting their own needs in society, if they still perceive that education will not help them achieve upward mobility.

As will be discussed later, psychologists face challenges in this case, to articulate moral or normative standards for evaluating relative functionality, in terms of the best ends. Often a judgement is implied, but not given outright, as the best path forward is assumed, rather than investigated, by such social scientists. The key questions here are whose or what functionality is to be prioritised, and what the implications are when it comes to intervention, in the situation.

Early psychological and related science on education emphasised intervention, in relation to these conflicts or mismatched expectations that would operate at the individual level, rather than at the societal level. This is due to the priority within these orientations towards increasing efficiency and utility in support of a capitalist economic system (Boler, 1999). In this vein, students were treated as akin to factory workers. Meanwhile, early occupational discourse focused not on employee welfare, but on system productivity and efficiency. Governments have likewise tended to 'gauge the quality of life of their citizens by observing economic barometers such as Gross Domestic Product (GDP)' although GDP does not reflect experiences of diverse individuals (Morris, 2012, p. 436). Moral and justice considerations are thus bypassed in these ways of thinking, as individuals are treated as factors in economic value, not as persons of inherent worth. This is reflected in an excerpt from a 1912 New York City High School Teachers Association Bulletin:

Comparisons between schools and mercantile establishments:

1. The teacher obviously corresponds to planning department, superintendent, manager of a factory.
2. The elements in the enterprise (the workmen, the raw material, and the finished product) are combined in the pupil. The other elements (tools, etc.) are the text books, charts, and apparatus . . . (cited in Boler, 1999, p. 46).

That individuals should improve themselves to function in line with what is good for the system also undergirds the more recent emotional intelligence (EI) movement (Goleman, 1995). EI is said to consist of traits related to understanding and regulating one's emotions and developing relationships, dispositions, and behaviours that enhance academic achievement and life success. Vital among these traits are self-awareness and self-regulation, motivation, empathy, and related dispositions and skills. EI is believed by proponents to be educable, meaning people can learn to recognise and understand the emotions of themselves and others, and use this knowledge to make decisions and act in more productive ways, to achieve personal and social goals. It is described as an intelligence by proponents, because it is said to not just correlate with but also lead to higher achievement by academic and other measures.

Positive psychologists also elaborate that people can learn to identify and manage their emotions to cultivate positive emotions and dispositions that can help them achieve their goals, develop a greater sense of well-being, and be more productive in society (Seligman, 2007; Allen et al., 2014). Against the backdrop of psychology's historical emphasis on what is dysfunctional or negative in people's individual cognitive and emotional experiences and expressions, positive psychologists emphasise what can enable an individual to function, and function better, and how to cultivate virtues associated with better functioning, focusing on the development of happiness and joy, gratitude, compassion, forgiveness, and other traits which are framed as positive and functional. Both EI and positive psychology emphasise the functioning of people to harmonise with systems rather than create social change. Daniel Goleman (1995) describes EI as equivalent to character and suggests that it is moral to teach it.

In relation to bolstering emotional regulation via positive psychology or EI frameworks, programmes and curricula have proliferated in the past few decades (Boler, 1999; Ecclestone, 2012). Recommended emotional regulation methods include (Jacobs & Gross, 2014): situation selection and situation modification (making choices to increase the likelihood of positive emotions), attention deployment (directing attention to and from situations to influence emotions), cognitive change (changing situation appraisal to influence emotions), and response modulation (influencing one's response, such as through an additional psychological or experiential reaction). EI has been found in some studies to enhance educational outcomes of students. Likewise, positive emotional traits highlighted in positive psychology have been found to correlate with factors and markers of personal, academic, and professional success.

Such findings are more common when EI and related emotional virtues education are integrated into a broad curriculum for social and emotional learning (SEL), school-wide initiatives to improve caring relationships, cooperation, and school safety. Some programmes for SEL have been found to enhance social-emotional and academic well-being of students and classrooms, including pro-social attitudes and behaviours, better mental health, and improved academic performance (Brackett & Rivers, 2014). As Maurice Elias and Dominic Moceri (2014, pp. 41–42) note, 'data from several school-based interventions designed to improve SEL, in so doing, also generated improvements in positive behaviours, learning-to-learn behaviours, self-efficacy and academic performance, as well as declines in problem behaviours such as aggression, withdrawal, anxiety, and substance abuse'. Similarly, positive psychology has been seen to positively impact young people and schools under the right conditions: with training of educators, and within a context of school and community support for enhancing well-being (Conoley et al., 2014). Amelia Aldao (2013) emphasises in relation the importance of flexibility in selecting emotional regulation strategies as a marker of well-being and healthy adjustment, and the teaching of flexibility in implementing strategies, as inflexibility and other forms of habituation can limit the benefits of using emotional regulation strategies over time.

2.1.3 Limitations

Although popular, EI lacks transparent conceptual bases. Some, both within and outside psychology, find EI to be an incoherent list of items, which 'does not make clear distinctions between emotions and general attitudes, desires, and moods, in so far as it aspires to be a holistic conception of people's emotional make-up' (Kristjánsson, 2018, p. 169). In this context, validly measuring EI is a challenge. In place of a single model, a variety of perspectives have emerged (Kristjánsson, 2007; Allen et al., 2014). None are free from methodological issues. For example, in the Bar-On model of emotional-social intelligence, test takers can attain higher scores by providing fake self-assessments (Grubb & McDaniel, 2007). This challenge can be somewhat ameliorated by providing force-choice models, where test takers choose between statements. Yet using this method decreases the capacity to meaningfully compare findings across people.

In addition, research designs do not enable studies to effectively trace whether progress in EI specifically provides for benefits over time (Allen et al., 2014). Interventions may give positive results which fade, or may be ineffective without meeting preconditions, such as being 'embedded within safe, caring, well-managed and cooperative classroom environments, as well as wider settings that provide equitable opportunities for positive participation and recognition' (Elias & Moceri, 2014, p. 44). What is measured across studies is also not uniform owing to diverse definitions of EI, as well as diverse educational aims (Allen et al., 2014).

These and other related conceptual challenges make it difficult to accurately and meaningfully evaluate the efficacy of many SEL programmes undergirded by EI and related frameworks, particularly as they are implemented to respond to particular issues in schools, rather than to broadly enhance student well-being. As Kathryn Ecclestone (2012, p. 466) observes:

> Promotions and evaluations of [positive thinking] initiatives have tended to reflect the slippery definitions ... often eliding conduct disorders, disaffection from formal class teaching, general lack of motivation, poor social skills, emotional difficulties, bad behaviour and lack of 'emotional literacy'. This means that claims about effectiveness and impact seem often to be about simple disciplinary training, such as making students more proactive in their learning, attend regularly, manage their homework and sports equipment and set realistic but challenging targets.

Thus, interventions may impact students as a kind of simple training, which helps to achieve particular immediate goals, but does not make a deep, positive impact. Such risks are prevalent when the interventions are add-ons, with approaches not reflectively and flexibly placed in the broader context of educational research, teacher training, school policies, and community conditions (Conoley et al., 2014).

Further, individuals are not all the same in their emotional processes and related self-regulation strategies (Grubb & McDaniel, 2007; Tian et al., 2014). What works for some may not work for others, and may even be harmful to them (Jacobs & Gross, 2014). Boler pointed out in 1999 that 'emotional intelligence is based on a universalized portrait of human nature and emotions which entirely neglects significant differences of culture or gender' (pp. 74–75). How gender, race, and class impact experiences of emotional regulation is still not well known (DeCuir-Gunby & Williams-Johnson, 2014; Pekrun & Linnenbrink-Garcia, 2014). While cross-cultural differences have been identified, those working in the fields of EI and positive psychology have thus far not adequately responded to the presence of such diversity, or developed frameworks that can be effectively used in diverse classrooms (Tian et al., 2014).

As mentioned previously, those with alexithymia, unable to 'normally' identify their emotions as required for EI, are normally distributed across populations. Yet Goleman discounts them (1995) as a 'tragic failing', 'a complete loss', and 'emotionally tone-deaf'. As others observe that people with alexithymia can indeed benefit from alternative forms of intervention (Taylor & Taylor-Allan, 2007), it seems clear that one view of normal

functioning has been unnecessarily idealised here, with troubling implications for educating diverse learners in a tolerant, inclusive, and equitable way. In sum, while it is known that emotional regulation strategies
should be implemented flexibly by individuals within healthy adjustment processes (Aldao, 2013), such findings tend to be neglected, while
particular strategies are brought into school settings in narrow, more
rigid ways.

In general, helping young people understand and manage their emotions seems to help some of them demonstrate that they understand and
can manage their emotions within an educational setting. And it remains
clear that educators do often make an important difference in the emotional lives of their students (although it may not always or necessarily be
a positive difference). Nonetheless, there are not many compelling
research claims regarding the generalisability of educational interventions for EI, positive psychology, and SEL to boost achievement or flourishing across diverse groups, despite their prominence among
contemporary approaches to educating emotions.

Proponents of SEL concede many of the above challenges. Marc
Brackett and Susan Rivers (2014) observe that SEL is often applied to
ameliorate particular challenges in a school, like bullying or drug use, or
used in a piecemeal way to decrease stress, while testing may be the cause
of stress, rather than EI deficiencies. Noting that the firmest theoretical
foundation for EI is self-determination theory, which regards meeting
individual needs as prerequisite for flourishing and independence, they
(2014) emphasise that enhancing the environment is integral for positive
emotional development (see also Bronfenbrenner, 1979; Deci & Ryan,
1985). Yet 'there remains a paucity of research at the mesosystem and
macrosystem levels' in positive psychology and other relevant research
areas, hindering the development of 'a sophisticated science of "what
works" for children and youth within the context of their schooling'
(Gilman, Huebner, & Furlong, 2014).

Emotional intelligence research and positive psychology aim to enhance
experiences for individuals, to help them succeed in achieving their goals
and related goals of organisations. But interventions for emotional regulation and positive emotional experiences do not necessarily aim at good or
moral goals, in contrast with bad or unethical goals, because they do not
typically include an explicit evaluation of goals from a moral view. What
tends to be assumed is that academic achievement (or labour or professional productivity) is good. But teaching for EI or positive psychology can
be instrumental, if mental health (or productivity) is sought in educationally troubling circumstances (i.e. stressful test-oriented environments).
Emotional intelligence or positive psychology approaches may help students achieve their goals and engage in pro-social behaviour. But they need

not lead to more just or caring environments, if students are not encouraged to reflect on their practices, in the case that prejudice and bias are common at school, for instance. As Boler (1999) notes, 'the classroom instances I observed engaged discussion of emotions without attention to political and cultural differences or analyses. Very few of the readings or literature in this area analyse social conflict in terms of social injustice' (p. 103). Students can learn to be emotionally healthy without learning to be better people.

Many psychologists are also critical in relation to the impact of EI and positive psychology on understandings of emotional regulation. Maya Tamir emphasises the diversity of influences on and motives for emotional regulation, beyond instrumental considerations highlighted by positive psychology and EI. She thus underscores the importance of cultural and social context in effectively theorising emotional regulation (2011). In particular, culture can be seen as an important factor in emotional regulation, as beliefs about controllability of emotions, and about values and goals, influence self-regulation approaches and strategies (Tamir & Mauss, 2011). Such work also bolsters the view that despite the prevalence of positive psychology approaches that regard the values of emotions in terms of instrumental and hedonic rationales, for many people goals are more eudeamonic and socially oriented (e.g. Parrott, 1993). Nico Frijda and Batja Mesquita (1994) also offer a view of the functionality of emotions that diverges from that emphasised by positive psychologists, observing that emotions serve social purposes within contexts and communities. Others in the field specifically argue against positive psychology, noting how researchers in the area tend to frame their solutions as evidence-based while lacking application of rigorous study methods and designs, thus offering solutions based on 'wishful thinking' rather than evidence (e.g. Coyne & Tennen, 2010).

Relatedly, Tamir (2011, p. 3) observes how emotional regulation research in childhood versus adult experience 'has continued somewhat independently within these two traditions' over time. In this context, the diverse experiences of children engaging in emotional development and regulation have been underemphasised within the positive psychology tradition, with interventions originally oriented towards adults being adapted to children, despite the diverse needs related to emotional regulation and personal and social development across these two groups (e.g. Brownell & Kopp, 2007; Koole, van Dillen, & Sheppes, 2011). Unfortunately, positive psychology's 'wishful thinking' has nonetheless found many receptive audiences among policymakers less concerned with its empirical bases than with its optimism in the face of complexity.

Governments have made well-being part of their educational agenda in societies such as the United Kingdom, Canada, and the United States, favouring and recommending positive psychology and EI approaches to enhance youth well-being. This can be seen as a moral act, in that it helps young people feel (and be) better, particularly if there is a crisis of well-being. On the other hand, from a behavioural, systems-level view, such interventions may also be promoted to keep populations working hard, obedient, docile, and resilient (Boler, 1999), when facing worsening economic prospects and less welfare provision from government bodies (Ecclestone, 2012; Ehrenreich, 2009). Bruce Maxwell and Roland Reichenbach (2007) discuss this as the difference between 'pedagogies of autonomy' and 'pedagogies of control'. While the former is oriented towards the intrinsic value of the positive development of young people as autonomous agents, the latter frames students more as passive objects to be manipulated (emotionally and otherwise), for some apparently 'higher' purpose.

There are some responses to such criticisms and concerns. In relation to charges that emotional education strategies individualise what should more properly be seen as societal problems and challenges, Kristjánsson writes (2013, p. 65):

> ... the question of what should logically come first, the cultivation of positive personal traits or the creation of positive institutions, is a chicken-or-egg question. The important thing is not to waste time wondering where to start but rather to start somewhere. And because it is usually easier to administer personal change ... than large-scale political transformation, there are good pragmatic reasons for starting at the individual level.

Changing systems and changing individuals are not mutually exclusive choices. Additionally, discourse critiquing psychological approaches as individualistic, or victim-blaming, can also, in a sense, dismiss the agency of ordinary people, who may be uncritically framed in such discourse as victims of the status quo. On the other hand, psychologists and other healthcare professionals are not necessarily pushing clinical diagnoses for environmental ills at students and patients. In some cases, people demand diagnoses for possibly environmental challenges from reluctant professionals. Thus, a top-down assessment appears to pit psychologists, politicians, and medical professionals against youth and ordinary people.

Nonetheless, positive psychologists, EI proponents, and others emphasising narrow views of emotional regulation, SEL, and the like focus on one side of the equation, when both individuals and organisational environments matter, to functioning, goodness, and justice. In school contexts, a broader view must be developed, as education has social and moral as well as personal development aims.

2.2 The Politics of Educating Emotions

As discussed in the previous section, predominant psychological discourses on educating emotions focus on individual functioning within
organisations and other social and institutional units. Interventions are
often put upon individuals, to change and harmonise their functioning
with that of the unit: the factory, the economy, or the classroom. By the
'politics of emotions' I refer to findings and perspectives in sociology,
social psychology, and other fields that conceptualise individual versus
societal functioning differently. These latter approaches explore the onus
of accountability and possibility for intervention in relation to groups and
systems, apart from the single individual. Although these views do not
primarily evaluate emotional experiences as morally good or bad, they
invoke questions of social justice because they draw attention to factors
beyond the individual that challenge functioning, moving beyond conflicting personal functions, to how systems and collectives can create
obstacles to individual functioning.

2.2.1 Antecedents

In contrast with positive psychologists, sociologists (and social psychologists, among others) aim to understand how groups fare interactively in
society, and how group and interpersonal relations are harmful or beneficial, or functional or dysfunctional, in patterned ways. Weber observed
how one aspect of social life, such as a religious or other culture, can
enable other systems to flourish, such as economic structures. In the
United States, he saw how Protestant work values and cultural systems
led people to work hard and persevere despite misfortune and challenges
(1959). Emotions thus play a role at a systems level in this view, and
systems of religion and more can relate dynamically to groups in
a society.

From a systems view, emotion has also been linked to dysfunction and
conflict. Durkheim (1951) found that people who are not bonded to others
within society can develop a suicidal sense, experiencing anomie and
alienation. For Marx, a religious work ethic was experienced as dysfunctional for individuals at the bottom of the system. He relatedly viewed the
separation of people into different classes in society as a means to hide
how social conflict is a part of the economic system.

Such thinkers sought to draw principles of justice for society from their
observations. That is, they used their insights to make recommendations
for enhancing society to benefit diverse individuals, rather than to
enhance individuals to benefit society (or some sub-section of it).
Durkheim envisioned sociology as a 'moral science' concerned with 'the

best forms of society' (Gorski, 2017). For Marx, the answer was restructuring the economy to equalise individual work requirements and living conditions.

Foucault further elucidated how institutions and social structures influence people's internal perceptions of self and world, in ways that can benefit institutions as much as, if not more than, ordinary people. Although not focused particularly on emotions, *Discipline and Punish* reveals how multi-pronged surveillance of individuals in society (by people in authority, and others with pastoral power, like priests, psychologists, doctors, and peers) influences people's sense of self, orienting people in many cases to identify deeply with the concerns of governments and institutions (1979). Like Durkheim, Foucault expressed interest in changing society in light of what he saw, and was critical of political processes that he saw as negatively impacting individuals in 'quiet' ways (1984).

Sociologists continue to struggle in diagnosing systems as healthy, moral, or functional, versus flawed, based on empirical evidence, as they show how people face different conditions and possibilities in society, and how social institutions (such as governments) may work towards different interests from those of diverse individuals. Contemporary sociologists thus tend to focus on conflicting functions across individuals and groups. Sociologists and other critical theorists (as well as social psychologists) also consider how emotions are influenced by media, to function for and against particular groups. In the Brexit vote and United States election of Donald Trump (in 2016), human data was used by *Cambridge Analytica* to change people's views (those identified through their data analyses as being more susceptible and impressionable) through targeted information (and misinformation) campaigns. Such targeting has immeasurable value to private and partisan groups, and while some see these processes as reasonable and justified ('the system is working'), others scrutinise them as mass emotional manipulation that can weaken or bend the will of a society, akin to an act of foreign interference in democratic processes (Cadwalladr, 2018; Jackson, 2019a).

Sociologists and other critical theorists of education have for a long time observed how schooling does not benefit all students (in a class, school, or society) equally, although equality of opportunity is a key principle for education around the world. The perpetuation of inequality of opportunity and inequitable achievement is continually traced in research to ascribed categories, such as race and gender, that are not related to merit or will. As achievement is related in patterns to such non-merit factors, such orientations elaborate that some benefit over others at the starting line, and that schooling does not particularly enable equity, despite this being one of its aims. Such work is particularly relevant to the politics of educating emotions.

2.2.2 Educational Applications

Sociological analyses consider how schools systematically reproduce disadvantage, while teaching students that they are meritocratic institutions, and that students are to blame for lack of achievement. Thus, schools shape and influence alienation experienced by some youth (e.g. MacLeod, 2009). As actors beyond the individual, educators are vital factors in school success, who impact students in different ways, intentionally and (often) unintentionally.

Characteristics related to achievement, which include personality and disposition, and other emotional and dispositional qualities, are often recognised by teachers to correlate with ascribed characteristics. A teacher may believe that poor youth, boys, and ethnic minorities are less likely or less motivated to succeed, such as by working hard, having the right attitude, and having emotional maturity or well-being (compared to middle-class and wealthy youth, girls, and ethnic majority young people). They may feel justified in their belief, as it may correlate with outcomes of examinations, educational research, and past experience. The causes of differences in achievement identified in educational research are not based merely in individual functioning or lack thereof. Nonetheless, apparent evidence backs up belief. People tend to prejudge others, based on beliefs as forms of bias (Eberhardt, 2019). In the classroom (as elsewhere in society), biases impact teachers' treatments of students and thus students' self-perceptions and educational circumstances.

When it comes to cultural differences, educators may be invited to engage in this sort of prejudgement as a kind of multicultural recognition. Being culturally aware, and understanding of diversity, is often considered a good thing in schooling and society (DeCuir-Gunby & Williams-Johnson, 2014). However, it is easy for such judgement to go wrong, particularly when it is prejudgement – not based on thoughtful discussions with an individual student but based on knowledge from past students, from first impressions, or in relation to other sources of information. Young people are not simply representatives of cultures, and cultures are not monoliths (Appiah, 1994; Jackson, 2014a). Furthermore, when students feel like they are being treated as different and as the 'other', it can be emotionally uncomfortable and educationally distracting, even if a teacher means well (DeCuir-Gunby & Williams-Johnson, 2014). Stereotype threat is a related emotional challenge, for women and ethnic minorities, 'wherein the performances of members of a stigmatized group are impaired simply by awareness of a pervasive, relevant negative stereotype' (Schutz et al., 2014, p. 363; Steele, 1997). Reminding students about stereotypes – about gender, race, or culture and achievement – can decrease performance, as anxiety and related emotions can be triggered through this recognition.

There are ways to ameliorate these challenges: things that teachers and students can do, think, and believe to try to combat stereotypes and related phenomena. However, often educator biases are not known or intentional, but operate on an unconscious level. These biases can also be experienced by students in an unconscious way. Jennifer Eberhardt (2019) observes that bias based on appearance and other difference is conditioned from infancy, with most people operating across contexts based on unconscious biases, in personal life and the workplace. Unconscious bias impacts women's opportunities in orchestra (with opportunities increasing with 'blind' auditions), and the treatment of people of colour in Western societies, in the public sphere, schooling, and criminal justice (Eberhard, 2019). Bias can be re-educated through training. However, many people intentionally or unintentionally reinforce biases in normal, everyday life, for instance by defending discrimination and differential expectations as normal, natural, or morally good, based on religious or other traditions, or political ideology. Teachers may assess students differently in maths based on gender, without meaning to do so (Riegle-Crumb & Humphries, 2012). Or they may do so intentionally, seeing it as 'natural', or best for society, for boys to be encouraged over girls in maths.

Psychologists observe differences in emotional expressions and experiences among men and women, and boys and girls. At the same time, there are stereotypes and different associations about gender (and race, etc.) and emotions. In this context, emotional virtues are expected of people discriminately, and young people's emotional expressions are judged according to norms which may be the result of prejudicial use of findings, differential expectations, or intentional or unconscious bias. This can be experienced as unequal and discriminatory, and impact people in harmful ways. Stereotype threat is one kind of emotional impact, causing anxiety for those identified with harmful stereotypes. For instance, in relation to maths education, girls express 'more maladaptive emotions, such as anxiety, shame, and hopelessness, and less enjoyment' (Pekrun & Perry, 2014, p. 129). This tends to lead to worse performance, and thus reinforces the stereotype in a vicious cycle.

Thus, a politics of educating emotions approach considers how different groups are expected or encouraged (or not expected or encouraged) to feel and express particular emotions. Such expectations are educational, whether found inside or outside schools. One may try to ignore or resist stereotypes and unfair norms and expectations. Yet the stereotypes linger as they continue to express popular visions of society, and hopes for individuals, to act in accordance with these visions. The expectations are thus also political, as they intersect with views about changing or preserving social orders and community and cultural norms. The expectations and norms of emotional relations and emotional difference impact people in different ways.

2.2.3 Feminist Theorisations

Gender roles remain powerful and prevalent across societies, and much research on emotional expectations observes differences based on gender. For Boler, the 'politics of emotion' is thus a feminist project, as women continue to face barriers in education and elsewhere related to social roles and emotional expectations. Boler's work (1999; Boler & Zembylas, 2016) relies in part on that of Arlie Hochschild. Hochschild (1983) explores how women in caregiving professions – in particular, flight attendants – engage in emotional work in their jobs. She describes this as 'emotional labour'. They do not actually feel like caring, and it is not 'natural' for them to care for customers. They get paid for it, after all. Yet people may assume it is natural for them, in contrast with men counterparts. While men flight attendants (and other men caregivers) are also expected to care about others in such social roles, the emotional expectation is often faced by women across fields as a requirement, while for men in these roles showing and sharing caring affect is more often deemed exceptional and morally praiseworthy (Jackson, 2017a, 2019b).

Hochschild found that flight attendants would over time experience their smiles and 'inner feelings' detaching from themselves and moving to others, in a process of alienation. It began to feel bad for them to work to 'feel good'. Hochschild articulates this experience in terms of 'feeling rules' that people face, when 'focusing on the pinch between "what I do feel" and "what I should feel"', in relation to other people's expectations (1983, p. 57). Experiences of feeling 'wrong feelings' thus reflect a conflict between social expectations and a person's own orientation towards their feelings. Such feeling rules, Hochschild notes, impact people across various kinds of social situations, not only in the workplace. And feeling rules can be applied beyond the workplace as in the workplace, in uneven, unequal, harmful ways.

For psychologists, such feeling rules reflect expectations to function in harmony with others in society. Thinking of people as individuals rather than as part of relations and communities, psychologists may see it as most crucial that people cope well or manage effectively the feeling rules they experience, without directly questioning the nature of these feeling

rules as social expectations, faced in unequal social relations and circumstances. Sociologists, on the other hand, may think more relationally
rather than individualistically, considering who or what perspective is
counted as most important, and reflecting upon who is said to be feeling
the 'right' or 'wrong' way in a situation.

Hochschild further elaborates the difference between a psychological
and sociological approach to understanding individual well-being in
relation to feeling rules, in the case of a woman who is nervous to get
married:

> A psychiatrist might respond to this roughly as follows: 'On the face of
> it, the young woman seems anxious . . . . The cause of her anxiety may
> lie in her ambivalence about marriage, which might be related to
> childhood impressions of her own parents' marriage or perhaps to
> the sexual aspects of it. I would need to know more to say for sure.'
> A sociologist would look at the wedding from quite another point of
> view. To begin with, he or she would consider the ceremony as a ritual
> event . . . . the sociologist could also be concerned with what happened
> in the realm lying between feelings and the external events of the
> ritual – the realm of feeling rules and emotional management . . . .
> When everything goes well, [the bride] experiences a unity between
> the event (the wedding), the appropriate way to think about it (to take
> it seriously), and the proper way to feel about it (happy, elated,
> enhanced). When that happens, the ritual works.   (1983, pp. 60–61)

Feminist theorists explore the possibly harmful experience of feeling
rules being applied based on gender, as a quiet means to maintain and
reproduce unjust, sexist status quos in society, such as lower pay for
caregiving work associated with women, rationalised as work that is
'women's work'.

Ahmed (2010) relatedly examines how discourses concerned about
women's and ethnic minorities' happiness reinforce sexist and racist
social relations. Ahmed traces this discourse in Rousseau's *Emile* (1762).
In *Emile*, the girl Sophie's future is as a happy wife who charms others. In
this framing, a good girl is happy, to make her parents happy, and then
her husband and children happy. Her (fictional) parents are quoted, 'We
want you to be happy, for our sakes as well as yours, for our happiness
depends on yours. A good girl finds her own happiness in the happiness
of a good man' (Rousseau, cited in Ahmed, 2010, pp. 57–58). Sophie's
happiness becomes a shared object of the family in this discussion. Her
potential lack of individual happiness is framed as precluding the happiness of the family. Here, Sophie might feel obliged to conceal possible
unhappiness, as she is encouraged to work to be happy, to maintain
others' happiness. Ahmed finds a similar discourse at work in the stereotype of the 'happy housewife', who is thought of as happiest while caring

for others, and whose foil, the 'feminist killjoy' ruins others' happiness, by refusing to cultivate her own inner happiness.

Girls and women are expected, in workplaces, schools, and elsewhere in society, to be happy as caregivers for others, and seen as naturally better *at* caring, and happiest *when* caring, compared to men (Jackson, 2017a, 2019b; Jackson & Peters, 2019). Such gender stereotypes, even if related to empirically based generalisations, ignore or dismiss diverse women's dispositions, and interests and capacities in various fields, and they can be used to justify gender differences in professional opportunities and achievements. Such stereotypes can encourage girls and women to express happiness they do not feel, potentially enabling in them a sense of alienation, rather than enhancing their emotional states. Happiness is one example. This book will consider a range of emotions discriminately desired and expected (or discouraged and not expected) within groups, in and across contexts, in relation to societal processes enabling inequitable relations.

2.2.4 *Comparing Accounts*

Like psychologists, sociologists and other thinkers exploring the political side of emotions use a combination of data gathering tools to decipher emotions, including interviews and self-report, triangulation with past studies and theoretical models, analysis of relevant texts, and observations. However, in contrast to many psychologists (particularly positive psychologists), those focusing on the politics of emotions do not make recommendations at the individual level, but observe how harms can be experienced in relation to feeling rules and related inequitable experiences in social situations. While psychologists tend to presume, in EI and positive psychology approaches, that feeling good has social and individual value, and therefore support interventions at an individual level that lead to such positive feelings, for the politics of emotions, the relationship of feelings with values is impacted by social roles and norms that create more challenges for some people than for others. The politics of educating emotions also shows how people can be influenced emotionally in problematic ways, to feel anxious, alarmed, disturbed, angry, and afraid (e.g. Sullivan, 2014), to benefit others, or to support and maintain problematic status quos.

These different focuses lead to different diagnoses and solutions. Within education, a sociologist (or a social psychologist) would part ways with a positive psychologist claiming that if students experience emotional challenges, they should work first on emotional regulation, to harmonise their emotional processes with the context (e.g. Miller, Nickerson, & Jimerson, 2014). Here, a sociologist would pay attention to how feelings rules are enforced and learned by students through their relationships with teachers and each other in the environment. They would also question which children (e.g. boys or girls?), in which situations, are expected and allowed by teachers to be angry or happy or sad, and how social expectations may be shaped more by the interests of educators and other stakeholders in society (parents, school leaders, partisan groups, etc.), than by interests expressed by youth themselves. An example of this way of thinking is articulated by Boler (1999) in her research on EI education:

> In this class exercise, each student was asked to mark on a scale on the board how they felt at the moment, from -5 to +5. One girl . . . ranks herself at -5 (and indeed in my estimation 'looked' very sad). The teacher responds to this, 'What do we need to know, class?' Before any student had the opportunity to respond, and without asking the girl herself what she needed or wanted, the teacher answered her own question: 'We want to give her space rather than tease her.' It seemed to me that 'what the class needed to know' was what the young girl herself wanted in response to her distress. The teacher's quick conclusion about how to react to an unhappy student is a fairly minor example of setting an arbitrary norm, which might have an adverse effect on the girl. But one can easily imagine other examples of arbitrary impositions of the educator's authority with much harder effects on students.   (pp. 100–101)

People's emotions, and capacities in regard to understanding and regulating them, can be impacted by experiences and situations beyond their control, such as poor economic conditions or developmental challenges. In this context, an approach cognisant about the politics of emotion does not focus on promoting the cultivation of personal well-being regardless of such conditions, but questions whether people should be asked or expected to adapt (or blamed for not adapting) to such systems, when the systems treat people differently in some cases, while often ignoring diversity, thereby structuring discriminately harmful environments. They thus scrutinise the system as much as individuals within it. This view gives space to attend to possibilities to change systems and conditions, rather than individuals. It also gives space to consider that systems may be harmful (emotionally and in other ways) to some students, and unjust. If a situation, like a classroom, is unjust, then bad feelings of a student may be a sign the classroom should change, not the student.

Thus, when it comes to the anxious student described at the beginning of this chapter, the politics of emotions prompts consideration of whether their anxiety could be caused not just by functional or dysfunctional personal factors, but by past experiences: such as of being bullied, of being marked as poor at presenting in the past despite efforts made, of seeing other students with similar personality or identity traits being poorly received by peers when publicly speaking, and so on. It encourages examination of how the student's anxiety relates to how they are treated by others more generally and to expectations of teachers and others towards them. The question is not simply whether the feelings are functional or not, but how functions may conflict with one another and how the classroom or school as an organisation structures and influences feeling experiences of students.

Research in educational psychology has recognised how cultural differences and bias play a role in educational success and the related development of emotional well-being. Yet the field has not thus far developed adequately for studying cross-cultural differences in emotional well-being (DeCuir-Gunby & Williams-Johnson, 2014). Thinking once more of the anxious student described at the beginning of the chapter, Jessica DeCuir-Gunby and Meca Williams-Johnson note (2014, p. 545) that most 'anxiety research takes a Western approach, including the methodology and assessments', while 'it is necessary to take cultural values into consideration when comparing groups – otherwise, any interpretations made will be questionable. Lastly, researchers cannot assume that different cultures view and experience anxiety in the same way.' Thus, there are various ways educational relations can be negative emotional experiences for young people, such as if they are misrecognised by teachers due to unconscious bias, conscious prejudice, or cross-cultural misrecognition.

Changing systems, like cultural norms, a classroom, or an environment, is more challenging and complex than changing individuals. In support of individual-based approaches, an individual is in a sense a smaller-scale, less complicated unit to analyse and interact with than macro entities. It is also difficult (if not impossible) to be scientific (generalising, validating) about 'what works' in intervening in environments which are complex, dynamic, and diverse. It is hard to diagnose a school simply as functional or dysfunctional, healthy or unhealthy.

Meanwhile, a dark cloud lingers over diverse societies, regarding the nature of gender and race differences, with continued debate about whether differences are somehow biological versus socialised, despite the fact that commonly held disparate social expectations and biases noticeably impact people (based on gender and race, among other factors) differently in real life. Thinking through the macro and micro again, such situations are not as simple as they are treated in the formulas for intervention provided by EI and related approaches. Positive psychologists and EI proponents have hardly done away with immoral and harmful individuals or environments in the world, or eradicated anxiety or depression, through individual-based models (which ideally take into account the environment people are in). Furthermore, that something is very complicated is not a moral reason to ignore or neglect its harmful impacts. The orientations of EI and positive psychology also tend to overlook some emotional processes, such as those of people with alexithymia, as discussed previously.

A 'politics of emotions' view thus prompts consideration of some aspects of individual and social functioning and well-being (and lack thereof) poorly understood from these mainstream psychological orientations. Actually, insights from critical political and sociological views of education are generally well-aligned with findings in social psychology. However, social psychology has been far less influential in education, despite its important observations related to such topics as stereotype treat and educator bias. In this context, reflecting upon the politics of emotions can help complement findings from social psychology in highlighting the significant limitations of individualistic thinking commonly applied to educating emotional virtues. These views have distinctive insights when applied to understanding emotional processes and educating emotional virtues, and they should not be neglected in place of an all-encompassing search for quick fixes and cures.

2.3 Conclusion

This chapter gave an overview of how emotions in individuals and in society are understood in two social science frameworks of relevance to education. In relation, it elaborated some pitfalls of social science-derived understandings of emotions. Many assume that 'we know what works' in educating emotional virtues. However, in psychology, emotions, emotional processes, and the results of interventions on emotions in education can be hard to understand and identify, given challenges of observation, self-report, and other means of gleaning the unconscious, undeveloped, and otherwise dynamic emotional experiences of people. At the same time, there can be a gap between understanding social practice as moral versus functional, from a psychological view. To be functional in a system, and psychologically well, is not necessarily to be good or moral. Furthermore, positive psychology and related approaches to educating emotional virtues have not been well developed as school-based interventions, as they have not been related systematically to experiences of diverse students, or across cultures.

In a politics of emotions perspective, the system or organisation of a classroom or society, and the relationship of teachers to students, may be scrutinised as not normal, natural, or just but as factors that shape disparate experiences across people (i.e. students in a classroom). As a result, thinkers with more political and sociological concerns may use similar data to that of psychologists to consider how systems, rather than individuals, are dysfunctional and, possibly, harmful or unjust. When applied to the topic of emotional education, this approach highlights how people's emotions are expected and treated differently, possibly in biased ways, which can be harmful and unfair. However, neither approach provides a firm foundation to understand school-based practices for educating emotional virtues as moral or immoral. Chapter 3 considers more philosophically based views on the morality of educating emotional virtues.

Views of Emotions in Moral Philosophy

This chapter continues to present an overview of major approaches to understanding the value of emotions in schools and society, turning to relevant orientations from moral philosophy and other related views of the good life. The perspectives explored here are intersecting, not mutually exclusive, with the approaches discussed in Chapter 2. On the one hand, the perspectives explored in Chapter 2 also dealt in part with the morality, goodness, or value of emotions, particularly those related to a politics of emotion which are influenced by political theory, feminist theory, and social justice orientations. On the other hand, the philosophical views explored in this chapter are also informed by empirical evidence. What distinguishes the views here from those in Chapter 2 is that the latter are based more on empirical understandings, rather than philosophical explorations. Chapter 2 discusses approaches based on systematic engagements with human data, observations, and texts. The work in this chapter explores the moral and human world more abstractly, with less basis in social and empirical examinations.

As seen here, philosophers throughout history have pondered how emotions, rationality, and morality intersect and its implications for education. This chapter presents an overview of basic points and issues of contention within and across philosophical perspectives related to these topics. Here, I consider particularly deontology, consequentialism, virtue ethics, care ethics and other relational views, and existentialism. I spend more time examining virtue ethics than other orientations, as virtue ethics is seen to philosophically undergird the majority of morally oriented social and emotional learning (SEL) and character education approaches in Western societies today. How emotions are understood in virtue ethics overlaps in some cases with that found in the social sciences, as well as that seen within some Eastern traditions. Confucianism, Daoism, and Buddhism will also be discussed here. This chapter thus summarises major insights and points of debate across some of the most pertinent philosophical traditions related to educating emotions.

3.1 Deontology

Deontology judges the moral worth of actions based on whether or not they follow moral principles or standards, derived from reasoning. Being rule-based and rationalist, deontology gives little to no space for emotions in reasoning, typically suspicious about their influence. Kant particularly argues against sentimentality, the excessive use of emotions. In contrast with personal autonomy, he elaborates heteronomy as being ruled by passions or others, in 'An Answer to the Question: "What is Enlightenment?"' (1784). When recommending activities to cultivate morality, Kant considers whether and how emotional experiences could interfere with rational thinking, discouraging tendencies to be more caring or compassionate than rational (Jackson, 2007, 2017b).

A deontological view of education aims at learning moral principles, which are believed to be attained through reason rather than through appeals to emotion or other forms of knowing (Crittenden, 1999; Rawls, 2000; Jackson, 2007). In this case, teaching for critical thinking about ethics is also valued, to develop students' capacities for arriving at autonomous judgements, working against the threats of conventionality, feelings, or other interpersonal, communal, or cultural values and biases (see also Maxwell & Reichenbach, 2007). Such a view contrasts with psychological views that regard good feelings as directly related to good actions, such as the positive psychology and emotional intelligence (EI) views examined in Chapter 2.

Lawrence Kohlberg supports a view of rational autonomy as an end of moral development, regarding interpersonal 'social-order maintaining' and other 'conventional' and normative perspectives as inferior (1981). Kohlberg studied how boys and men reasoned, to argue that moral education should be focused on learning to make decisions based on abstract principles, rather than feelings or cultural values (Colby & Kohlberg, 1987). Kohlberg argues that students exposed to his stages of moral reasoning at school – to a view of justice as ruled by abstract, universal principles – would most effectively develop civic character (1981). He thus claims that moral development leads people from (1) emotional, self-interested orientations, to (2) interpersonal and conformist orientations, then towards (3) depersonalised social contract views, and, finally, (4) universal ethical principles.

Hand also defends teaching moral standards with little regard for feelings or emotions. Hand does not identify as a deontologist, noting that he leaves 'open the question of whether there is more to morality, and hence more to moral education, than moral standards and justificatory beliefs' (2018, p. 27). However, Hand is sympathetic to Rawls' and Kant's views in his work. Hand (2011) regards emotions as risky in civic and character education, as they can 'cloud' civic and moral judgement about standards for decision-making and action.

The influence of Kohlbergian thinking can be seen in both informal and formal lessons focusing on rational moral principles – to tell the truth, to act fairly – as well as in slogans, such as 'think for yourself', and the encouragement of other attitudes related to independent, impartial judgement (although virtue ethicists could also claim influence here). Kohlberg also recommends learning through case studies and in democratic school communities in his 'Just Schools' approach (Power, Higgins, & Kohlberg, 1989; D'Alessandro, 2015). One of Kohlberg's case studies considers whether or not a man should steal an expensive drug when he is unable to pay for it to save his wife's life. The student's answer is evaluated according to the rationale given. Commitment to impartial use of principled reasoning is seen as moral progress, over consideration of more partial or subjective factors or reasons.

In a sense, this model and Kohlberg's views have influenced educational thought and practice in Western societies, particularly as schools have over time become more commonly regarded as akin to democratic communities, where student autonomy is highly valued (D'Alessandro, 2015). Although not identifying with any fundamental moral theory like deontology, Meira Levinson also takes up the ideas that schools should engage students as collective actors (2014), and that teaching for and in a democracy can progress through the use of substantive case studies (Levinson & Fay, 2016, 2019). On the other hand, Kohlberg's suggestion that moral education should be a key focus of schooling, with educators as advocates of justice and moral reason, has not found mainstream popularity, as the specific moral purposes of schooling have remained more contentious in and across societies (D'Alessandro, 2015).

In relation, many are sceptical of the notion of universal moral positions and purely rational moral reasoning implied in Kant's and Rawls' work. A well-known critique is communitarian (MacIntyre, 1989). One part of this reply is that universal moral rules described in any substantive manner do not capture and reflect a common will across humanity, or even that of people in the same society, as they are biased towards cultural and other characteristics that shape all people's thinking. Furthermore, so-called communitarians note that such orientations are overly individualistic, suggesting that people can and do reason and think of themselves as separate from others in the moral domain. (I examine this claim in Jackson, 2007.)

Kohlberg promotes his views as empirically confirming a process of apparently universal, linear moral development (Kohlberg, Levine, & Hewer, 1983). Yet evidence of ordinary people normally developing as stipulated is weak. Kohlberg's initial studies focused on the experiences and expressions of a rather homogenous group of white boys and men. Other studies using Kohlberg's framework show differences across cultures and societies. Furthermore, 'even in the most favourable conditions, no more than 2 to 4 per cent' of subjects achieve the highest 'stage profile' (Crittenden, 1999, p. 176). Such a challenge need not spell doom; Kohlberg (among others) intended to develop aspirational moral ideals and exemplars in his work which can motivate people, even if they are not entirely achievable. Nonetheless, these findings contradict the claim that morality develops from emotionality to impartiality in practice.

A related critique of Kohlberg's model is feminist in orientation. When Kohlberg's framework was applied to research with girls and women, they were found to develop less in relation to his stages. To effectively regard boys and men as more morally developed or morally capable than girls and women implies, as Carol Gilligan (1982) argues, that girls and women are deficient in relation to universal moral stages. As an alternative, Gilligan argues that women have a different kind of moral experience, which is more caring and relational, and less independent, impersonal, and rational, not captured in Kohlberg's schema. For Gilligan, this is not due to any essential or biological difference between girls and boys, but due to social structures and expectations that place women in caregiving roles in families and elsewhere in society.

Another more general line of attack against deontology is that deontological judgements are based on emotions, even if Kant (and Rawls and Kohlberg, etc.) denies it. Susan Moller Okin (1989) notes that assumptions about caring, benevolence, and empathy underlie Rawls' principles of justice despite his apparent attempts in some of his work to follow Kant in separating morality from feelings. Joshua Greene argues in relation to Kant with reference to brain activity studies that 'emotional response predicts deontological judgment' (2007, p. 68). Greene and colleagues thus charge that emotional feeling normally guides morality more than is usually presumed in rule-based theories (Greene et al., 2004, p. 397).

A final charge against deontology is that it paints a cold, unattractive picture of the social and moral landscape. As Paul Crittenden (1999) describes it, 'this is a world of impersonal principles and fundamental rights and duties, in which caring about the people one loves might appear problematic or to lie outside the moral domain altogether' (p. 179). Eamonn Callan, though supportive of a Rawlsian-based framework for ethics in education, argues that Kohlberg's theory is inordinately abstract, lacking 'commonsense recognition that contextual sensitivity is crucial to the interpretation of rights' (1997, p. 74). Similarly, John White (1990) describes Hand's view as an overly strict and uncaring ethics: a 'combination of rigid adherence to favoured values, unwillingness to compromise, and the pervasive tendency to blame oneself and others for moral defects' (p. 53).

This latter challenge has been recognised, and dismissed, by those favouring a rationality-based approach to morality and emotions. To White, Hand replies, 'the unloveliness of moral emotions hardly compares with the unloveliness of the conduct it is their function to prevent. Violence, theft, deception, cruelty and injustice blight human lives much more profoundly than guilt and blame' (2018, p. 114). Hand emphasises once more: 'Children's sympathies can certainly be educationally extended, but they cannot be so far extended as to change the circumstances of justice' (2018, p. 121). For Callan, the limitations of Kohlberg's work do not detract from the merits of a Rawlsian theory of justice. In Callan's view, Kohlberg simply gets the judgement wrong, abstracting humanity out of the picture in a way that leads to 'ridiculous' moral conclusions (1997, p. 74). Nonetheless, Callan (1997) continues to argue that relational feelings are never superior foundations for action or justice, even if they are more palatable to some.

Though dominant in the 1970s and 1980s, Kohlberg's views have decreased in influence. Many now see deontology as unrealistic and unpalatable. Relatedly, some hold that there is no need for anyone – scholar or layperson – to select and comply with one particular moral stance in life, like deontology (among others), which is too restrictive and limited in its view to be helpful in everyday moral decision-making (Prinz, 2007; Levinson & Fay, 2016). While some still find its sense of justice as impartiality compelling (e.g. Nagel, 1979), others discard deontology in favour of views seen as less rigid, and more relational and contextually sensitive.

3.2   Consequentialism

Consequentialism is also basically rule-based. It holds that moral duty is related to the consequences of rules or actions. Such consequences could be related to emotions, thus compelling people to seek pleasure or happiness, such as in the hedonic utilitarian stances of Bentham (1789) and Mill (1861). However, consequences are normally considered at a broader level than the good (or pleasure) that an act (or principle) might produce for a single person. Thus, utilitarians consider what actions or principles maximise good or well-being across a community, calculating the morality of options in terms of costs and benefits, overall. A common tool for teaching this view (particularly alongside deontology) is the trolley problem (Foot, 1967). In the trolley problem, five people are tied to a trolley track and about to be killed by an approaching trolley. The trolley has a lever, however, that can be pulled, to direct the trolley to another track, to which only a single person is tied. One thus has the choice to act by pulling the lever and kill one person to save five others. Alternatively, they can 'do nothing', as five people are about to die. Deontologists and other rights advocates typically see it as wrong to intentionally harm anyone (thus refusing to pull the lever), while consequentialists will see it as better to act (pull the lever) to save five lives and sacrifice one.

The most influential variant of moral consequentialism encourages a focus on duties to the greater good, over one's own inconveniences, discomforts, or other negative feelings in making sacrifices. Singer (1972, 1993) argues that well-off people should make personal sacrifices (greater sacrifices than they are normally expected to make, such as giving substantial financial donations to charity) that can make a big difference in the lives of those less fortunate, in the context of global inequality and widespread poverty. In one of his latest texts, he appeals to readers to track the negative impact of emotions on their behaviour in such cases. As he writes, 'reasoning may tell you that you ought to be doing something substantial to help the world's poorest people, but your emotions may not move you to act in accordance with this view' (2019, p. 257). He argues here that people tend to act too quickly in relation to their feelings, and not act based on relevant reasoning processes, when attempting to act morally in society.

People at times express an intuitive resonance with consequentialism and utilitarianism, particularly with the simple set-up of the trolley problem (Navarrete et al., 2012). Furthermore, utilitarian cost–benefit analyses can often be seen to play a part in institutional decision-making by governments and other actors. In the United Kingdom, Richard Layard argues for social policy that enhances well-being, claiming that mental health interventions should be supported by the government because they will lead to a stronger economy, as many people suffering from mental health issues are of working age, but need to recover to become healthier and participate more effectively in society (Layard & Clark, 2015; Clark et al., 2018). Relatedly, nudge theory (Thaler & Sunstein, 2008) argues that 'health, wealth, and happiness' can be enhanced in society through altering the landscape for people to make personal choices, so that people can act more to support their own and others' best interests in the future.

There is also a sense in which positive psychology and EI are consequentialist. After all, their proponents promote the development of cognitive and emotional traits not (precisely or explicitly) because they are intrinsically moral, but because they are instrumentally useful, as they are regarded generally as benefit-producing, and as 'what works' (Guha & Carson, 2014). Psychologists in their work do not typically defend certain emotions specifically because they are morally good, but rather they justify their benefits by discussing what they cause or enable that is good in the future.

Schools also teach partly for a consequentialist way of thinking, at least in some informal manners. In relation to teaching virtues of compassion and generosity, schools might encourage or facilitate young people donating or volunteering in support of less advantaged people and social justice causes (Jackson, 2019a). Teachers may, following an EI or positive psychology orientation, teach students EI or about positive emotional dispositions, in order to benefit those students or others in the future. Doing homework which does not inherently bring joy is often connected to future well-being, as receiving good grades early on and habituating studiousness are seen by parents and educators as important means for obtaining professional qualifications later in life. Teachers also generally want young people to develop capacities to understand consequences over time, and make choices related to them.

However, as a kind of overall code for making moral decisions or living moral life, consequentialism is not commonly defended or favoured in moral or civic education. Some critics of Singer argue that his recommendations are morally overly demanding and psychologically burdensome, expecting all people to take responsibility for serious structurally based injustices they cannot possibly resolve as individuals (Corbett, 1995; Pettit, 1997). In relation, Greene (2013) notes how people with alexithymia, unable to identify their emotions, are more likely to make utilitarian judgements, as they are less likely to experience issues with empathy or other kinds of emotional discomfort that may plague others, in cases such as the trolley problem. Greene and colleagues thus argue that, as in the case of deontology, emotional processes (and lack thereof) inevitably play a role in utilitarian decision-making, including in evaluations of better and worse outcomes (2004).

Others question the assumption that one can predict the outcomes of actions adequately. Noddings makes this point about the epistemology (and possible biases therein) of utilitarianism, also questioning Singer's calculating process:

> It is presumptuous to suppose that we can determine the greatest good for large numbers of people with whom we have no direct contact, and it too easily passes over the assessment of the acts themselves. We are not behaving morally if we turn our backs on the present other in order to give some good to a large number of others. At best, we are behaving expediently. (1984, p. 185)

Singer dismisses such concerns, defending an idealistic view of human capacity as a means to broaden people's minds, to at least lay a foundation towards more compassionate ways of living, even if his view may appear to ask too much of ordinary people (1972). Nevertheless, although clearly influential in shaping public policy, utilitarianism is not emphasised in the field of moral education as much as other frameworks.

3.3 Virtue Ethics

Virtue ethics encourages a sense of a moral mean state between deficient and excessive states, when it comes to dispositions, cognitive evaluations, and emotions. For instance, to be thoughtful is better than its deficiency – thoughtlessness – or its excess – obsessiveness. The main virtues are those associated with treating others well, such as beneficence, generosity, compassion, gratitude, patience, tolerance, and humility.

Among virtue ethicists, not all hold the same view of the relation between virtue and emotion. But there are common trends. For Aristotle, 'emotions and emotion-like states are, along with actions, important "outputs" of virtues' (Roberts, 2017, p. 22). For most virtue ethicists, a subjective feeling is important in having a virtue. People should not tell the truth only on the rational basis that they know it is judged as right in society, or due to a desire to appear good to others. They should not even do it merely because they believe (or know) it is good to do so. Rather, they should tell the truth out of an internal appreciation for the virtue (of honesty) and with a subjective feeling related to desiring to be honest. Moral beliefs are thus related to feelings and actions in such an account. This is in contrast with a deontological or utilitarian view, in combining rational judgement and feeling.

For Aristotelian virtue ethics, an emotion should be rationally formed within a mean state between excess and deficit, as the basis for moral judgement. Emotion should not be prioritised over, or dismissed against, evaluative judgement in practical wisdom. Rather, a fusion of rationality (or reason) and emotions should be strived for. Kristjánsson (2018) describes this view as soft rationalism, as reasoning is of value separately from emotional experience here, while emotions still play a fundamental role alongside reasoning in the good life (see also Roberts, 2003, 2013).

In education, according to Aristotelian virtue ethicists, young people should, and normally do, cultivate morality through habituation initially. In this process, caregivers and educators first 'hone' children's character. Over time, young people (ideally) develop a more independent capacity to make reflective choices, as they develop the intellectual virtue of *phronesis* (Kristjánsson, 2018). Following this, a virtue ethics approach encourages children and young people to emulate role models and habituate good behaviours, before they internalise reasoned ways of being virtuous, over a variety of situations (Sherman, 1999). It is thought that

through emulation and habituation, through engaging in virtuous behaviour repeatedly over time, one can become better at acting virtuously,
and develop a sense of enjoyment in performing virtuous acts, motivating
more virtuous behaviour in turn (Sreenivasan, 2020).

Nancy Sherman (1999) highlights the role of emotions in virtue. She
writes, '[E]motions play a crucial epistemic role in the moral life in their
function of recording information' (p. 40). In addition to facilitating
reflection on moral matters, emotions shape communication. By implication, understanding one's emotions must be part of exercising practical
wisdom, lest one communicate feeling without reflection. Apart from
instrumental uses, emotions provide for virtuous relations and for flourishing of individuals and those around them (Sherman, 1999).

Virtue ethics thus defines as virtuous states and acts coinciding with
a full experience of a virtuous feeling. In the real world, such virtue 'will
involve multiple dispositions, modes of receptivity, and concern', 'deepening of understanding, increasing subtlety of discernment and judgment', and 'enlarged moral imagination, maturing deliberative ability,
and a firming of certain motivational propensities' (Jacobs, 2017, p. 136).
The cultivation of virtue requires continuously developing emotional
habits and reflections, so that emotion is 'cognitively informed'. At the
same time, 'an ethically decent person will see that virtue and practical
wisdom are always incomplete, that there are always ways in which
virtues can be more fully integrated, and that experience can provide
reasons for striving to revise some of one's reactions, perhaps some of
one's desires, and making adjustments in one's self-conception' (Jacobs,
2017, p. 139).

Yet in reality people often experience a mixture of states and do not
always feel a sense of virtuous certainty. At the same time, people's
behaviour varies from one situation to the next (Sreenivasan, 2020).
These features of virtue ethics make it difficult to fully attain, for
Aristotle recommends moral consistency as part of virtuous development. More generally, virtue ethics is often seen as not as operationali-
sable as rule-based theories, as which factors are most important in
decision-making is not clear in real-world situations (Johansson &
Svensson, 2018). Thus, virtue ethics is regarded as more complex to
practise in everyday situations, in comparison with deontology and
consequentialism.

Christian Miller articulates such concerns as part of virtue ethics'
'realism challenge' (2014, p. 22). While the main goal of virtue ethics is
to become virtuous, most fall short in reality, tending to be virtuous or not
based on situations, and even moods. In this context, it is in line with
a virtue ethics view, Miller claims, to nonetheless continue to work
towards virtue, considering obstacles to virtuousness, and looking to

saintly role models, even if emulating them fully is not realistic. Miller argues relatedly that 'it would take a serious revision of our ordinary thinking to claim that we should not try to emulate the characters of our moral heroes and saints such as Jesus, Gandhi, or one of our friends or family members' (2014, p. 24).

Virtue ethics is more aligned with positive psychology and EI than the other approaches examined thus far in this chapter, in that feelings are regarded as central to a good moral life. However, virtue ethics differs in its underlying justification. While virtue ethics emphasises that which makes thought and behaviour moral, positive psychology emphasises what makes feelings and judgements productive and beneficial to oneself and/or others. EI and positive psychology give no specifically moral justification for cultivating an emotional state or disposition, viewing positive feelings as functional, productive, and healthy. For example, positive feelings are said to provide medical benefits, while negative feelings cause harm, such as high blood pressure (Goleman, 1997, pp. 168–177).

Nonetheless, EI proponents and positive psychologists use the language of virtues to describe their views. Furthermore, despite their different foundations, for many educators virtue ethics and positive psychology (or EI) go hand in hand, as both focus on the goodness of emotional states and similar strategies for their cultivation. Nancy Snow argues that the value of 'social intelligence' (SI) as 'the cognitive and affective knowledge, skills, and sensitivities needed to deal with people and effectively navigate social life' can serve as justification for cultivating virtue ethics, as virtues can be seen as forms of SI (2010, p. 118). For Snow, SI and EI education could be part of character education for virtue ethics, but not constitute such a curriculum entirely.

Virtue ethics is popular in philosophy and education, as it is seen as resonant with how young people are thought to develop moral character (e.g. Carr, Arthur, & Kristjánsson, 2017). Adults expect young children to form habits, and follow elders in moral matters, before desiring that they think more deeply and develop more independently as they mature. Virtue ethics has been incorporated particularly into the work of the Jubilee Centre for Character and Virtues, founded in 2012 at the University of Birmingham School of Education. Along with promoting character education, Centre publications conceive and endorse 'virtue literacy' as 'virtue perception' and understanding, and 'virtue reasoning' (Jubilee, 2017). The centre recommends a virtues education that encourages students to reflect on emotions and how they intersect with perceptions. Emotional management is part of learning critical thinking and reasoning skills, in this view (Harrison, Arthur, & Burn, 2016).

As one Jubilee guide for emotional virtues education notes, 'developing the virtues involves becoming emotionally skilful ... This is a demanding process which begins with an awareness of feelings' (Harrison et al., 2016, p. 135). The guide presents a 'mood map', which indicates how adrenaline and serotonin interrelate with feelings in 'zones' of performance, recovery, burnout, and survival:

> If I identify that I am in the survival zone and that my adrenaline levels are high, this tells me that if I want to move zones, I need to do something to reduce my adrenaline (e.g. mindful breathing) or something to increase my serotonin (e.g. time with good friends, or seeing something funny), or both. By building up a repertoire of activities which I know to affect my emotions in predictable ways, I can start to become more skilful in the way that I experience emotion.
>
> (Harrison et al., 2016, p. 135)

Much such work in translating virtue ethics into character education is well conceptualised, using insights from psychological and philosophical perspectives. However, there are some limitations to these approaches and to virtue ethics philosophy.

First, as is the case with other orientations, this framework tends to suggest a universal perspective, as people are implicitly seen as roughly equal or the same. Virtue ethics remains dominated by public, and men-authored situations and viewpoints. However, 'women encounter dilemmas which are not typically part of men's lived experiences' (Berges, 2015, p. 5; e.g. Jackson, 2017a, 2019b). Character education is meant to function to benefit the school community as a whole, but in this community not all students are the same in their experiences or perspectives (Suissa, 2015, 2016). Nonetheless, the 'I' in the extract above has no context, culture, or social position. In relation, while Miller defends virtue ethics as it is 'ordinary thinking ... to emulate the characters of our moral heroes and saints such as Jesus, Gandhi, or one of our friends or family members' (2014, p. 24), this takes for granted a substantive cultural context. From cultural views that emphasise disparate and hierarchical social roles and relations (such as Confucianism), it may appear arrogant (or inept) to work to emulate saints as individuals, or particular family members.

Jubilee authors recommend that virtues guides be contextualised before being used and do not suggest importing their texts to other societies (Harrison et al., 2016). The importance of cultural difference is acknowledged in much work on virtue ethics which considers how virtues may be expressed or seen differently across cultures (Carr & Steutel, 1999; Kristjánsson, 2007). Kristjánsson (2018) additionally examines the difficulty in applying Aristotelian thought to justice issues particular to communities and societies, as he concedes that: 'Care ethicists, who understand the self-goals of emotion education explicitly in terms of improving self-*relations*, may have the strongest weapons in their arsenal . . . Aristotle did think that human character must be cultivated at the individual and family-level before being extended to society at large' (p. 175, emphasis in the original).

However, people within a context experience different situations and social positions relative to one another in the same instance, while cultural diversity is not an unusual situation across educational settings today. These environmental and political aspects are not foregrounded, even within promotions of situated virtues development. The primary emphasis in virtue ethics is cultivation of the self (Berges, 2015; Tessman, 2005). Thus, civic virtues become secondary to individual inner landscapes. As Sandrine Berges (2015, p. 123) notes, 'although we need others around to learn and practise our virtues, the focus is always on ourselves and our development'.

Examining Nussbaum's (2016) Aristotelian-inspired recommendations for people to work through anger, for the good of themselves and for that of society, demonstrates the limitations of this primary focus on inner cultivation. In Nussbaum's framing of the moral role of emotions, she extracts personal feelings, experiences, and behaviour from power relations in a situation. In exploring anger, she distinguishes 'taking something personally' and being inappropriately vengeful, from a good, more impartial, 'not-quite-angry' response. Yet because her focus is self-cultivation, other critical issues drop from her analysis. In her (2016) discussion of a woman's response to discovering that her friend was raped, Nussbaum considers the woman friend's response, apart from the injustice of the rape. In this case, Nussbaum claims that feeling vengeful and wanting to lower the status of the rapist is inappropriate (2016). She argues that preventing future rape is not served by such feelings, so exercising practical wisdom would encourage the woman friend to be less angry, or not angry. Others also prioritise self-cultivation over more angry and intolerant responses to harm and injustice in their work. Patrick Fitzgerald (1998) argues that people should follow the Dalai Lama in striving to cultivate gratitude when they have been severely harmed, physically abused, or politically oppressed, because anyone, or all people, can cultivate gratitude, even in such cases of extreme harm.

It is not self-evident that practical wisdom requires such responses. Alternatively, within a social context, working at the outset to maintain a constructive, positive attitude in response to these issues may communicate acceptance and tolerance of injustice, and express acceptance of the status quo in relation to these challenges. (These points will be further

62   *Views of Emotions in Moral Philosophy*

considered in Chapter 9.) Thought experiments of Nussbaum and Fitzgerald seem to ask abused and raped women (in major examples that they give) to 'grin and bear it' to some degree, but other approaches which are more tolerant of upset and outrage may be less harmful in relation to abused and raped women's well-being (and for preventing future cases of rape and abuse). Virtue ethics thus tends to err on the side of the status quo, rather than encouraging action against harm or wrong-doing, due to the primary focus on self-cultivation, and developing as a highly (perhaps overly) reasonable person at the individual level. Virtue ethics does not encourage 'doing nothing' in cases of injustice. But at the same time, it also does not specifically encourage doing any-thing or viewing direct action as valuable in such cases, due to the inward turn initially encouraged in a situation, and the framing of character strengths as morally and politically neutral (Suissa, 2016).

Virtue ethics is therefore not particularly constructive when it comes to addressing and responding to political and social problems (rather than personal ones). Of course, for most people the personal, political, and the social are not always easy to distinguish from each other in real life. In relation, Lisa Tessman (2005) describes being troubled that 'as I tried to think . . . which character traits could be recommended as virtues within the context of liberatory political movements . . . [I saw] virtues that, while practically necessitated for surviving oppression or morally necessitated for opposing it, carry with them a cost for the bearer' (p. 4). As she writes, virtue ethicists such as Aristotle acknowledge that virtue is not sufficient for flourishing, and how demanding virtues can be, and yet:

> Aristotle did not anticipate that such virtues would be pervasive, because he did not theorize how the bad luck that produces adverse conditions (for basically good people) could be systemic and unrelent-ing. This unlinking of virtue from a good life can take place under conditions of moral conflict, where the competing demands produced by great injustice force even the most virtuous agent to leave some 'ought' unfulfilled and to subsequently be regretful or sorrowful or ill at ease with her/himself; and a similar unlinking can follow from maintaining character traits that are praiseworthy due to their efficacy for a politics of resistance, but that forfeit their bearer's well-being because they are self-sacrificial or corrosive or crowd out other valu-able traits.   (Tessman, 2005, p. 5)

Nussbaum (2016) and Fitzgerald (1998) distinguish unhealthy and immoral acceptance of injustice from healthy and moral responses. Yet their accounts overlook how those with bad luck in the context of struc-tural social injustice, such as rape or abuse victims, nonetheless remain at risk of further serious damage to themselves, through trying to meet (and possibly meeting) social expectations to cultivate virtues of forgiveness, releasing feelings of anger in cases of harm, as they suggest. Tessman describes virtues as 'burdened' in these cases, which are not particularly unusual, but part of the realm of everyday concerns for some people (rape and abuse of women is not particularly rare; see CPS, 2019), although they may not be common experiences for virtue ethicists.

The burden of virtues is neglected in most approaches to educating emotional virtues, because they urge students to work on personal responses to problems, rather than (or before) working on the problems themselves, as interpersonal or social. As a result, the value of critically evaluating and responding to social injustice and harm is deemphasised. Jubilee Centre-developed curricula praise Anne Frank for humility, and Rosa Parks for bravery, leaving aside the value of learning more specifically about the horrors of the Holocaust and Jim Crow (Jubilee Centre, 2014). As Judith Suissa notes, this 'shifts the emphasis away from … collective political movements and the hope and belief they embody that the political system can be radically changed' (2015, p. 115; 2016). The political and sociological context of decision-making becomes invisible in these approaches to moral and civic education, given their orientation towards practical wisdom within oneself.

Such approaches may also whitewash history to emphasise self-cultivation. Nussbaum (2016) cites King, Gandhi, and Mandela as examples of not-too-angry people, to promote her stance against anger. Yet these individuals spoke of and expressed anger, and channelled it into their work, rather than lacking it, despite Nussbaum's claims (see Chapter 9). Anyone learning from these cases, as framed by Nussbaum, would be deceived about the nature of 'moral sainthood', and disempowered from understanding the actual conditions under which these heroes cultivated themselves, while also organising with others to systematically change society. Such approaches also do not enable young people to understand how virtues may be 'burdened', and how and why they should take actions against harms and injustices faced.

Virtue ethicists concede the 'realism challenge', and may also emphasise that intentionally harmful education, and 'efforts at the *indoctrination* of traits are inimical to' developing practical wisdom (Kristjánsson, 2018, p. 174, emphasis in the original; also 2007). Kristjánsson (2013a) also argues that while some approaches to Aristotelian character education may be politically conservative and individualistic, this need not be at the heart of such character education. Nonetheless, character education which focuses on traits apart from social circumstances and relational issues orients young people towards the status quo at the outset, given also that traits are first to be habituated and modelled, before being regarded as demanding the exercise of individual practical wisdom. As a kind of character education, such an approach can thus be paternalistic, as young people may be told that others (i.e. teachers in a classroom setting) know better than they do what they should feel and what is good for them, at the outset. Practical wisdom is thus risky to teach, given burdened virtues and students' needs to become social actors, not just people of virtue, in society.

In relation, texts describing virtue ethics and their cultivation rarely if ever discuss political or social participation in a sustained way, apart from what individual character traits should be developed, modelled, and idealised (e.g. Arthur, 2019; Harrison & Walker, 2018). As moral worth is associated with 'the extent to which (people) have made the virtues of action and emotion their own', the value of general equal treatment of others is also downplayed in such approaches (Kristjánsson, 2007, p. 179). Here, the focus is more on one's own virtue, not on the moral value of action (or inaction). For example, for Kristjánsson (2018), a major challenge of service learning is that it does not result in 'lasting changes in the emotional make-up of most students ... the reflective element was missing ... hence, also the opportunity for young people to digest and make sense of the experiences' (p. 178). That service learning might have other purposes, of enhancing social justice or equity across groups, is not treated as worth critical reflection from this virtues-oriented view.

A final limitation of virtue ethics concerns its treatment of those unable to identify their emotions, such as those with autism and alexithymia. While autism is well known, alexithymia is more common; it is normally distributed across societies, and experienced by some as a stable trait and by others as state-dependent (Panaite & Bylsma, 2012; Goerlich, 2018). People with autism can feel empathy (Brewer & Murphy, 2016), while those with alexithymia 'display clear moral concerns and a conscientious approach to their dealing with others' (Kennett, 2017, p. 371). Yet from a virtue ethics view, people with these conditions are often framed as morally deficient or incapable, since practical wisdom requires emotional self-awareness and coordination. Andrew Pinsent, for example, discusses how autism may obstruct the formation of virtue (2017). In this context, one can imagine people with these experiences striving to bring their emotions to the surface as virtue ethicists advocate, to be good people (and to be recognised as good people) in vain, due to the urgings of those who equate lack of emotional awareness with deviancy. Troubling, unnecessary implications for conceptualising and educating emotional virtues can thus arise from such perspectives.

3.4   Care Ethics and Relational Views

Gilligan's observations about how psychology and philosophy have largely been domains of men prompted her recognition of 'a different voice' in ethics, associated with women's experiences (1982). Care ethics and relational views take up women's and others' diverse experiences, to develop ethics to be relevant and resonant to people across society, beyond the context of public politics usually explored by philosophers. Drawing on Gilligan in part, Noddings asserts that caring relations form the foundation of ethics (1984). She contrasts her view with others (such as variants of virtue ethics) by emphasising that an experience of relation is the basis of her view, with there being little sense in self-cultivation apart from relationships. Thus, departing from an Aristotelian view, home relations and other non-public, private-sphere situations are foundational (Noddings, 1984; Berges, 2015). A rational cognitive view is also deemphasised, in contrast with developing oneself based on relational experiences of caring, where people appropriately and effectively care for each other. Reasoning is essential, but secondary, in Noddings' view, as she characterises appropriate caring as responsive, attentive, and respectful. Virginia Held likewise argues that care should be prior to justice, as it is necessary to human life more so than justice (1995).

Noddings focuses on interpersonal relations and caring, understood as a process and practice of caregivers, such as parents and educators. She also elaborates that traits of caring are applicable to a sense of care in distant relations. For example, she notes that caring was not respectful or attentive, when people donated clothing after an earthquake in Afghanistan, when building materials were needed (Noddings, 2002; Jackson, 2017c). Seeing ethical relations as stemming from experiences of caring, Noddings prioritises that people learn to care and be cared for as fundamental to flourishing, within families and other associations like schools. In relation she promotes the cultivation of happiness in education, arguing that Western education has for too long justified experiences of suffering to the neglect of happiness. Cultivating happiness, she writes, has intrinsic and instrumental purposes, to enhance education in subjects and increase the value of education to life (2003). Though Noddings does not outline a curriculum, she argues that people should learn how to decrease their own suffering and that of others, seeing happiness as beneficial to society. She observes, in relation, unhappy and uncaring practices of schooling, such as practically irrelevant curricula and practices of punishment and shaming (2003). She also argues for teaching about home life, and family and home making, given their centrality to caring and good life (2003).

Such care-focused views are popular in education. Teachers are normally seen as caregivers, especially in early years (Jackson, 2019a). Within school settings, being caring, compassionate, and respectful to others are regarded as major emotional virtues, while caring relations in families and with friends are celebrated. As will be discussed in the next chapters, given resonances of Noddings' views with positive psychology (particularly in promoting happiness), care ethics can be seen as a philosophical frame for SEL initiatives aimed at promoting individual and community well-being. Many find care ethics palatable and intuitive. People like to think of teachers as caregivers and schools as caring communities.

However, although Noddings aims to promote caring as undervalued and misrecognised in a masculine-oriented society, her writing often appears to reinforce gender stereotypes. She regards mother–child relations as foundational, and references the 'mother's voice' as reliant on emotion, and the 'father's voice' as rational. Such conceptualisations hardly help ameliorate dualistic, sexist thinking (Thayer-Bacon, 2019). Instead, they reinforce gender stereotypes about good relations of boys versus girls. Such stereotypes can negatively impact girls (and boys), encouraging girls to potentially care too much for others, ignoring their own needs (Houston, 1990; Applebaum, 1998). Such stereotypes can also lead to the framing of good teaching by women as essentially the work of selfless caregivers, limiting possibilities for other perceptions of what it means to be a good teacher, as a woman or otherwise (e.g. Tamboukou, 2000; Jackson, 2017a). The focus on binary views of gender also enables a sense of gender essentialism that neglects how gender experiences and expectations are 'performed' rather than 'natural' (Butler, 1990), and how expectations also differ across culture, race, ethnicity, and class (hooks, 1989; Suleri, 1992). In relation, caring and other discourse on happy families in schools can overlook cultural differences in expressions and norms of caring (Kang, 2006). Such discourse can also fail to recognise the diversity of healthy families, with damaging impacts for youth and families not identifying with heterosexual or 'nuclear' family norms (Mayo, 2014).

The value of caring and learning to care and be cared for is intuitive to many people. It is backed up by psychological views of well-being and fits into the predominant script of family relations: that is, that one is first cared for (and in a sense, must be cared for), and learns to care for others, as they progress from babies and children to adults and elders. However, not everyone experiences caring in this ideal way. Thus, to the extent that Noddings' conception seems to idealise what caring is, it can be seen to overlook how mixed, not entirely positive emotions may undergird normal and unfortunate experiences of caring relations, which complicates the notion of caring as an inherently moral practice and experience. In parallel with Tessman's (2005) articulation of burdened virtues, Berges (2015, p. 120) asks whether prizing caring across diverse experiences can require heavy lifting among some people that is not closely considered in Noddings' account.

> For a certain portion of humanity, memories of care are inseparable from memories of abuse ... Unfortunately, being in charge of a small defenceless child, which one is expected to feed, clothe, educate and live with at all times, can be an intensely frustrating experience, and even an average well-disposed adult may at times lack patience not to abuse the power he has over a dependent. In cases where the adult has no good will toward the child or in cases where the adult is so deeply disturbed that what good will he has cannot withstand the harm he causes, the experience of being cared for can become deeply traumatic. For it is still an experience of care, if the person doing the abusing is also the person keeping you alive.

Because caring as an idealised quality is not as universal (or as easy and simple to enact) as Noddings' writing sometimes suggests, Berges recommends (2015) a different framing of care, which regards it as inseparable from justice. Others see care ethics as ungrounded, as 'cherry-picking a small set of emotions from the standard virtuous-emotion repertoire' (Kristjánsson, 2018, p. 169), or as otherwise unpalatable in the context of social injustice issues. As Callan relatedly notes, 'persons have a worth that is not reducible to the relationships in which they are embedded, and their worth creates peremptory claims on the aid or forbearance of others, moral rights in other words, whose significance does not wax and wane according to the affections they may or may not elicit from others' (1997, p. 83). Such views are further discussed in Chapter 5.

Another relational view is communitarian, emphasising that one's subjective sense of self is significantly impacted by their community, thereby rejecting the depersonalised deontological tradition, among other views (Sandel, 1981; Taylor, 1985; MacIntyre, 1989). Although communitarianism is normally conceived more as a response to liberalism than as a fully fleshed alternative orientation, Charles Taylor's account of multicultural recognition emphasises the importance of interpersonal recognition in society and institutions such as schools (1992). As Taylor notes (1992), one's sense of self is significantly impacted by how they are recognised, or seen by others around them. In relation, he observes that to be misrecognised in a community, as not of initial equal dignity or respect, can cause grave harm, thereby serving as a discriminatory act that entrenches social hierarchies and inequities (see also Fanon, 1961). This view theoretically undergirds multicultural education, in emphasising cultural identity as dialogical, and articulating that interpersonal relations and education should enable greater positive cross-cultural recognition and respect (see also Banks, 2008).

According to relational multiculturalism, it is moral for institutions such as schools to enhance people's self-respect via appropriate cultural recognition. This position is applied in contexts where multicultural literacy is promoted, such as students learning to see people who seem 'different' with positive recognition, thus encouraging tolerance and pluralism and teaching against discrimination, bias, and prejudice (Jackson, 2014a). One's feelings towards others clearly matter in this view. Students are taught to have sympathy in place of hate or fear towards others, and compassion for others around the world, rather than apathy. Communitarianism also informs views of schools as places to reflect the values and cultural norms and relations of communities, in place of other rationales for schooling, such as for individual or political-economic functioning.

Many appreciate as a basic insight of this orientation that people need respect and adequate recognition, while disputing the cultural emphasis of multiculturalists and communitarians (Appiah, 1994). While people need self-esteem, this does not necessarily require deep cultural recognition, which in some cases might be harmful, as some students may want to be seen as normal and like 'everyone else' (Appiah, 1994; Jackson, 2014a). When it comes to multicultural education for broader aims, for example compassion towards others in society or around the world, some consider whether a justice orientation may be more useful. Virtue ethicists may also share with communitarians a basic appreciation for the way in which virtues are cultivated and understood within particular communities, yet see virtues nonetheless as more basic and held in common across cultural groups (e.g. Kristjánsson, 2007). These insights will be explored more in relation to educating particular emotional virtues (such as compassion) in later chapters.

3.5   Existentialism

Thinkers described as existentialists focus on feelings as basic to human experience, while not emphasising particular feelings as generally better than others, as virtue ethicists and care ethicists do. Like communitarians (and Taylor is sometime described as an existentialist; see Crowell, 2015), Sartre (1943) and de Beauvoir (1949) explore how people are perceived by others differently than they perceive themselves. Heidegger (1962) elaborates this experience not as something to be resolved (as Taylor's recognition approach suggests), but as an essential part of experience, to be in some sense accepted, or 'dwelled with'. Heidegger describes this as part of being not 'at home' in the world, as a person becomes alienated from their self-understanding with more engagement with others. Existentialists do not focus on relations in this case, as in care ethics, but explore what it means to come to grips with oneself, and transcend and go beyond limits to experiences of being, from one moment to the next. The recommendation in this context, if there is one, is the pursuit of authentic being (Crowell, 2015). Thus, so-called negative emotions, like fear, anger, and anxiety, are not regarded as necessarily morally problematic, but signify aspects of the self which may be essential.

Sartre (1943) observes how people sense the existence of virtues, and seek to understand and order them, through making right choices. Yet he also notes that people face anguish in thinking deeply about the ultimate justifications for their choices, as virtue ethicists also note. Seeking a deeper engagement in the situation is the only way 'forward' or 'out' in his view. Related to authentic engagement, historicising and politicising one's situation, and contextualising and relating oneself to the world around them in space and time, is also explored by Sartre and Heidegger. Such a stance finds resonance with sociological views and the politics of emotions, as what sociologists describe as 'feeling rules' are, to the existentialist, inevitably encountered and worked through. However, existentialists would characterise experiences with feeling rules and related issues as essential, as they can be experienced regardless of one's position, while their flavour will also critically depend on particularities of the situation, and therefore are not open to a generalised form of moral evaluation of the right response or future action. Thus, an existentialist might respond to the politics of emotions by emphasising that no one can evade conflicts between personal subjective experiences and cultural and other feeling rules through appealing to general moral principles.

Existentialism is not a mainstream orientation. It is regarded by most as unstraightforward and not helpful for good living. It rejects answers, certainty, and knowing as a perpetual striving for something that can never be fully attained, given what it means to be a person. Yet some thinkers, like Peter Roberts (2013, 2016) and Andrew Gibbons (2013), develop existential themes in relation to education. Roberts (2013, 2016) considers how some existentialist (and Daoist) thought can be brought to bear in examining calls for happiness in education, as in positive psychology and Noddings' work. (This will be discussed more in the next chapter.) Roberts observes here how mainstream psychological (and philosophical) arguments for ameliorating negative emotions of despair and alienation in schools are idealistic and unrealistic, existentially framed as 'inhuman'. As Roberts writes, promotions of only 'positive' feelings in schools deny and dismiss the value of 'negative' emotions, which are inevitable parts of experience, not simply inconveniences to be resolved.

Roberts attributes the popularity of 'positive feelings' orientations in education to their pragmatism, and an optimistic view that social ills and negative feelings can be solved through the right form or focus of schooling. To Roberts, a sense of the world as fixable and solvable undergirds the popular focus on cultivating positive emotions, which neglects essential parts of human experience that are not just 'negative'. As he goes on (2016, p. 113):

> Also problematic is the concept of finitude that underpins the idea of cure. The very act of addressing one situation of despair can lead to the recognition and experiencing of other, new forms of despair. Despair does not 'go away' so easily. As human beings, we undergo constant change, and in our unfinishedness our perceptions of, and responses to, despair as well as hope and happiness can change.

Roberts does not try to remedy, ignore, or evade 'bad' emotions, and does not characterise emotions as 'bad' and 'good'. With a focus on authenticity and engagement, such a philosophy applied to education would entail challenging instrumentalist thought. As Roberts (2016) observes, this means becoming less certain of what one knows, and less confident and simplistic about what one feels, and growing awareness of suffering and its potential value, rather than avoiding it. By implication, instrumentalist thinking regarding so-called good emotions in education would be avoided, in contrast with psychological views, among others. If authenticity is of value, then such attempts to educate emotions as virtues would not be helpful, as they can interfere with what is natural or personal to the student as an individual (see also Maxwell & Reichenbach, 2005).

Such a view resonates with aspects of human experience not well-considered in other philosophical views. In education, an existentialist perspective could help students not 'feel bad' about feeling 'negative' emotions. It could also help young people make sense of and recognise in a more balanced way experiences of feeling frustrated or despairing, about burdened virtues, seemingly impossible feelings rules, or other emotional regulation challenges (Jackson, 2019a). A student might grow more frustrated when they are taught they should avoid bad feelings, or if they feel bad while doing the 'right thing'. Such feelings are ultimately not entirely controllable, and they therefore should not be regarded simply as things to be avoided, although they are dynamic and changeable. Thus, seen from this approach, conflict resolution discourses that moralise anger or sadness may compound difficulties, if they regard the feelings as bad rather than as normal parts of human experience.

Existentialism also provides a theoretical understanding of dynamic, distinctive emotional experiences, such as alexithymia, as found in psychology, by underscoring how it can be normal, not deviant or disordered, to experience changing, hard to decipher states. While this insight is appreciated by researchers who work to effectively identify emotions empirically, it remains largely ignored in mainstream models of emotional virtues, which focus on their malleability, and ideal moral consistency. Existentialism thus enables a reconsideration of what is ideal in terms of emotional experience and directedness.

In *The Stranger*, Camus defends his strange character Mersault as deep and appropriately passionate, with unwavering commitment to his sense of inner truth, despite his consistent failure to follow the emotional norms of those around him, or be appropriately attuned to his circumstances. As Robert Roberts (2013) notes in relation, such a metaphysical attunement to one's own sense of truth apart from circumstances of life is key to fulfilment in some other moral epistemologies and is not unique to the character of Mersault (Roberts particularly considers Christian metaphysics). Thus, Camus' story of Mersault, among other explorations of emotional deviancy, highlights diversity of human emotional experience, encouraging critical reconsideration of what is normal and ideal, and their value in light of other aims of education.

As discussed in the previous chapter, Boler (1999) observed a teacher telling her class to leave a student alone, because the student expressed that she was feeling bad. Such an approach might make sense from an instrumentalist psychological view, which regards avoiding conflict and encouraging functioning of individuals and the classroom as primary. Yet from an existentialist view, the needs of the girl and the rest of class to have negative feelings recognised as normal and acceptable could be met through an alternative strategy, where the student is not isolated or alienated from others due to confessing to feeling bad. On the other hand, like existentialism, some variants of psychology and virtue ethics do recognise and accept some negative feelings (more so than is often emphasised when they are applied in education). Nonetheless, tolerance for negativity is not promoted in education with the label 'existentialism', as existentialists are framed as rather amoral, in emphasising no grand method for morality, apart from experiencing life authentically, and accepting despair and other challenging feelings in experience.

3.6 Confucianism, Daoism, and Buddhism

The ideas discussed so far are not exhaustive of mainstream views within and across societies, while they are also not alien to non-Western perspectives. In many ways, prominent Eastern understandings of morality, feelings, and relations intersect with Western ones (Ng, 2018). While there is no singular Confucian way, Confucianism has been a centralised system of thought in China and elsewhere in Asia, in contrast with the relative pluralism of Western philosophy (Hall & Ames, 1995). Confucianism is often regarded by Western thinkers as akin to virtue ethics, with its emphasis on situational ethics and practical wisdom at the individual level (e.g. Cua, 1998; Van Norden, 2007). Like Aristotle, Confucian thinkers highlight circumstances, moderation, and reflection.

For Mencius, the Confucian way entails aligning one's feelings with what is right through cognitive and emotional development, which can be taught and trained (Liu, 2004; Sim, 2017). However, Confucianism is also routinely observed to differ from Western virtue ethics, in also focusing on familial and private relations, and the intricacies of situations and interpersonal relations, which allow for few generalisations. Discernment and self-awareness are key features of emotional self-monitoring encouraged by Confucianism, in private life and public life:

> One must be conscientious of oneself as an actor in the social world. This explains why the *Analects* is a preoccupation with seemingly minute matters of conduct, such as one's posture, countenance, tone of voice, choice of words and attire, and overall comportment. Crucially ... these aspects of one's visible person were thought to affect how *others* behave and how interpersonal situations unfold.
>
> (Sarkissian, 2014, p. 184).

Because care within relations is emphasised in Confucian ethics, Chenyang Li (1994) traces overlapping of Confucian ethics with Noddings' care ethics. Shirong Luo (2007) relatedly observes that feelings of empathy and compassion are a focus of ethical idealism in both philosophies (see also Epley, 2015). Yet given the complexities of Confucianism, it is not generally helpful to assimilate Confucian ethics with virtue ethics or care ethics, as a matter of course. Confucianism also emphasises moral standards and rules, stressing 'the significance of the unity of virtue and rule, a possibility which has been largely neglected by contemporary Western philosophers' (Liu, 2004, p. ix; see also Herr, 2003). Such combining of different ways of moral thinking (i.e. deontology and virtue ethics) is not out of line with how people ordinarily think, across societies (Prinz, 2007; Levinson & Fay, 2016). (Nor is it out of line with critiques of virtue ethics that question its independence from traditional rule-based views; see Nussbaum, 1999; Angle & Slote, 2013.)

Educational recommendations of Confucianism, virtue ethics, and care ethics are not entirely dissimilar, despite their divergent theoretical foundations. In education, Mencius emphasises modelling and guiding behaviour (as in virtue ethics) in interpersonal relations. However, Confucian ethics is more substantive and hierarchical educationally, in focusing on the significance of social roles, and filial piety, obedience, and respect of young people towards elders (although this should be reciprocal). In relation, Confucian ethics has been accused of encouraging oppressive patriarchal and subservient paternalistic and patriotic practices (Herr, 2003). Some lessons emphasise gender roles (with wives being subservient to husbands in some accounts), and the importance of supporting government structures and leaders, to promote and maintain social harmony (Sarkissian, 2014).

Thus, another point of contrast between Western educational philosophy and Confucian teaching is in treating the family as akin to the nation. This is due to the emphasis in Confucian thought on relationality, which can be seen as far deeper and more extensive than in the conceptions of any mainstream Western thinkers such as Noddings (1984). As Zhuran You, A. G. Rud, and Yingzi Hu note (2018, p. 17): 'This cultural inclination is characterized by a centripetal force of family upon individuals just like roots upon leaves, a basic feature of a root-like network of human relations, and the derived cultural characteristics such as collectivism, conformity, and interdependence developed in the patriarchal clan society of ancient China.'

Confucianism, as a state-cultivated view, reflects the relations of people in Chinese (and other) societies that did not transform as Western societies did, from clan-based or feudal to strongly individualistic and liberal. Thus, on the one hand, these views are deeply relational, and the familial is essential to morality, in contrast with traditional Western philosophies. On the other hand, moral understandings about familial care and relations are directly applicable to societal relations in a Confucian account. This conceptualisation of care as societal is at odds with mainstream care ethics views, which are not particularly decisive about societal issues, given their grounding of morality in interpersonal caring acts, although some do posit care as having specifically public value (e.g. Tronto, 1993).

While Confucianism is a major ideological force across many Eastern societies, Daoism's social influence is not nearly as obvious. In contrast to Confucianism, 'the way' in Daoism is not developed through role modelling and instruction on principles or virtues. The Confucian Mencius emphasises teaching virtues, stating 'if [people] are full of food, have warm clothes, and live in comfort but are without instruction, then they come close to being animals' (Sim, 2017, p. 113). In contrast, Daoist Laozi focuses on learning through authentic engagement in the world, not through recognising and directly learning about 'the way':

> When the Way was lost there was Virtue
> When Virtue was lost there was humaneness
> When humaneness was lost there was righteousness
> When righteousness was lost there were the rites.
> The rites are the wearing thin of loyalty and trust,
>   and the beginning of chaos.
>
> (Sim, 2017, p. 113)

From this perspective, the way, as an authentic experience and purpose, is superior to formal education and ethics of virtue, or other formulas for goodness, which essentially boil down into rules for conduct and on social mannerisms. Also in contrast with Confucianism, for Daoism, negative experiences, emotions, and relations are not to be rejected. This can be seen to be in alignment with existentialism (see Hung, 2014; also Roberts, 2013, 2016).

Like existentialism, Daoism is not taught in schools or endorsed by other mainstream institutions promoting morality and well-being. Indeed, Daoism does not clearly promote its own teaching, but primarily rejects schooling and formal forms of education, in favour of diverse experiences of more natural or unguided personal development, where sages may be present, but should still 'let go' (Maki, 2016, 2018). Daoism can thus be seen in part as a response to the influence of Confucianism, as many Daoist texts are critical of Confucianism, arguing against Confucian views of good behaviour and propriety, which they describe as 'forms of self-imprisonment', and manipulations of people for questionable purposes that can harm human nature rather than simply correct it (Sarkissian, 2014, p. 185; Hung, 2014). However, Daoism continues to have cultural influence and philosophical resonance, sometimes seen as a counter position or corrective to the centralising, unidirectional influence of Confucianism in Chinese societies.

Buddhism is taught in many parts of the world, with an emphasis on meditation and a virtuous Buddhist lifestyle. Diverse Buddhist leaders vary in their worldviews and what they promote, so one can describe the overall educational implications of Buddhism only through over-generalisation. Buddhism has a reputation among Western thinkers for being relatively unemotional and pacifistic. Some (e.g. Kupperman, 1995; Nussbaum, 2001) associate it with 'stone-like' Stoicism, while others commend the immense, but somewhat socially distanced, inner gratitude and compassion observed of the Dalai Lama (Fitzgerald, 1998). Practices associated with Buddhism, particularly meditation, are seen to promote individual tranquillity as key to enlightenment. More broadly, the Vedic tradition from which Buddhism and Hinduism (and Jainism) arose also encouraged yoga, used across cultures to (among other things) 'clear the mind', 'take away negative energy' or thought, and develop a peaceful, accepting, smiling disposition (Jackson, 2019d). In relation, mindfulness is popular in psychology and promoted by Jubilee research among others, while yoga and other physical training, specifically for relaxation and learning of emotional self-regulation, is also increasingly encouraged in schools across societies (Ergas, 2019; Jackson, 2019d; see Chapter 7).

However, the reputation of Buddhism as pacifistic or stoic may be due to the popularity of the Dalai Lama among Westerners, as these features are not necessarily inherent to Buddhism. Bell hooks tells of an encounter with Vietnamese Buddhist monk Thich Nhat Hanh, wherein she was surprised to discover that he was not 'Mr. Calm, himself, Mr. Peace', but rather he encouraged and recommended that hooks not discard her anger, but use it 'as compost for your garden' (Yancy & hooks, 2015). While arguments against anger are found in some Buddhist texts, in others there is a place for anger, in a Buddhist life that is aware and socially committed (McRae, 2015). Thus, some Buddhists may be compared more to existentialists than Stoics, and to more sociologically inclined thinkers (McRae, 2012, 2015).

Others note the similarities between Buddhist views and virtue ethics, given the incorporation of feeling into wisdom in dispositions and situations, and an emphasis on individual cultivation apart from societal or relational issues. Buddhist aims across literature highlight the need to overcome negative feelings and dispositions while developing virtues, regarding positive character traits and related feelings as good regardless of their consequences (MacKenzie, 2018). Buddhist views will be considered periodically in this text.

3.7 Conclusion

This chapter examined various Western and Eastern philosophical and moral traditions for their framings of the role of emotions in society and school. As shown, not all traditions and philosophies are prevalent today or commonly found in schools. Still, some aspects of many of the orientations can be seen in schools. There may be values characterised as deontological and consequentialist in some informal or formal lessons, in schools. Meanwhile, virtue ethics is regarded as particularly promising for education (alongside care ethics), and is more aligned with prevalent psychological views of educating emotional virtues. A blend of approaches is perhaps often used in schools, as societies are not characterised as oriented towards one's single philosophical approach to good life. People ordinarily borrow across diverse traditions depending on the situation, with many possible interplays across traditions. Likewise, ties across Eastern and Western traditions can be seen, while particular Eastern views also have distinctive features and insights. This chapter concludes the first part of this book. In the next part these philosophies come to life, as they inform approaches to particular emotional virtues in schools.

CHAPTER 4

Happiness, Eudemonia, and Well-Being

Happiness has been a major topic of philosophical and other forms of investigation throughout history. Happiness has often been held as an end and a means to good life. People have generally sought happiness, and happiness is related in common and academic discourse to progress, success, and value. However, not all traditions prize happiness, and the definition of happiness and its implications for social life and education are contested. How to measure it, whether one can measure it, and how to know it when you see it are some puzzles psychologists and philosophers (among others) grapple with. This chapter gives a brief history of the concept of happiness alongside other concepts, of eudemonia and well-being, from philosophical orientations, in psychology, and from the perspective of the politics of emotions. It traces how these views have shaped educational aims and strategies. The analysis here emphasises the need for consideration of more critical approaches to happiness as an educational aim, despite the praise of happiness as a good in itself in much of Western philosophy and psychology.

4.1 Happiness in Philosophy

There are two major framings of happiness in philosophy, which can be seen as competitive or complementary approaches. The first emphasises pleasure, while the second emphasises virtue. Historically, these are exemplified by the views of Epicurus and Aristotle. For Epicurus, the goal of life was freedom from pain and the pursuit of the experience of pleasure, both bodily and mentally. Epicurus' hedonist account differentiates human happiness from that of animals. However, the experiences and engagements that any person could pursue were emphasised, including simple pleasures, apart from reflections on achievement or realising projects in a deeper manner (Konstan, 2012). For example, Epicurus speaks about how a simple, ascetic diet is underrated in its capacity to free from pain and enable pleasure. Virtues in this account, and other moral and just behaviour, are instrumentally valued to enable happiness (O'Keefe, 2019).

Modern hedonists such as Bentham (1789) argued for the greatest happiness for the greatest number of people as the aim of life, defining happiness as a balance of pleasures over pains. Most find this approach simplistic, however, as such happiness can occur alongside wrongdoing to others (if not also to oneself), from a broad view. As Mill notes (1861), there is a sense of better and worse ('higher' and 'lower') pleasures, and many feel that people should critically reflect as part of cultivating and experiencing happiness, not just seeking pleasure in a crude way.

Thus, other definitions emphasise living in a virtuous and reflective manner, with pleasure as a secondary consideration. The modern term 'happiness' denotes 'good hap', or good fortune (Haybron, 2011). Yet good fortune in an external sense, such as material and basic bodily comfort and security, is not something that all people can easily secure and sustain. Life involves struggle and suffering for most people. In this context, philosophers elaborate happiness as a positive or content state of mind, marked by reflective moral evaluation (Haybron, 2011). Various thinkers across philosophical and religious traditions emphasise happiness as related to the capacity to grapple with fortune or misfortune in a good, pleasant, or peaceful way, with moral value attached to emotional contentment, whether one is lucky or unlucky (McMahon, 2006).

For Socrates, Plato, and Aristotle, a sense of contentment and evaluative judgement are intertwined, as virtue is reflective practice and experience that corresponds with understanding. Thus, some evaluative judgement is expected in a sense of happiness as *eudemonia*. Equated by philosophers with happiness or flourishing, eudemonia is an objective state of virtuousness and the aim of moral life in this view. For Aristotle, various virtues were part of eudemonia, as well as ongoing character states and dispositions. Happiness includes pleasure in this account, but not 'every kind of pleasure ... the pleasure felt by a human being who engages in theoretical activity' (Kraut, 2018).

A related understanding of happiness as part of sustained moral reflection and resilience despite obstacles is also common in Jewish and Christian views. Again, these views are less concerned with happiness as a pure emotional state or experience of pleasure, and more focused on seeking meaning and purpose from experience (Pett, 2012; R. Roberts, 2013). Confucian texts similarly emphasise happiness as 'finding a "fit" between ourselves and the environment', with exercise of the capacity to reflect critically and deliberatively on facing and making choices (Wong, 2013). In this case, happiness is dependent upon living well in harmony with others, discounting any value to hedonism (Morris, 2012).

Other Eastern views focus less on fitting in than on accepting circumstances of life. Such views are no more hedonistic than Christian or Confucian views, but may be described as focused on mental or spiritual detachment, rather than on spiritual 'attunement' (R. Roberts, 2013). Hinduist and Daoist conceptions both regard general detachment from personal circumstances as virtuous (Wong, 2013). Hindu Vivekananda states that 'What we want is neither happiness nor misery. Both make us forget our true nature; both are chains, one of iron, another of gold' (cited in Pett, 2012, p. 61). Daoist contentment also involves leaving behind the search for happiness, given its fleeting nature. Zhuangzi emphasises the need to align oneself with a larger cosmos, beyond good and evil, in which one is just a small part, in a reflective and rather passive way (Wong, 2013). Similarly, existentialists emphasise the fleeting nature of happiness, wherein the very search for it disables one from truly experiencing it, so that one is better off observing and accepting one's experience in a free and open-minded manner, rather than pursuing it more strategically (Gibbons, 2013; Roberts, 2016).

The eudemonic, Aristotelian conception of happiness resonates with many (Western) moral philosophers today. Nussbaum considers a moral sense of happiness as a subjective emotional quality cultivated with appropriate judgement or evaluation. Contrasting her account with hedonism, Nussbaum notes that 'if I ever notice myself feeling feelings of satisfaction, I blame myself and think that, insofar as I have those I'm like Mill's "pig satisfied" or Aristotle's "dumb grazing animals," and thus, reflectively, I report *dissatisfaction* with my life as a whole' (2012, p. 345). When it comes to what is required to develop such happiness, Nussbaum emphasises capabilities a person is entitled to develop that can help them cultivate 'enrichment of the soul or a deepening of self-knowledge'. Nussbaum identifies that such capabilities include being able to experience 'at least some pleasure and the relief of pain', as well as freedom from hunger, violence, oppression, and other abuses 'that seem to have no positive educative function' (2012, p. 350). There is a place for pleasure here, but Nussbaum cautions against a view of subjective well-being that lacks reflective moral judgement.

Noddings also promotes an Aristotelian orientation towards eudemonia (2003). Yet in contrast with Nussbaum, Noddings also argues for happiness specifically as a subjective state of mind. In the course, she diminishes the importance of the sorts of detached or attuned reflection on one's life emphasised in transcendent and religious traditions, and by Nussbaum. As Noddings sees it, failing to recognise a moral value for happiness in the subjective sense, suffering has been too often accepted, if not endorsed as key to good life, particularly among early and modern Christian thinkers (Noddings, 2003). Noddings sees the sense of optimism and acceptance despite struggle being promoted by such traditions as enabling subservience and misery among ordinary people. She argues, in contrast, that pleasure, fun, and play are essential, as such experiences of subjective happiness are intrinsically good, and instrumentally valuable, for learning and developing character. Noddings justifies her view, observing that 'Happy individuals are rarely violent or intentionally cruel, either to other human beings or to nonhuman animals' (2003, p. 2).

Despite theoretical distinctions of their views, Nussbaum and Noddings come to similar educational conclusions. Both argue for the cultivation of happiness alongside other moral traits in education. Both see happiness as requiring a relative lack of what they regard as needless suffering, so that people's inferred and expressed needs (what Nussbaum describes in terms of capabilities) can be met. In schools, both argue that children's physical and emotional needs should be looked after, including needs for pleasure, fun, and play. Play and imaginative experiences and related carefree opportunities are explored in part in Nussbaum's capabilities view, while Noddings particularly stresses such points. As Noddings observes, fulfilling emotional wants and needs enhances learning of subjects, as pleasure, fun, and play enable students' desire to sustain attention, dwell and reflect on perception, and gain intrinsic satisfaction from learning, with instrumental gains (2003).

Noddings' views (and Nussbaum's) have receptive audiences in educational contexts. They are to some extent in line with common views in Western societies about childhood as a time for fun, games, and joy. Nonetheless, their views have also met with some challenges. Some critique Noddings' (and Nussbaum's) tendency to write from a universal position, despite the fact that their views, particularly when elaborated into educational or life strategies, are historically and culturally situated (Walzer, 1985; Stewart, 2001). Despite Noddings' emphasis on relations in much of her work, she tends to describe happiness as a personal characteristic and experience, important to cultivate for oneself (as Nussbaum also tends to do). This is at odds with the profoundly relational orientation towards the self as embedded within a community that is cultivated in Confucian philosophy, for example. Noddings explicitly defends a hedonistic kind of happiness, articulating play and fun for its own sake. In contrast:

> ... all major Chinese philosophical schools advocate abandoning personal desire and engaging in activities and thoughts that are focused on and directed toward the fulfilment of others' well-being. They also regard such realization of human potential as the way to happiness. Furthermore, people in collectivist cultures are more sensitive to social norms in their pursuit of happiness than are people in individualist cultures, and this would in turn predispose them to take others' well-being into consideration ... hedonic balance is a stronger predictor of life satisfaction in individualist cultures than in collectivist cultures.
>
> (Ho, Duan, & Tang, 2014, p. 218)

Relatedly, Hanan Alexander explores how Noddings' (interpersonal) relational orientation leads her to ignore the moral place of broader cultural communities in shaping deeply held views and related personal experiences (2013). As Alexander argues, Noddings tends to dismiss culture and community as factors in a person's moral life, as she often writes from a kind of universal position, in discussing interpersonal relations. To Alexander, this universalism is problematic, as it pertains to her understanding of human freedom and agency. Noddings critiques Victor Frankl's (1973) understanding that some inmates in Nazi concentration camps found a sense of freedom and meaning in suffering. In her critique, Noddings describes Frankl as glorifying suffering (1984). Yet according to Alexander, Noddings here lacks attention to how views (her own, and others') are historically and culturally situated. She describes people's capacity to assess their situations as vital in her ethics of care, and yet fails to appreciate Frankl's description of that same sort of freedom, failing to recognise the cultural contexts framing her understanding of possibility and agency in relation to that of Frankl (Alexander, 2013).

Similarly, Robert Roberts describes a painful life as happy in the case of metaphysical attunement, even if one is otherwise poorly adjusted to their circumstances (2013). Acknowledging its departure from simpler, more modern notions of happiness as life satisfaction or as feeling good, Roberts (2013) defends this sense of happiness as richer and as worth preserving, defending it as a more virtuous conception of happiness. As he contends, 'many serious and reflective people do not want to be satisfied with their life under just any conditions. For example, they would not want to be "happy" under conditions of religious illusion, even if it were seamless' (Roberts, 2013, p. 188).

Peter Roberts (2016) similarly urges reconsideration of the insights of transcendental and existential thought among those promoting happiness as feeling good, particularly in education. Arguing that suffering is unavoidable to some extent, he suggests that educators should not overlook its possible value, and should therefore enable acceptance, if not a more enthusiastic embrace, of suffering experiences as essential parts of being human. In distinguishing the glorification of suffering from what she regards as a necessary capacity for unhappiness and related acceptance of some unhappy and painful moments, Noddings fails to recognise the intrinsic value of suffering in religious and existential views. Noddings seems to imply that tolerating suffering enables undue suffering, unless any such unhappiness has a clear purpose (2003). For Roberts, this view implies a sense of certainty and finitude, and a related desire for freedom from suffering. Roberts views these expectations and desires as unnecessary, unhelpful, and unrealistic.

Despair can be productive for Roberts, as it can be seen as encouraging criticality about challenges in life, whereas if people aim primarily to avoid suffering, they can effectively close themselves off from such kinds of critical reflection. Such reflection can, in turn, lead to greater understanding and related positive and meaningful experiences in the future, even if it can also lead to moments of despair. On the other hand, as Roberts observes:

> We might say that developing a critical, and in that sense despairing, consciousness is better than deliberately 'dumbing down' the curriculum or simply seeking to pump facts into students' minds … A pedagogical system that works against the formation of critically conscious beings allows social injustices to continue without contestation … and closes off the possibility of new forms of experience that demand greater intellectual sophistication.   (2016, p. 115)

The view that happiness is an essential end, to the exclusion of experiences of unhappiness, can close a person off to issues of social injustice, which can cause despair and distress, and are likely to, especially in the short term. Deontologists (and consequentialists) similarly worry about the value of emotional experiences, in relation to making critical evaluations of issues of injustice in society, noting how emotions can cloud judgement about uncomfortable and disturbing social issues, as discussed in Chapter 3 (e.g. Hand, 2018). Psychologists, and those concerned about the politics of emotions, also consider how the unbridled pursuit of happiness and related positive thinking can enable social harms, even if they can at the same time have some personal and social benefits.

4.2 Happiness in Psychology

William James notes that positive thinking and the search for happiness can have negative social impacts, and enable a turn from injustice. As he writes,

> since evil facts are as genuine parts of nature as the good ones, the philosophic presumption should be that they have some rational significance, and that systematic healthy-mindedness, failing as it does to accord to sorrow, pain, and death any positive and active attention whatever, is formally less complete than systems that try at least to include these elements in their scope.   (1982, pp. 170–171)

However, many later psychologists ignore the value of painful experiences and feelings, and the accompanying risks and challenges related to happiness, instead framing feeling happy and satisfied with life as key to well-being. In relation, psychologists often study individuals' objective and subjective senses of happiness and well-being as part of quality of life research for governments and other institutions. In this research, they use self-reports alongside other personal data, such as on economic well-being, to evaluate trends in happiness and well-being within and across populations. In this research, unlike philosophical scholarship on the topic, life satisfaction, happiness, and subjective well-being are often treated as synonymous (Frey, 2008). Given the positive relationship assumed between quality of life and happiness, this research aims to elucidate factors leading to greater happiness and life satisfaction.

Positive psychologists focus particularly on how to develop positive feelings like happiness, seeing positive feelings as instrumentally valuable to a person's subjective and objective well-being and flourishing, and to spreading positive social benefits towards others. Positive psychologists argue that experiencing happiness is beneficial to achieving in society (and in schools), to being a better person, and doing greater good. In positive psychology and the 'science of happiness', researchers and theorists examine what might cause people to exhibit and report experiencing happiness, holding such factors as potential keys towards developing a happier, better, more productive world. Based primarily on different forms of self-reports, positive psychologists find that manifestations of, or dispositions towards good feelings such as happiness, well-being, fulfilment, and optimism correlate with one another and with morally good traits like altruism, compassion, and tendencies towards pro-social, self-directed, and productive behaviours. Studies on subjective happiness and well-being around the world show correlations with age, wealth, employment, marital status, and more. They indicate that happiness is increasing within and across societies, bolstering views that social progress is occurring.

Martin Seligman (2002) emphasises the benefits to a person of being happy, and indicates many pathways towards happiness. Expressing that he aims not to be prescriptive or normative in his description, he notes that one can seek happiness by pursuing pleasant emotions, engaging in gratifying experiences, developing meaning in relations with others, or dedicating oneself to achievements. Seligman (2002) struggled not to rank or directly recommend these pathways from a moral viewpoint. He conceded that a limitation of his view was a lack of capacity to critically evaluate pathways to happiness, observing that this 'is a consequence . . . of its descriptive, as opposed to prescriptive nature' (Jayawickreme, Pawelski, & Seligman, cited in Kristjánsson, 2013b). Later, Seligman moved away from promoting happiness (2011) to a sense of flourishing more aligned to well-being. This concept was framed as less subjective and experiential, as more related to leading a meaningful life. Others similarly prioritise well-being over happiness, including happiness as one constitutive element of well-being, which might also include confidence, a sense of autonomy, positive relationships, and the development of cognitive capacities (Pett, 2012).

Educational interventions undergirded by such research aim to enhance student happiness and well-being. Often such programmes involve emotional literacy as a central component, and are part of social and emotional learning (SEL) curricula (Boler, 1999; Bywater & Sharples, 2012). Such curricula aim to help students recognise emotional experiences and expressions in themselves and others, as prerequisite to working to control their emotions, avoid problematic and so-called negative emotions, and cultivate positive ones related to well-being and happiness. Students in this context learn to see their feelings as their responsibility, to themselves and to others. They also learn to exhibit expressions recognisable as positive emotions and train themselves to do so.

One example is the School Speciality (2018) Premier Esteem curriculum 'planner' for young children in North America. The handbook asks students to articulate what makes them happy and sad, with the statement, 'Your feelings can change your actions. Know why you feel the way you do. This will help you make good choices' (p. ES-7). Understanding emotions is taken here as something one can do correctly or incorrectly. Such curricula can be cast as morally neutral, but pragmatically useful, for learning and being productive. They are justified by supporters to promote 'equality of opportunity for happiness' (Ecclestone, 2012), given reported rises in some societies in mental and emotional disorders, and their disproportionate impact on youth from socio-economically deprived and disadvantaged backgrounds. As Layard puts it, 'Happiness is good for you ... What if it really is possible for individuals and whole societies to shape and boost their happiness?' (cited in Ecclestone, 2012, p. 465).

However, some criticise both these mainstream psychological views of happiness and the related educational interventions. Richard Bentall challenges the view that happiness is beneficial psychologically (1992). In contrast, Bentall argues that happiness can be classed as a psychiatric disorder, because it is statistically abnormal, and has significant associations with disordered characteristics and tendencies (see also Parrott, 2014). While happiness is normally associated with well-being and prosocial behaviour, Bentall also notes its association with being carefree, impulsive, and unpredictable (1992, p. 94). He additionally observes 'clinical evidence of an association between happiness, obesity, and indulgence in alcoholic beverages', thus indicating that happiness poses 'a moderate risk to life' (p. 96). Finally, happiness is associated in research with difficulty in facing 'mundane but essential tasks' and 'retrieving negative events from long-term memory', preventing happy people 'from acquiring a realistic understanding of their physical and social environment' (1992, p. 97).

While Bentall's view may seem extreme, others also note that a lack of personal distress plays a key role in psychopathy, as unpleasant experiences are met without distress, whether they impact oneself or others (Kennett, 2017). Relatedly, Lauren Alloy and Lyn Abramson (1988) defend 'depressive realism' as a more negative mind-set more attuned to reality. Optimism in the face of hardship can be seen as a dysfunctional emotion when it distorts a worrisome reality (Parrott, 2014). Optimistic and non-depressed individuals can thus rely unhelpfully on appraisals of the world which are positively biased and less accurate or inaccurate.

From a measurement perspective, it can also be difficult to accurately measure well-being or happiness for psychological research or intervention purposes (Haybron, 2008; Ecclestone, 2012). The emotions and correlative experiences can be fleeting, dynamic experiences, while measurement of 'judgments require an unrealistic aggregation of a great many factors' (Alexandrova, 2016, p. 397). Happiness and well-being also vary according to transient mood, and they are otherwise contextual to a person's situation (Greco, Holmes, & McKenzie, 2015). In this case, self-reports that interventions work in education may indicate results that do not last over time.

Furthermore, some SEL curricula for happiness have backwash effects. Interventions for emotional virtues tend to frame those with negative feeling experiences as vulnerable or susceptible. This can result in interventions in a sense stigmatising youth for expressing or indicating apparent deficiencies in 'good' feelings like happiness, thereby potentially exacerbating negative feelings of those already feeling 'bad' (Ecclestone, 2012). As Boler (1999) found in observing SEL practices (as discussed in previous chapters), such curricula can increase the sense of vulnerability of already-vulnerable youth, who may be treated by well-intentioned but uncritical educators as exemplars of happiness deficiency (or general emotional deviancy) in their classes. Such experiences can have long-lasting negative impacts on some students and their relations with peers and educators. Particularly in contexts where young people are anxious to perform, succeed, or act in a respectful and productive relation with educators and peers, emotional suppression could be a strategy implicitly encouraged in these contexts, which can make future emotional self-regulation more challenging, thereby ultimately making it harder for some students to feel happy and do well (Sarkissian, 2014). When constant happiness is hardly a normal (or necessarily the most functional) state, students can learn unhelpful lessons from happiness curricula that are effectively (although it may not be intentionally) designed to critically evaluate their happiness or lack thereof.

Meanwhile, psychologists are typically focused on the adaptive nature of happiness for individuals. Morality is a secondary concern in much of this work, and may be neglected, particularly in some positive psychology approaches, in favour of the direct pursuit of more obvious manifestations of happiness. As Ecclestone puts it, prominent 'discourses of well-being and character both recast virtues and moral values as psychological constructs that can be trained without requiring moral engagement' (2012, p. 475). Larger moral considerations can be ignored here, apart from one's responsibility to engage in emotional management and the cultivation of happiness, when such psychological views are foregrounded. Ruth Cigman relatedly observes the possible pitfalls of such individualistic orientations towards emotional cultivation: 'Consider self-esteem. The Social and Emotional Aspects of Learning programme teaches children to reach positive conclusions about themselves, saying things like "I accept myself for who and what I am". But a child who has just bullied another child should not necessarily be encouraged to say this; it could reinforce a dangerous arrogance or conceit' (2012, p. 453).

As discussed in Chapter 2, positive psychology situates happiness, well-being, and other feelings at the individual level. Emotional intelligence (EI) and positive psychology frame happiness as a disciplinary technique and individual responsibility. Assessments of success are individual, rather than relational or communal, in such studies (Cigman, 2012). Thus, positive psychology regards it as a 'thing' people have the capacity to possess. Happiness is a descriptor for people as individuals, and psychological views that interventions 'work' consider the cultivation of happiness as a freestanding choice – as something a person can (and should) develop regardless of the world around them. Although this approach might make happiness seem easy to attain, it diverts attention from issues of relating to others in communities, in just or unjust ways. When happiness is a personal choice, unrelated to social context, people can be blamed for unhappiness or bad attitudes, while their other actions, views, or choices – or the environment they experience – can be neglected (Ehrenreich, 2009). Thus, unhappiness is framed as an individual deficiency, while the larger context is ignored, normalised, and held as acceptable, natural, and not worth sustained focus and consideration. This line of thinking can then result in unhappy individuals being blamed, in a sense, for challenges, should they fail to 'put on a happy face' (Cigman, 2012).

Educational and social leaders who promote psychologically based happiness and well-being interventions tend to assume these feelings 'work' in a moral way, but no research clearly links a particular form or experience of happiness to moral behaviour, across diverse people and situations. One can intuitively claim (like Noddings) that being happy and well leads to benefits to oneself and others. Studies indeed show correlations between happiness and well-being and (generally self-reported) pro-social tendencies, of being generous, optimistic, kind, and more (Veenhoven, 2008; Kesebir & Diener, 2014). But happiness can also lead to harm, as discussed here: There is no necessary or essential link between feeling happy and doing good things. One can be happy and well according to psychological measures and not be a good person. A person can be happy, and selfish and unkind. On the other hand, one can also be unhappy and unwell, according to psychological measures, and do and be good in the world around them.

4.3   The Politics of Happiness

Sociological and politically oriented theorists and researchers explore how happiness is (a) socially constructed and (b) relational. Sociologists articulate how social processes play a role in people's experiences of happiness, related to their understanding of what happiness consists in, and their understanding of their inclusion and belonging in society (Greco et al., 2015; Cieslik, 2016). That social institutions help define and educate people about happiness is one aspect of its social construction. Marx, Marcuse (2002), and Adorno (1941) observe how modern life (in Western societies) leads to alienation from a sense of belonging, and how social and commercial institutions encourage a narrowed, artificial conception of happiness, through consumerism and popular culture (Cieslik, 2016). The idea is that one must engage in certain consumptive practices in order to reach personal fulfilment, as needs are constructed through media and advertising, as new personal problems to be resolved through participating in commercial transactions (shopping). Relatedly, therapy talk has replaced moral talk in the public sphere, as people learn through social institutions (schools, media, and so on) that seeking out their own well-being and happiness should be their primary purpose (Furedi, 2004).

A relational view questions from whose perspective happiness or well-being is defined and understood as functional in a situation and good. Such an account considers power relations behind appeals to particular others' (such as students') happiness, and how some might see happiness and well-being interventions as less costly substitutes for changing social structures, which can often be more important factors in people's experiences of unhappiness, suffering, lack of attention in schools, and so on. Many calls for well-being interventions in education reflect desires for equal opportunities for happiness, while simultaneously linking them to social productivity and maintaining classroom, school, and/or broad social order (Cigman, 2012; Ecclestone, 2012).

Ahmed (2004a, 2010) scrutinises discourse on the personal and social value of happiness, examining who is identified in such discourse as vulnerable to unhappiness, or as deficient or lacking in happiness, and how happiness is associated in popular views to particular identity traits, rather than to social relations of diverse people in a community. For example, in large-scale studies, it has been found that marriage leads to happiness. However, such research is based upon and reflects men's experiences more accurately than women's (Davies, 1987). Studies, both in Western societies and in East Asia, suggest that the extent of emotional benefits in marriage is generally greater for men than for women (Hori & Kamo, 2018). Some may simplistically deduce here that differences are gender-based (i.e. women are less happy than men in marriage due to their gender). In popular culture, the difference is often regarded as individual deficiency, impacting women more than men. Yet psychologists systematically exploring this experience gap consider how marital relations are part of the equation. Blaine Fowers observes that these different outcomes may be 'produced at the level of marital interactions that favour husbands in some way', such as 'differences in marital tasks and power' (1991, p. 209). Discourse that suggests that cultivation of happiness is an individual capacity or responsibility, rather than an outcome related to relationships and environments, thus enables possible victim blaming, as women are recommended to make themselves happy, despite and within potentially negative and harmful situations they may face.

In this context, Ahmed (2010) analyses the tropes of 'happy housewife' and 'feminist killjoy' to understand how feeling rules (as discussed in Chapter 2) demand women to be happy in situations that are treated as positive (such as traditional heterosexual marriage) but may not be experienced as positive by particular women. Ahmed notes that the model of the happy housewife is 'a white bourgeois fantasy of the past, a nostalgia for a past that was never possible as a present for most women' (2010). However, the model remains prevalent underneath the surface of much popular discourse, as women are still encouraged to find happiness in pleasing others, as good wives and mothers.

As explored in Chapter 2, this discourse is reflected in the training of the girl Sophie in Rousseau's *Emile* (1762). *Emile* frames Sophie's future role as that of a happy partner. Her parents are quoted, 'A good girl finds her happiness in the happiness of a good man' (Rousseau, cited in Ahmed, 2010, p. 58). Ahmed describes this as a 'happiness commandment: it is for the sake of her happiness and the happiness of her parents that she *must* find happiness in the right place which is in the happiness of a good man' (2010, p. 58). While Sophie must be redirected from reading and thinking, towards simple contentment and happiness, feminist troublemakers are seen as the cause of their unhappiness, in their focus on social problems, and failure to be content with gender roles in families and in society. As happiness is regarded as a social responsibility to a greater good, such women are encouraged to appreciate having their basic needs (possibly) met and develop their capacity to find happiness within themselves – to 'just smile', rather than to face and express sourness, dissatisfaction, and negativity (Jackson, 2019b). When everyone is seen to benefit, and enjoy the gender status quo apart from feminists, feminists are framed as the source of bad feelings in social spaces, apart from the issues that feminists raise. Feminists are thus regarded as killjoys, who refuse to be happy and therefore make things worse for everyone, ruining the 'naturally happy' context. As Ahmed (2010, p. 65) elaborates:

> In the sociality of everyday spaces, feminists are thus attributed as the origin of bad feelings, as the ones who ruin the atmosphere . . . Say we are seated at the dinner table. Around this table, the family gathers, having polite conversations, where only certain things can be brought up. Someone says something you consider problematic. You respond, carefully, perhaps. You might be speaking quietly; or you might be getting 'wound up' . . . The violence of what was said or the violence of the provocation goes unnoticed. However she speaks, the feminist is usually the one who is viewed as 'causing the argument,' who is disturbing the fragility of peace.

In the case of the feminist killjoy, there is a discrepancy between an individual assessment and a relational evaluation of the situation. In the former case, because having happiness is good for individuals, it becomes difficult or unhelpful to describe the unjust relations possibly shaping her unhappiness. In contrast, when one looks at the relationality of emotions, they consider not only who has happiness, but how happiness circulates. From an individualist view, the feminist killjoy is wrong, deviant, and deficient, because she has failed to be happy, and thus detracts from the happiness of the group. But if one sees happiness as relational, they must look at the social circumstances of the so-called troublemaker.

Sophie and the happy housewife are to find happiness through rela-tionships: in creating happiness and recognising it in their loved ones around them. This sense of happiness is not a bad thing in itself. This view of happiness is similar in kind to happiness models valued in Chinese societies. In Mainland China and Hong Kong, in alignment with Confucian views of filial piety, people hold a two-factor structure under-standing of happiness. People more often evaluate their happiness according to both personal, individual experiences, and in relation to interpersonal evaluations, of the experiences and conditions of family members (Ho et al., 2014, p. 221).

In contrast, in Western societies, happiness tends to be understood more as individual … except in the case of the happy housewife. Here, the feminist killjoy emerges as a liberal individual who seeks out her own happiness and well-being, but as a woman she is discouraged from doing so, in something like a Western variant of Chinese scripts of ritual propriety (e.g. Sarkissian, 2014). Thus, two orientations towards happiness are applied at once in a group, based on gender. In contrast to Sophie, Emile does not have to devote himself in the same way to his partner's or his family's happiness. If Emile is unhappy, he is not discouraged from exploring the possible roots, internal or external, of his unhappiness, and seeking to improve his experience, through changing relations and situations.

In Confucian filial piety, there is an expectation that both parties have roles and responsibilities to play: husbands and wives, and parents and children. Husbands and parents thus also have to sacrifice for the greater good of the group, although these contributions will look different based on their different social roles. Unfortunately, this system does not appear to always (or often) work in the ideal way, in practice. Usually, the children and wife are expected to be more self-sacrificing (Herr, 2003; Sarkissian, 2014). Worse, some understandings of Confucianism are blatantly patriarchal, framing women as subservient to and virtuously obedient to men (Wei, 2007).

As filial piety and ritual propriety also influence civic relations of individuals and families with the nation-state, one can continue this line of thinking by considering who in the society, beyond the family, is expected or required to be self-sacrificing and sensitive to others in the formation of 'social' happiness, and who is not. Likewise, Ahmed does not only consider gender in her analysis of happiness discourse, but also explores the case of the 'melancholy migrant', the ethnic minority who is accused in postcolonial Western contexts (e.g. the United Kingdom) of clinging to the past in ways that appear problematic to mainstream members of society, who want them to more fully assimilate (2004a; also Jackson, 2019c). In this case, there is again an expectation for some people to be expressly happy within a situation that might be discriminatory or harmful towards them. Ethnic and racial minorities may be asked to give up what makes them happy and fulfilled (such as cultural traditions) to make mainstream members of society feel safe and happy, as if the minorities are responsible for mainstream people's possibly paranoid sense of threat, simply caused by their discovering diversity in their community.

Thus, what makes the mainstream members of society happy is often regarded as the only real or important happiness. In this vein, the idea that society should be more open, diverse, equitable, and pluralistic is regarded as causing less happiness, because it is not desired by mainstream members of society who fear change (including change to their own status in society; see Kinnvall, 2013), even though toleration would lead to greater happiness among ethnic and racial minorities. These views find resonance with the experiences of minorities in many Western societies, where some find that they are regarded as inherently threatening if they are not always smiling, demure, and fully and enthusiastically assimilated (see also Chapters 9 and 10).

A political account of happiness thus enables recognition of some pitfalls and risks of expecting particular emotional performances from people, across social contexts and in the midst of problematic power relations. It also sheds light on potentially pathological forms of happiness, which might be the result of expectations for happiness in inequitable and harmful circumstances. In contexts of domination, less empowered people are expected to take the perspective of more privileged people (Young, 1988; Bartky, 1990). Psychologically, this 'cultivates feelings of incapability and denies the values and experiences of the oppressed' (Superson, 2012). In societies marked by patterned violence, such as the normalisation of gender violence and racial discrimination, this can lead to pathologies related to seeking happiness in situations where it is not a rational response to experiences of threat. People can develop diminished confidence and reinforce their own negative feelings about themselves and their relations in this context, leading to 'deformed desires'. Such desires may include internalised views among women that 'a woman's place is in the home', which maintains stereotypes and inequities, and 'thereby perpetuates oppression' (Superson, 2012; see also Cudd, 2006).

Gendered emotional expectations for happiness are particularly found in traditionally feminine occupations, or 'women's work'. As Hochschild (1983) notes, service professions that involve extensive interpersonal relations and rely on some kind of customer or client satisfaction come with expectations that impact women employees in particular to express happiness to enable that of others. In education, women may be asked to do more service and emotional work and more teaching than men, because it is expected that this work makes them happier, as they are seen as more naturally sociable. Such views are also reflected in student evaluations of teaching, wherein students judge women teachers' effectiveness more in terms of their performing positive emotional dispositions such as caring, kindness, niceness, and friendliness, traits associated with expectations that women play nurturing roles (Tamboukou, 2000; Jackson, 2017a, 2019b). Educators', and particularly women's, happiness is thus expected as part of pastoral care giving.

Furthermore, under educational frameworks focused on the promotion of happiness, teachers are expected to perform happiness as models for students, and within social contexts where aspiring towards happiness is seen as a moral responsibility. They are also expected to teach students in ways that can enable happiness. Lessons that can be emotionally upsetting may be avoided in this case, if they present challenges to the image of the classroom as a happy community (Mayo, 2016). In this context, education that focuses on issues of injustice can be framed as enabling emotionally 'deviant' classroom experiences. As will be discussed more in the next chapter, empathetic and compassionate responses to the unfortunate circumstances of others are often seen as requiring a sense of personal moral distress. A lack of moral distress, as mentioned earlier, is seen as a sign of psychopathy in such contexts (Kennett, 2017). Unhappiness may be a more reasonable outcome, and the result of accurate appraisal, when learning about bad things in life, such as racial oppression, war, or gender violence (Alloy & Abramson, 1988). However, students may experience having such 'mixed emotions' as a bad thing, if happiness is framed as a larger, primary educational goal.

Thus, it may be difficult for a teacher concerned with social justice, or identifying social problems such as oppression, to teach with an orientation towards enhancing happiness, as experiences and expressions of anger, resentment, despair, and distress might be seen as inappropriate, or as departing from more 'productive' emotional engagements, which are calm, focused, and at least moderately cheery. In such a context, as Roberts notes (2016), 'the goal is to keep students or viewers happy; discomfort should be avoided wherever possible. And where this breaks down, and students or viewers become bored, or restless, or angry, those who provide the teaching or the programming are punished with lower ratings and, where necessary appropriate disciplinary action' (pp. 104–105). When happiness is prioritised and valued above all else, a teacher can lose authority or face penalties for not being happy (or not appearing happy, even if they are), or for not emotionally managing students so that they are also happy, or seem happy. Furthermore, in such situations teachers can become alienated from their work, when being authoritative is tied to happy performance despite challenges of personal life, vocation, or tragedy in the world generally (Hochschild, 1983). In this case, teachers may not feel allowed or empowered to ever have bad days, or experience uncertainty, or despair. Yet these situations cannot necessarily be avoided, and they can also be functional.

Students also face challenges in seeking effective and meaningful educational experiences while being expected to perform happiness before peers and teachers. Students, and particularly girls, are implicitly asked to trust in their educators as authorities of emotional management in curricular promotions of happiness. They are encouraged to manage their feelings and perform the right ones with each other and with educators, to have the 'right attitude'. Their experiences and expressions of happiness are then treated not just as feelings, which can be fleeting, changeable, dynamic, and related to all sorts of external causes. Rather, their experiences and expressions become reframed as a part of their moral or educational duty. Here, a focus on happiness, to the exclusion of tolerating or even exploring in an open-minded way the value of negative emotions and experiences, risks obscuring the real challenges in the world and significant challenges the students may themselves be facing. Students may also be led to think that a happy, carefree space is a 'safe' space, when it can be unintellectual, personally harmful (in the case that they develop pathologies related to happiness), and miseducative.

Alternatively, an attitude more tolerant towards expressions of unhappiness may be vital to an education oriented towards improving the world, rather than maintaining status quos that can be harmful and unjust (Ahmed, 2010). As Roberts summarises (2016, pp. 117–118), 'Happiness, for most of us, is a vital component of a good life – but it need not be *the* goal to which we should always aspire . . . Happiness in its commodified form, as a kind of drug to be marketed and administered in regular doses, takes us not closer to our humanity but further away from it.' Uncertainty and discomfort can accompany being open-minded, while despair may be a constructive response to considering the plight of others with empathy and compassion.

Depression and related experiences, as sustained long-term negative feelings that disable meaningful living and action, should surely not be promoted over well-being in education. Yet given the uncontrollable and dynamic nature of feelings, squashing negative feelings may also come at a cost. While exploring challenging situations and social problems may lead to emotions like anger, resentment, and distress in the short term, it may, in the longer term, lead to deeper feelings and a different sense of meaning, fulfilment, and joy, through effective engagement with social injustice in the world. There can also be an important place for despair and uncertainty in education.

*****

Youth self-harm, including suicide, is a pressing matter around the world, clearly linked to emotional well-being. Hong Kong, marked by extremes of wealth and poverty, limited opportunities for mobility, and extreme educational competition, has a particular challenge with youth suicide. Between 70 and 90 young people aged 6–25 commit suicide yearly, or about 8–9 per 100,000 (Education Bureau, 2017), with many more attempting suicide and engaging in self-harm. While acknowledging that suicide should be considered from an ecological perspective (as with any other psychological issue), the Hong Kong Committee on Prevention of Student Suicides identifies as relevant 'multiple factors (including mental illness, relationship and personal problems, family discord, academic concerns, etc.) and *there is no substantial direct link between student suicides and the education system*' (2016, p. 81, emphasis added). One university student on the committee argued that during the course of the committee work she identified the educational system as a factor in youth well-being and lack thereof. She claimed her view was ignored by the rest of the committee, however, as 'not evidence-based' (Wong, 2017), as if schools were somehow detached from other factors such as academic concerns, and family and personal relationships.

This is just one example which echoes what Ecclestone (2012) and Cigman (2012) observe in the United Kingdom, where government institutions treat young people as de-contextualised, as students without schools, in their final assessment of happiness and well-being. Such a framing significantly shapes the direction of interventions, effectively placing the onus of responsibility on individuals (students) to demonstrate happiness regardless of situations, as if this is the only way to enhance one's well-being and lot in life. As in Hong Kong, committees for handling youth well-being in Western societies, comprised mostly of politicians, ignore possible backwash effects of well-being interventions, as well as the lack of compelling evidence backing up suppositions about the efficacy and justice of the individual-based interventions they promote. Government institutions such as schools thereby dismiss and reject the idea that politics or social structures in society have anything to do with happiness or unhappiness. Well-being and happiness are indeed vital in society. However, their significance is not well reflected in the narrow way they are treated and promoted as educational and social aims in many societies.

4.4 Concluding Thoughts

Thinkers focused on happiness are by and large concerned with improving quality of life and cultivating fulfilment. They seek to ensure that greater numbers of people have access to a life where they feel a sense of inclusion, satisfaction, enjoyment, and meaning. Proponents of interventions to increase happiness in schools note unequal opportunities in society for these experiences, and the possibility that greater happiness for more people is attainable through interventions. They also see this happiness as instrumental for making communities more functional, prosperous, and positive, overall. Interventions to enhance moods and positive attitudes work in many cases, in the eyes of therapists, teachers, and patients and test subjects. If it works, then what is the problem?

Political examinations of happiness show how it is socially constructed, often in ways that dismiss the importance of external, relational, and communal factors. This benefits organisations and social institutions and their leaders, who do not want to change their practices, or be regarded as accountable for happiness and well-being in communities. Many schools providing emotional literacy programmes and related curricula have not had as their primary aim improvement of the lives of students from a holistic view, but have rather only effectively worked on improvement of students' attitudes and outlooks to enhance learning (Boler, 1999; Ecclestone, 2012). Brackett and Rivers (2014) similarly note how SEL curricula are employed in some cases to decrease stress caused by high-stakes testing, which is also seen to negatively impact teacher well-being (see also Tye & O'Brien, 2002; Abeles, 2015). These trends are particularly common in some East Asian societies, such as Hong Kong, where student suicide related to academic stress is on the rise. While some small degree of test anxiety is not necessarily unhealthy, schools are in many cases implementing practices which clearly increase unhealthy stress levels of students (and staff), while effectively holding students (and staff) accountable for their coping.

In this context, schools should not teach that happiness is simply a good thing, as if it is unrelated to the dynamic circumstances of life and the challenges people face. Challenges in life are to some extent unavoidable, and happiness can never be (and should never be) a permanent state. Acceptance of some unhappiness should therefore also be encouraged, as unhappy feelings are a part of life. Otherwise, students may find themselves in a place of hiding their feelings, seeing their feelings as bound up in impossible feeling rules to never be unhappy. In some cases, unhappiness should also be seen as a reasonable response to negative situations and as a sign that something external should change. Given such cases, student unhappiness can also be accepted and explored as intrinsically and instrumentally valuable towards enhancing well-being. Students should not be encouraged to put on a happy face in every situation. Instead, cases of unhappiness can be contemplated and learned from, as students develop their sense of the full range of human emotions and experiences, and learn to see themselves as active parts of dynamic environments, where making things better is not just a personal matter.

CHAPTER 5

Caring, Compassion, and Altruism

This chapter focuses on some of the most prized virtues for cultivation in education: caring, compassion, and altruism. Related traits are empathy, sympathy, and pity. These qualities are widely held to be important to develop among people, across traditions around the world. They are typically seen as foundational traits to being a good person and doing good deeds. As such, they have been discussed at length by philosophers over time, and are broadly regarded as vital characteristics to develop in young people through schooling and other education and cultivation. However, there are contexts where these feelings and related emerging dispositions and practices are controversial or undesirable, challenging a blanket positive assessment of these feelings as always good.

This chapter examines major views of caring, compassion, and related emotional virtues, fleshing out divergences and convergences across traditions and disciplines, and exploring different understandings of their significance for education. In this chapter, views on these topics are organised in relation to their orientation towards the 'empathy-altruism' thesis. The empathy-altruism thesis generally contends that empathy, sympathy, compassion, and the like can lead to emotional experiences of fellow feeling and positive relationality towards others, altruistic motivation, and benevolent deeds (Batson, 1991; also Cialdini et al., 1997). It then follows that education should strive to cultivate these other-oriented feelings. Many philosophers, psychologists, and educators support this perspective. However, it faces challenges, also from across fields, among those who focus on the thesis's limitations and possibly problematic educational implications.

When it comes to caring, compassion, and altruism, this chapter shows that while there appears to be a consensus view on the merits of these feelings and related dispositions and actions in education and society, the blanket promotion of these emotional virtues is not altogether unproblematic. In this case, a more critical perspective on the empathy-altruism thesis is defended, as the over-optimistic view of these feelings and dispositions can fail to recognise the risks and challenges that accompany them.

95

5.1   The Empathy-Altruism Thesis

The interrelated emotional virtues of pity, sympathy, compassion, and empathy are explored by a variety of thinkers. Pity is sometimes seen as condescending today, but it did not have the same connotation historically. In the past, pity was regarded as similar to what one might call sympathy or empathy today: an essentially relational feeling, where one feels connected, particularly to the pain of another (Nussbaum, 2013). However, Aristotle does not emphasise pity as a virtue, because he regards it as excessive, writing that 'for example, no good person would be distressed when parricides and bloodthirsty murderers meet punishment' (cited in Kristjánsson, 2018, p. 70). For Aristotle, pity is a pain without judgement that can be felt for those with *deserved* bad fortune. A more reflective pain, reserved for those with *undeserved* bad fortune, is different. Aristotle does not name or promote a specific virtuous state here. For Nussbaum (2013) and Kristjánsson (2018), an emotional virtue can be elaborated following Aristotle's logic, however, which is roughly akin to contemporary understandings of compassion. This is described, although it is not named, by Aristotle, as 'a feeling or pain at an apparent evil, destructive, or painful, which befalls one who does not deserve it, and which we might expect to befall ourselves or some friend of ours, and moreover to befall us soon' (1984).

Sympathy is emphasised as an emotional virtue by Hume and Smith. Like pity, sympathy is described by Hume as a kind of 'emotional contagion', which can progress towards compassion (or empathy), in acts of benevolence (or care), upon a 'vivid impression' of suffering (Ilyes, 2017). Smith (1759) envisions cases for sympathy more broadly, claiming that sympathy can 'denote our fellow-feeling with any passion whatever' (p. 49). He critically observes in relation that sympathy tends to be partial, typically experienced towards directly related others, such as a friend, family member, or other 'fellow' person or group. Smith claims that an ordinary European man would lose more sleep over the loss of his finger than over an earthquake in China. Only by incorporating a 'love of virtue' in this place could the man morally develop his basic sympathy, to create a more impartial view, which Smith held as essential for moral judgement and action (Ilyes, 2017, p. 106).

Writing in the same time period, Sophie de Grouchy has a slightly different view. She argues that a person can be naturally or reflexively sympathetic, as an emotional response, for others not connected to oneself, by applying a sense of general sympathy in considering matters of social justice. As de Grouchy sees it, 'a properly developed human being who lives in a society that does not actively discourage sympathy, one with good laws and no massive inequality, will feel sympathy for anyone who suffers regardless of who he is. This is so because we learn not just to feel for others like us but how to feel for others, for humanity in general' (cited in Berges, 2015, p. 96).

These views, which idealise broadening conceptions of care from close others to distant others, contrast with those encouraged by Confucianism. In Chinese societies, altruism, *ren* as a kind of benevolent love, and *li* as a ritualistic expression of internalised loyalty, respect, and deferential care, are stressed as central to morality and virtue (Dubs, 1951; Herr, 2003). Yet Confucian thinkers err on the side of favouring those close to oneself, defending it as morally better and natural (Dubs, 1951; Munro, 2002; Epley, 2015). *Li* is framed as an other-serving disposition enabling benevolent behaviour to be encouraged primarily of children towards their families (Herr, 2003). In contrast with de Grouchy and Smith, Confucian texts encourage care and altruism based more on family connection, in the forms of filial piety and ritual propriety. In Ancient China, Mozi criticised this exclusive approach to love as a factor in the rise of clannish and criminal behaviour in society. However, Mencius (among others) emphasised in contrast that it is alien, or even non-human to fail to recognise special duties in close interpersonal relationships, over any kind of more generalised feeling of care or altruism (Dubs, 1951; also Munro, 2002; Herr, 2003; Wei, 2007).

Contemporary Western thinkers tend to endorse a more all-encompassing ideal of empathy, care, and compassion, when it comes to the question of for 'whom' one should care. Nussbaum references Aristotle's view, in identifying compassion as occurring when a person observes that someone suffers something serious through no fault of their own, which could happen to their self (2013). She contends that eudemonistic evaluation in relation to such emotions can lead to just action. Compassion, according to Nussbaum, extends from empathy, which she defines as 'participatory enactment of the situation of the sufferer ... combined with the awareness that one is not oneself the sufferer' (2001, p. 329). One can, on the other hand, be empathetic without being compassionate. Nussbaum gives the example of a juror who 'may come to understand the experience of a criminal without having compassion for the person's plight', upon reaching a guilty verdict (2001, p. 329). Empathy that leads to compassion, Nussbaum argues, can motivate altruistic action.

This connection between empathy, compassion, and altruism is also defended by Lawrence Blum. As Blum argues, 'a sympathetic, compassionate person is more likely to act to foster the good of others. This is part of what it means to be sympathetic and compassionate, insofar as these involve dispositions to have certain emotions, and these emotions involve a disposition to act for the sake of the other's good' (1980, pp. 132–133). Blum relatedly emphasises and defends the value of altruism as an emotional disposition towards moral action on behalf of others, which (he argues) qualifies as a good in itself. According to Blum, one gains something from experiencing another's altruistic emotional orientation towards them. He states that this is possible even in a situation where one seems unable to do any good for another. As Blum writes: 'It might not be so obvious whether someone is suffering, nor so clear whether there is something one could do to help . . . Encouraging compassion and concern, rather than always a focus on duties of beneficence, can, among other things, reveal greater needs for and possibilities of beneficence' (1980, p. 110). He further argues that feelings like sympathy enhance a totality of good given through altruistic acts, regardless of duty, or the consequences (or lack thereof) of such acts (1980).

Blum gives some examples to elaborate his views (1980). Blum imagines a husband Bob visiting his dying wife Sue at the hospital. Blum argues that it would make a difference to Sue if she found that Bob did not visit her out of a sense of care, but out of objective duty. Though 'the visit would probably bring about *some* good to Sue . . . [this] will be mitigated by her discomfort, anger, or disappointment', upon recognising Bob was motivated by duty rather than by emotion (1980, p. 143). In another example, Blum considers citizens striking against Californian fruit growers in support of farmworkers. In this case, 'the sympathy and human support' of citizens has a value independent from any 'concrete assistance' (Blum, 1980, p. 145). Blum thus argues that an expression of emotional concern 'constitutes a kind of totality which is the bearer of the good to the recipient' (1980, p. 146).

Noddings (2002) and Michael Slote (2007) relatedly frame caring feelings as foundational to justice. Noddings states that 'feeling what [another] feels as nearly as possible, is the essential part of caring from the view of the one-caring'. Similar to Blum's emotional altruism, she goes on that 'in the deep human sense that [occupies] us, I cannot claim to care . . . if my caretaking is perfunctory' (1984, p. 16). In Noddings' work, care has relational, emotional, and 'rational-objective thinking' components. Caring cannot be 'perfunctory', or based only upon a sense of rational, objective duty, as caring requires an emotional relation (2002). This positions Noddings' care ethics view (as well as Blum's view) as at odds with Confucian ethics, as the concept of *li* frames care as a matter of relational duty, expressed through norms implying communal social standards (Herr, 2003; Epley, 2015).

Noddings emphasises the intrinsic or inherent value of care, arguing that because relationships of care are a fundamental good, essential in childhood for appropriate human development, people are morally obliged to care for others in a way that is recognisable to those others as care. The relationship is essential to care, as it enables mutual recognition of care giving. Noddings also indicates that a caring response may not follow rules, as it is particular to a situation, not subject to Universalist ethics (2002). In relation, in giving care as an act or within a relation, one must be respectful, attentive, and responsive. Respect is recognition that another person is an end in their own right, with their own world view, and not an extension of oneself. Attentiveness is an active-listening orientation towards others, which entails considering needs or causes of dilemmas below the surface in seeking to understand others' situations. Responsiveness relates to the appropriateness of a reaction. Caring is not like charity or broad generosity. Noddings (2002) notes that it was not responsive when people donated food and clothing to Afghanistan after an earthquake, for example, when building materials were what was needed.

Noddings signals that caring interpersonal relations should undergird ethical thought, while principles of care can also inform broader social practices (Noddings, 1999). Nussbaum similarly argues that compassion begins with direct relations, before ideally branching out cross-culturally and globally, as people tend to develop compassion initially towards those close to them (e.g. 1994). Sigal Ben-Porath (2008) argues that just as interdependency in the lifespan obliges people to care, so does global interdependency justify a global ethics of care. Ben-Porath observes that it may seem strange to discuss care of social entities such as nation-states. She thus elaborates that 'caring relations among groups refer broadly to the common understandings they have about possible ways to perform caring acts. The way the other is portrayed . . . and the self-understanding of each group as related to its role with the other . . . generates the basis for the relationship among the groups' (2008, p. 65).

These accounts of care, compassion, and altruism intersect with, and are echoed by, some findings and perspectives in psychology. Caregiving is regarded as essential for psychological adjustment and well-being, generally speaking. Care and compassion are typically classified as 'positive emotions' and regarded as good and moral in psychological accounts (DeCuir-Gunby & Williams-Johnson, 2014; Shuman & Scherer, 2014). Empathy is considered a key element of emotional intelligence that people develop during childhood (Graham & Taylor, 2014; Immordino-Yang & Christodoulou, 2014). Empathy is considered by most psychologists to lead to altruistic behaviour, and many studies evidence that people normally make sacrifices to their own well-being as part of empathetic responses to observing others' suffering (Stueber, 2019). The empathy-altruism thesis is particularly associated with the work of Daniel Batson, who found that perspective taking leads to empathetic concern, and that empathetic concern leads people to engage in altruistic behaviour to improve life for others around them (1991). Others contend that it is not specifically altruism manifested in this case, but a sense of self–other overlap that develops from empathy; such overlap could indicate that apparent altruism is not purely other-oriented, as it can also be seen to be beneficial to oneself (Cialdini et al., 1997).

Psychologists also break down empathy into two basic kinds: cognitive and emotional. Cognitive empathy is a capacity to understand another's experience and take their perspective, while emotional empathy is the feeling of what another feels: 'an emotional response that stems from another's emotional state or condition and that is congruent' with it (Eisenberg & Strayer, 1987). There has been a great deal of debate in the field about whether cognitive and emotional empathy are distinct and separate, or whether both are component parts of empathy, properly understood (Eisenberg & Strayer, 1987; Davis, 1996). In relation, psychologists associate the failure to develop and exhibit empathy as developmentally irregular and deviant, given its importance to realising emotional intelligence and giving appropriate responses to others in society (Hoffman, 2000). These emotional virtues are likewise highlighted in social and emotional learning approaches, which regard the ability to recognise, understand, and label emotions of others as beneficial to interacting with others effectively and appropriately, interpreting situations from others' perspectives, and reducing misunderstandings (Brackett & Rivers, 2014).

Many educational recommendations stem from these philosophical and psychological perspectives. For Nussbaum, empathy and compassion are the most crucial emotions related to social justice that educators should develop in students (2001). Nussbaum elaborates that these emotional virtues are vital capabilities for understanding what justice demands in relation to social policy and welfare (1995). As an implication of her view, she posits (2001, 2013) that people should read multicultural literature to develop their productive sense of human relation, empathy, and compassion, and to learn to extend their sense of sympathy from those close to them to those further away, who they may see as 'different'. Educators therefore should encourage empathy and compassion in civic and moral education, by sharing literature that invokes students' empathetic responses and critical reflections on others' suffering (Peterson, 2017), in cases that are both easy and difficult to imagine. Nussbaum contends that such engaged reading can invoke deeper reflection on social justice issues in society and around the world (2013). Such a view, which intersects with other multicultural orientations towards civic and moral education, is intuitively attractive to many people, and reflected in educator practices in many parts of the world (particularly in Western societies).

Noddings relatedly states that people should learn to care for each other in education, as caring relations are foundational to a good life (1984, 2002, 2003). She also argues that schools should be caring institutions, where educators are responsible not just for teaching content, but also for caring for and developing caring relations with and alongside students (2002). This means educators should attend to young people's needs – emotional, psychological, and physical, as well as intellectual – in schools, and encourage similarly caring dispositions among students. Others also emphasise the need for educators to cultivate empathy towards their students as part of professional practice, as 'to relate successfully, we need to be able to draw on each other's emotions as well as taking their perspectives' (Demetriou, 2018, p. 280; also Peterson, 2017). Such recommendations are in line with many common practices, particularly in primary education across contexts, and also in Confucian-heritage societies, where educators across age groups are seen to be like caregivers and 'important others' for students – like a second family of mentors and elders (Jackson, 2019a).

Beyond exposing students to multicultural stories and caring for them, some recommend direct instruction for understanding and encouraging caring, empathy, and compassion, as well. This can be part of a broader curriculum for emotional intelligence and social and emotional learning, involving self-awareness and self-regulation of emotions, or developed into a focused curriculum on valuing and exhibiting empathy, compassion, and caring. The Jubilee Centre provides instructional materials so students can learn at primary stages that, for instance, 'without caring, people would get sick and there would be no-one to help them get better' (n.d.). Jubilee materials also take a virtue ethics approach in part, encouraging students in one guide to think through the mean state for exhibiting compassion (Kristjánsson et al., 2017). The Centre also recommends Buddhist Loving-Kindness Meditation, among other forms of perspective taking, for young people to develop compassion for a broader group of people, as discussed in the below extract (Kristjánsson et al., 2017):

> In the first stage, you feel metta [love] for yourself. You start by becoming aware of yourself, and focusing on feelings of peace, calm, and tranquillity. You can use an image, like golden light flooding your body. In the second stage you think of a good friend. Bring them to mind as vividly as you can, and think of their good qualities. Feel your connection with your friend, and your liking for them, and encourage these to grow by wishing them well. If it is helpful, you can use an image such as shining light from your heart into theirs. Then think of someone you do not particularly like or dislike. Your feelings towards this person are 'neutral'. This may be someone you do not know well but see around, such as your

> postman or someone who regularly serves you in a shop. Include them in your feelings of metta. Then think of someone you are currently having difficulties with. Trying not to get caught up in any difficult feelings, you think of them positively and send your metta to them as well.

Such a method aligns with Buddhist meditative practices and recommendations for moral training, particularly in Indo-Tibetan Buddhism, and has been found, in some studies, to increase the ability to feel empathy and compassion towards others (McRae, 2017).

Interestingly, this approach does not emphasise compassion as a mean state, as an Aristotelian might advocate, or a more critical view, such as Nussbaum's limiting of compassion to those who do not deserve their harsh fate. Aristotle or Nussbaum could counter here that they may have reason to dislike someone, so developing deep empathy towards them could be wasted energy in some contexts. Noddings also would not advocate for this approach, as caring is found in relation to others (where one is receptive, attentive, and respectful); meditating on a person at length without relating to them is hardly the same thing as her ideal of caring practice. On the other hand, such a universal notion of compassion, as is seen in Loving-Kindness Meditation, is also found in Christianity, where the individual cultivation of feelings of compassion is advocated not only in relation to those who are held as blameless for their suffering, and not only in relation to those who are close to oneself (Roberts, 2013, also 1989).

In contrast, Andrew Peterson (2017) argues that dialogue is important for developing compassion in education. As a form of intersubjective communication, which can involve both verbal and non-verbal communicative exchanges, students can learn to recognise each other and share interests, with the development of more caring tendencies as an expected outcome. When students engage in dialogue that is authentic and sincere, they can learn to see beyond themselves and engage in listening and practising eudemonistic judgement (Peterson, 2017). Relatedly, Maxwell and Reichenbach identify 'requests to exercise imagination, namely to engage in moral role taking', as a common strategy of emotional education used by parents and teachers alike, holding such empathetic engagement with others as 'a precondition of the possibility of moral agency as such' (2005, p. 194). This strategy also engages students more dialogically and relationally in cultivating empathy as a virtue.

Another recommendation for developing student empathy and compassion is to facilitate students' service learning or exchange trips. Noddings (1984) writes in favour of this approach, noting that 'wherever students might be assigned – to hospitals, nursing homes, animal shelters, parks, botanical gardens – a definite expectation would be that their work be a true apprenticeship in caring' (pp. 2–3). Relatedly, international exchanges are widely endorsed and valued for their capacity to enable students to reflect on their lives in comparison with those of others (Gallwey & Wilgus, 2014; Nesterova & Jackson, 2016). Often, there is a focus in exchanges or service trips on understanding the plight of disadvantaged others, to develop a broader sense of empathy and compassion among students, who can see through first-hand travels the struggles other people face (typically through no fault of their own) and develop themselves more as 'global citizens' (Jackson, 2013; Peterson, 2017).

Such strategies stem in part from recognition of a key challenge with cultivating compassion, care, or empathy as emotional virtues: people do not tend to develop as much compassion or empathy towards people they do not see as 'fellows'. That is, they can struggle to identify with and have compassion for people who do not seem similar, or close, to themselves (Sreenivasan, 2020; Roberts, 1989). They may also fail to imagine that others are in situations they could someday find themselves in, given deep inequities within and across societies. This decreases the likelihood of an experience of fellow feeling, and related effective evaluative judgement and responsive action. Moreover, developing young people's emotional and relational aspects as recommended in the previous paragraphs does not necessarily lead to their becoming good people and serving just ends. These challenges and others, and alternative orientations towards caring and compassion, will be discussed in the next section.

5.2 Challenges and Alternative Views

Many challenges in appropriately cultivating the emotional virtues of caring and compassion in relations with others relate to the use of eudemonistic or other reflective judgement. First, people tend to have compassion more towards loved ones and others who they think are more like themselves. As Nussbaum concedes, one may feel more strongly towards a friend stuck in traffic than a homeless person (2001). This possibility challenges the premise that empathy leads to altruism, as empathy and empathetic altruism can therefore be racist, sexist, and ethnocentric. Most people have unconscious biases towards different groups that go unrecognised in the use of moral judgement and evaluation (Eberhardt, 2019). In relation, compassion occurs when one sees another's suffering as undeserved. People tend to more clearly see suffering as undeserved when they feel empathy for people who are 'like' themselves. Stereotypes significantly influence people's evaluations here. For instance, when psychologists remind subjects of racial stereotypes about delinquent boys, subjects more often judge them as responsible and blameworthy, and thus 'more deserving of punishment than participants in an unprimed control condition' (Graham & Taylor, 2014, p. 113).

Nussbaum, Noddings, and others interested in civic education, such as Taylor (1992) and Callan (1997), argue that because of this tendency, the work of cultivating civic fellow feelings towards others in society should start small and broaden over time, to extend compassion from unknown to known others (Jackson, 2019a). This view of the value of broadening one's perspective gradually seems to be reflected in Buddhist meditative practices (as discussed above), where a person develops loving kindness, from friends to acquaintances, and finally to people they do not like. Yet the capacity to imagine oneself in another's shoes across social difference is also required here, to know what diverse others are going through, effectively evaluate their possible culpability, and appropriately recognise their suffering (Kukar, 2016). This can be challenging in the best of cases, given individual differences. As Nussbaum notes, 'even appropriate compassion is unreliable and partial' (2001, p. 403). People's emotional responses can be unreasonable or disproportionate for a variety of personal or interpersonal reasons. When it comes to educating young children, requests for empathetic perspective-taking, although common, are often found to be ineffective (Maxwell & Reichenbach, 2007).

Meanwhile, there are also noteworthy cross-cultural differences in expressions of emotions and in judgements of normal responses to situations that challenge the process of understanding others (Graham & Taylor, 2014; e.g. Wong & Tsai, 2007). So-Young Kang (2006) compares views of caring among white and black US people and Koreans. Kang finds significant differences in expressions and articulations of relations of care across the three groups, which imply divergent understandings of requirements and appearances of care. Kang also notes that gender and other factors are involved in people's views about appropriate expressions and behaviours of care within these groups. Likewise, as previously discussed, Confucian views of appropriate expressions of caring in various kinds of social relations differ from those in Western virtue or care ethics, and other mainstream Western conceptions (Herr, 2003; Wei, 2007; Epley, 2015). Christian views of compassion may also contrast with Aristotelian ones (R. Roberts, 2013). Empathy and related altruism and care thus require substantial respect and attention across cultures, if one is indeed to understand another's experience, rather than ethnocentrically judge them. In this case, it can be unhelpful to simply imagine oneself in another's shoes. One can get judgements wrong through ignorance and inept attention, even when trying.

Other challenges, including pathologies of empathy, are obscured in the empathy-altruism thesis. One is the possibility that egoism rather than altruism informs so-called caring or compassion-based altruistic action, as empathy can be used to benefit oneself. The most extreme variant of this process in Western culture is categorised as psychopathy. Although psychopaths often seem to exhibit lack of empathy, they may have empathy and be able to imagine others' experiences of suffering (Kennett, 2017, p. 367). What they more precisely lack is distress related to such empathy, which involves a moral judgement about suffering, in the case of others or themselves.

In relation, 'tactical empathy', wherein one develops empathy in order to manipulate others, is 'under-reported and under-studied because of the assumption among many researchers that empathy is inherently virtuous' (Hollan, 2017, p. 347). Broadly across societies, 'poker players, police profilers, military strategists, con artists, Internet scammers, method actors, and everyday romantic Casanovas' work to understand others' views and feelings, to win them over for personal, self-serving, rather than altruistic, ends (Hollan, 2017, p. 347; Ta & Ickes, 2017). As Maxwell and Reichenbach (2007, p. 152) note, 'perspective-taking, of course, has no moral value in and of itself for it can be used also for morally dubious ends'.

Empathy can therefore be abused in educational contexts, to benefit students and teachers and make them feel better about themselves, rather than to engage in altruistic action, or develop broader compassion. As Boler observes, students reading multicultural literature can enjoy engaging in passive empathy that is not intensely felt, even when reading about the Holocaust, failing to develop moral distress in relation to others' suffering (1999). As Boler writes, the 'palatable permission of pleasure motivates no consequent reflection or action, either about the production of meaning, or about one's complicit responsibility within historical and social conditions. Let off the hook, we are free to move on to the next consumption' (1999, p. 164). Boler notes that such reading, rather than causing distress, can more simply make students feel good about their own place in the world. They may feel like (and 'learn' that) they are becoming better people, simply for enjoying multicultural literature.

Relatedly, international exchanges and service learning trips, where students serve communities by volunteering in schools and other social institutions in disadvantaged areas, are often justified as a means for developing compassion and empathy. Yet most evaluations of such experiences only examine their impacts for students. They consider the trips successful if students learn about the experiences of others (and enjoy themselves). Often, there is little concern for whether the students positively impact communities or develop themselves as moral agents (Kristjánsson, 2018). Such forms of engagement reflect and teach messages that any cross-cultural (or cross-town) engagement is beneficial, if it is seen as such by privileged parties (students and educators facilitating trips). Meanwhile, the challenges and significance of empathising across difference in a moral way in these cases remain largely overlooked (Cook, 2012; Jackson, 2013; Nesterova & Jackson, 2016).

In this context, a deeper approach advocated for moral and political education emphasises that such approaches should specifically involve witnessing suffering in the world, and experiencing related emotional discomfort (Boler, 1999; Zembylas, 2008; Applebaum, 2016). Yet educators observe that students may resist such approaches when they become uncomfortable, complaining that the lesson is encouraging their guilt or shame, which are hardly ideal responses (Peterson, 2017). At other times, witnessing trauma can lead to resentment, when students feel powerless or complicit in relation to challenges that seem to be well beyond the scope of their personal capacity. Such approaches have also been found to lead to desensitisation (Zembylas, 2008). For some students, they can lead to moral disgust and cynicism.

Faced with such possible experiences, students may reflexively express that they want to 'do something' when faced with the evils of the world around them, in lessons intended to cultivate empathy and compassion (Hytten & Warren, 2003). Some students want to transform their shock into action, so that they do not have to feel uncomfortable about discovering unearned advantages over others. Such action may be experienced as, and believed to be, other-serving. But since this 'doing something' is a response to one's own experience rather than a change in experience necessarily impacting others, it may be self-serving, as the needs and differences of others are still not effectively attended to through rash action. These observations are supported by work in psychology, where empathic *concern* is seen more specifically to motivate caring actions for others, while emotional empathy is not as motivational. As Jean Decety and Keith Yoder (2016, p. 12) note, 'emotional sharing with the misfortune of others ... can lead to personal distress and not necessarily a motivation for upholding a principle of justice for all'.

Feelings of pity and empathy may lead a person to volunteer for service learning or exchanges experiences, to attempt to work towards correcting the wrongs of the world. Yet in this context some volunteers face resistance, because local people recognise them as patronising, culturally inappropriate, and self-serving, rather than attentive and respectful (Jackson, 2013). María Lugones and Elizabeth Spelman (1983, p. 581) write that in such a case, 'We become the vehicles of your own redemption .... You should stay out of our way, respect us and our distance, and forego the use of whatever power you have over us – for example, the power to use your language ... to overwhelm us with your education.' Such examples make it clear that empathy or compassion cannot be virtuous or just without the critical use of judgement, which requires reflecting on a range of moral considerations within a situation, rather than orienting oneself towards compassion at every opportunity (R. Roberts, 2013; Sreenivasan, 2020).

Psychologists have identified a related, but distinct form of pathological 'egoism-altruism'. It is not intentionally manipulative like psychopathy, or a simple form of egoism masquerading as altruism. Instead, this egoism-altruism stems from a blurring of the experiences of self and other, which has unhelpful outcomes. This is the tendency towards developing a strong fellow feeling for others, where 'the conception of self and other are not distinct but are merged to some degree', which causes people to sacrifice themselves in experimental conditions for the benefit of others (Cialdini et al., 1997, p. 490). From one perspective, selflessness is a moral ideal, often invoked in religious traditions (and in Confucianism), and in everyday discussions of the benefits of empathy, compassion, caring, and altruism. However, seen from another angle, it can be harmful to oneself to feel too much empathy for others, with one's feelings not well anchored to a stable sense of and respect for oneself (May, 2017). Such radical altruism stemming from a deep form of empathy, where the lines between self and other are blurred, can render one useless and helpless, unable to benefit oneself or others, and prone to despair.

Another challenge related to promoting empathy involves the common use of disparate expectations for empathy and care, based particularly on gender. People tend to assume that women are naturally more empathetic and caring than men. This impacts conceptions about compassion and care in Western societies, and in Confucian-heritage contexts (Wei, 2007). As has been mentioned in previous chapters, Noddings' care ethics relates caring to a maternal rather than paternal role, and describes the use of emotion to guide moral action as using the 'woman's voice'. Neuroscientific and self-report research also suggest that women are more empathetic. Simon Baron-Cohen (2003) depicts 'male' and 'female' brain types, which are apparently 'hardwired' for 'systematising' and 'empathising', respectively.

Yet Baron-Cohen's methods for gathering evidence and his biological framework for understanding such differences have been found by other researchers to be highly problematic, exaggerating statistical significance to deliberately elaborate gendered types (Bluhm, 2017; Rippon, 2019). More systematic research finds that social expectations play a significant role in apparent gender differences in empathy. In studies, men demonstrate more empathy when they are rewarded for it, highlighting that the perceived value of empathy influences its cultivation at the individual level (Ta & Ickes, 2017). In relation to studies based on self-reports, researchers note that 'women assume that it is expected to be more empathetic as a female and thus are more likely to describe themselves according to this gender stereotype' (Derntl et al., 2010, p. 79). Furthermore, the impact of 'gender stereotypes might even extend to neuro-biological responses ... when subjects, in particular females, assume that it is expected to act according to a certain stereotype' (Derntl et al., 2010, p. 79).

In this context, it is likely that uneven expectations for caring and empathy are often encouraged across many societies based on gender. Indeed, women are more likely to 'care too much' in contexts where their subservience is encouraged (Card, 1990). Caring is traditionally regarded as women's (unpaid) work. In this context, the intrinsic value placed on caring in education should be problematised, as 'caring may not always be good', particularly when 'certain social groups feel guilty about not caring', when others face no such predicaments (Applebaum, 1998, p. 421; see also Jackson, 2019b). Disparate expectations of empathy and care, and their possibly harmful consequences, should be considered, in evaluating the benefits of promoting these emotional virtues in diverse classrooms, among both teachers and students.

More generally, some observe that given the cognitive and emotional demands of emotional regulation and the seemingly infinite possibilities for witnessing suffering in the world, care and compassion as human resources are scarce, given 'the public's bounded ability to feel and act on behalf of distant others' (Chouliaraki, 2010, p. 120). Organisations such as Oxfam can be seen to manipulate people's tendencies towards empathy and compassion, to gain donations from people who feel guilty when they experience these feelings and are reminded of the suffering of others (Jackson, 2014b). Yet there are limits to the human capacity to witness suffering. Compassion fatigue (Kavar, 2010; Peterson, 2017), over-functioning (Norwood, 2008), empathy overload, and other dysfunctional traits are observed in cases where people care too much, and fail to recognise their own needs due to their (often taught or trained) dispositions to be overly oriented towards others. In relation, empathy can be seen as 'a limited resource that we need to use wisely', as desensitization to suffering can be facilitated though widespread perception of senseless, hopeless, pervasive suffering (Leighton, 2011, p. 226).

Finally, there are emotional experiences wherein people are not able to attune themselves to others emotionally in the way prized by proponents of empathy and compassion. Research on autism and alexithymia, both known to limit one's particular capacity to '*feel* what things are like for another person' (Kennett, 2017, emphasis in original), contradicts the empathy-altruism thesis, problematising the link between empathy and morality. Relatedly, people with caring attachment problems, stemming from childhood relationship challenges (a population intersecting with those with autism and alexithymia), are also hindered in engaging in empathetic relations, due to early experiences where their responsiveness to others was demanded and manipulated in abusive, neglectful ways (Denham, 2017; Demetriou, 2018). Research with these groups shows that people can lack fellow feeling – and many do so, through no fault of their own – while they can nonetheless still cognitively work to understand others' views and needs to care about others in a moral, if not emotional, way. Jeanette Kennett thus concludes (2017, p. 374):

> While there is no question that empathy is important for participation in moral communities, regulation of behaviour, the sharing of norms and acquisition of morally relevant information . . . an examination of psychopathologies in which empathy is impaired indicates that there are other pathways to moral concern and moral understanding and other processes that are important to moral judgment and moral agency. These other pathways and processes are not just compensatory mechanisms; they operate and are important in the ordinary case.

As discussed in previous chapters, people with limited capacities for identifying their own emotions and those of others are framed as deviant in discourses on educating emotional virtues that hold emotional self-awareness as essential. Yet these experiences are not far removed from tendencies of ordinary people. All are vulnerable to having difficulty with emotional awareness and empathy at times. No one is perfectly and ideally empathetic all the time. Thus, while such people and experiences may not constitute majorities, they should not be regarded as morally deficient, or deviant in educational contexts (among others). Lessons in schools should not stigmatise such normal experiences and challenges, by suggesting that morality requires constant emotional attunement. In this context, it is bad moral luck for some that empathy and compassion are linked, in Western discourse, to moral cultivation and social justice education.

Thus, one can care and feel fellow feeling, with bias and partiality in relation to others, or with inaccurate perceptions across lines of difference. They can do so in self-serving, egotistical, immoral ways. Or they can do it too much, or to the point of fatigue, harmful guilt, or with an oppressive or otherwise unhelpful sense of radical selflessness. People's empathy can be manipulated for good or bad ends; others can be moral but lack the capacity for fellow feeling that compassion demands. For all these reasons, empathy, care, and compassion are emotional virtues that should be educated about in a cautious way.

Some philosophies notably diverge in view from the empathy-altruism thesis, given such concerns. Stoicism is one of the earliest traditions known for a concern with resisting action based on 'passions' (emotional responses and impulses) or personal attachments (or fears). Stoics observe the value of experiencing good feelings, such as a basic kind of warmth towards others, and they do see a role for emotions in life (Jackson, 2017b). However, their view of the role of emotions is limited, in relation to rational judgement, given the tendency of people to be biased towards those closest to them (Nussbaum, 1994). Buddhists are also known for their aim at releasing desires for particular forms of caring attachment, while they may still see a positive role for a less attached form of compassion (Kupperman, 1995; McRae, 2012). Some Muslim and Christian thinkers also identify risks of inappropriate partiality towards loved ones (Jackson, 2017b). Early Christians wrestled with the place of marriage and love in society, recognising that such deep interpersonal attachments could be possible distractions from other commitments of a Christian life. As mentioned previously, the Chinese philosopher Mozi saw commonplace Confucian dedication and loyalty to personal family connections as problematic, enabling criminal behaviour without attachment to larger society (Dubs, 1951).

In his early writings Kant articulated moral feeling as the base of morality (1797; Jackson, 2018a). He argued that people should observe the situations of the disadvantaged to cultivate empathy and develop their orientations towards justice. However, his later work emphasises the dangers of rashly acting on sympathetic or benevolent feelings (Jackson, 2017b). Rawls (2000) similarly claims that principles derived from neutrality and impartiality should guide action and moral education. Thomas Nagel (1970) defends 'pure rational altruism' as a deontological duty of benevolence based in objective, impartial understanding of humanity. As Nagel claims, 'without question people may be motivated by benevolence, sympathy, love . . . but there is also something else, a motivation available when none of those are, and also operative when they are present, which has genuinely the status of a rational requirement on human conduct' (1970, p, 80). Following Kant, Nagel argues that rational altruism requires that people 'view ourselves from both the personal and impersonal standpoints' and develop altruism as an interest in objective good (1970, p. 144).

Callan (1997, pp. 80–81) argues in parallel that an emotional good of care is not necessarily better than a rational good. To elaborate this, Callan considers the case of an illiterate husband and wife. The wife wants to learn to read, but the husband forbids her. Finally, he accepts her wish. Callan asks if it matters here whether the husband's change of heart stems from love, rather than his sense of his wife's rights and his duties. Callan argues that the man's respect for his wife as a person is morally better than his fulfilling her needs due to his interpersonal emotional connection, as a 'fundamental part of our self-conception is a worth we possess that does not depend on the affection of others' (1997, p. 80). Callan also gives a second example, of a slaveholder and a slave. In this case, it is hardly morally superior, or better for the slave, if the slaveholder frees the slave out of love, affection, or interpersonal concern, rather than duty. Because moral rights are independent of, and should come before, desires related to partial affection and care, 'to be freed out of love would remain degrading' (Jackson, 2017b, p. 413).

That one's sense of justice should be primary to any sympathetic emotional response also echoes evidence from interviews with rescuers of Jews in Nazi Europe, who often expressed their motivations in terms of their sense of injustice, rather than in relation to sympathetic, emotional feelings and particular relations of interdependency (Konarzewski, 1992; Monroe, 1996). Many rescuers stated they had no close feelings for the Jews they helped, nor did they imagine that they themselves could be placed in the same situation in the future (Monroe, 1996). Instead, they more often mentioned a perception of shared humanity as the basis for action, which framed their deep altruism as a kind of reflex (Monroe, 1996). Other psychological research also downplays the role of relationships in altruism, emphasising the sense of injustice faced by others who are basically similar to, but unknown by and unrelated to, oneself (Stueber, 2019). While empathy is about extending feeling and perspective from oneself to others, altruistic action can also be encouraged by basic appreciation of shared humanity and a sense of implicit connection among all people, for better or worse (Peterson, 2017).

Blum defends emotional altruism, arguing that the feeling of care is a good that is qualitatively better than a rational duty. However, in Blum's example of Bob visiting his wife Sue on her deathbed in the hospital, it is not difficult to imagine, in contrast to Blum, that Sue might not be particularly concerned with Bob's inner desires and motives, if she wants to keep the relationship positive, rather than grapple with complexities of care in her grave situation. Indeed, in close relationships, couples sometimes helpfully draw 'benign misconceptions' of their partners in place of empathy, to 'avoid making accurate inferences that are likely to result in more harm than benefit' (Ta & Ickes, 2017, p. 360). Bob may be extremely drained from the experience, to the point of not being able to feel much at all, let alone a deep and sustained feeling of care. Or he may not be a very emotionally aware person. None of this must spell doom for Sue, or annoy her when she is facing her own death.

On the other hand, farmworkers may not appreciate a strike in support of their plight, which they may regard as patronising, disrespectful, or self-serving, if they did not ask for that action, over other, possibly more consequential actions, even if the strikers mean them well. A compassion that trumps all else may not be so virtuous; what Sreenivasan (2020) describes as 'cleverness' is also part of a virtuous exercise of compassion. Teaching for such moral and reflective capacity may require taking a step back from first impressions and fast actions in many cases, rather than regarding compassion as if it should always be prioritised over other considerations (Hytten & Warren, 2003).

In sum, that empathy is required for altruism, and that compassion and care are better foundations for just action than more reflective, rational pursuits or other perspectives or forms of awareness, is not entirely compelling, given complicating and conflicting evidence and views across fields. Educators in this context should not hold care, compassion, and altruism as moral goods beyond critical consideration and reflection (Kukar, 2016). While many who promote these emotional virtues are broadly aligned with a virtue ethics (or care ethics) moral philosophy tradition, there is a risk of overlooking how too much of an emphasis on empathy or compassion can also be problematic in society and education. These emotional virtues should therefore not be treated as absolute goods. In light of the possible harms, intentional or unintentional, of invocations of care, empathy, and altruism, a more nuanced approach can be of greater benefit, particularly in learning about these feelings with young people in moral and civic education.

5.3   Concluding Thoughts

Much work has been done to explore how and when people become empathetic, compassionate, and caring, syncing their emotional experiences with their perceptions in ways that encourage them to be good to others around them. The empathy-altruism thesis (in a rough form) is held by many, and it is reflected in educational interventions to encourage empathy, sympathy, caring, and altruism. This view appeals to a variety of philosophers and seems grounded in various psychological studies. Yet conceptual difficulties underlie neat assessments, that it is altruism, rather than egoism or self-serving interest, that translates feelings about others' suffering into just action, and that altruistic action based on compassion is always or normally beneficial. Practically, educators focused on social justice in the classroom observe that not all lessons for caring and empathy go as planned. Students may find equating their position with that of disadvantaged others unpleasant, unsafe, and undesirable (or impossible), or they may resolve to enact quick fixes that simply alleviate their own experiences of unpleasantness, failing to develop an empathy that is respectful towards others as persons.

A virtue ethics or care ethics view of caring and compassion can be more beneficial than others given the need for reflective judgement and appropriate responsiveness. As Nussbaum and Noddings note, and as is reflected in Jubilee curricula in part, one's judgement can go wrong, so they should be encouraged to reflect on how their feelings relate to their potential actions. Yet a challenge such frameworks tend to not critically consider is the significance of profound social difference and social injustice in everyday cases where suffering is found. Reflecting on social (and cultural) difference and on bias is essential to getting judgements right. These challenges can be alleviated to some extent by reflection or meditation dedicated to developing compassion across difference. However, these approaches still fail to recognise the relational and institutional aspects of social injustice, which go beyond individual dispositions and mean states. For one, caring and compassion are not universally prized, but sought from girls and women disparately. Here, the inward-looking orientation of virtue ethics (and care ethics), even within situations, makes it difficult for students to recognise potentially problematic interests behind some calls for compassion and sympathy, as well as the political and moral implications of public discourse demanding individual altruistic and caring action. Virtues-based approaches encourage students to reflect on what is going on at the personal level, but are less likely to encourage a deep understanding of a situation at a societal level. More critical societal reflection is required in this context, rather than blanket endorsements of compassion, caring, and empathy, to engage in emotional virtues education that benefits society.

In relation, educators should take a step back from discourses of humanitarian aid that are employed to do good, but are not necessarily effective in doing so, or for benefitting diverse people equitably. Those involved with exchanges, service learning, volunteerism, and partnerships with international organisations should reflect on what is being learned and gained and by whom, to not unwittingly teach students that a voyeuristic exploration of difficult circumstances is good, while at the same time ensuring that engagement with suffering does not lead to other negative consequences, such as cynicism, desensitisation, or paternalistic, unproductive practices. In such settings, educators can engage students in debates about the utility of empathy and compassion that are critical, not simplistic. A sense of moral ambiguity (at least initially) can be regarded as a reasonable, critically informed alternative to 'doing something' in some cases, while feeling for others in a world at crisis (Boler, 1999). The possibility of refraining from quick action is also worth considering here. The value of examining the concept of shared humanity and more duty-bound views about rights and justice can be explored in such cases. Caring and exercising empathy and compassion should not be ultimate goals of education, but should be incorporated into critical reflection on how one can be a just actor in a complicated moral and social world.

CHAPTER 6

Gratitude

In the history of philosophy, some have extolled gratitude as a virtue or matter of ideal duty, while others have conveyed more ambivalence towards the trait and experience. Today, the vast majority of philosophers emphasise its goodness. This reflects broader views about gratitude in society. Generally, people assume gratitude is beneficial to oneself and others, and is morally good. Feeling thankful for what one has is conceived as virtuous across fields, while acts expressing gratefulness to others are regarded as morally praiseworthy, if not expected. Ingratitude, as a lack of gratefulness in situations where it is seen as praiseworthy or expected, is regarded as distasteful, harmful, and a moral defect. Very few question gratitude's value in society or in education.

In psychology, gratitude is also normally valued as a positive feeling and expression. In relation, it is becoming commonplace to embrace practices of cultivating gratitude that have been identified and elaborated in positive psychology, such as gratitude journaling and chronicling, and related cognitive training. However, most work on gratitude is not focused on its political use or misuse. Additionally, the value and risks of gratitude in cases of inequity and social injustice, and pathological conditions for gratitude, have not been a major focus of scholarly literature.

This chapter examines the emotional virtue of gratitude in society and education. First, it explores some commonly accepted and more controversial understandings of gratitude found in philosophy and psychology that elaborate what gratitude is and why it is called for. The practices encouraged for cultivating feelings and social experiences of gratitude, by psychologists and educators, will also be discussed. Then, the chapter will turn to critical views of gratitude that question its moral value, its psychological utility, and its place in education. While teaching feelings of gratitude in the classroom may not necessarily be harmful, there are risks and challenges in doing so that should not be overlooked by educators (among others) interested in the moral and social development of young people.

6.1 Promotions of Gratitude

Gratitude is generally praised as an individual's favourable, thankful response to receiving something desirable, necessary, and/or beneficial, as a free gift rather than as an object of exchange. It thus involves a feeling of appreciation and goodwill, and a related disposition to act positively in response to someone or something in the future. However, from this general view, debate surrounds the value of 'stricter' versus 'broader' accounts of gratitude, particularly related to when (in what situations) it may be viewed as expected, praised, and/or required. One way of dividing views of gratitude is based on whether gratitude is 'targeted' or 'generalised'. In other words, gratitude can be a general positive disposition about one's good fortune, or more specific, and based on a concrete situation and benefactor (Lambert, Graham, & Fincham, 2009; McAleer, 2012). According to such different views, gratitude can be an individual experience and feeling, or a relational and social one.

Gratitude is 'targeted' when there is a benefactor (target) who appears to possess agency and intentionality and who aims to do or does do something that both the benefactor and beneficiary see as good and desirable in the situation (Lambert et al., 2009; McAleer, 2012). Such targeted gratitude is regarded as morally ideal or praiseworthy, because it aligns with principles that one should act reciprocally towards others and reinforce beneficence (McAleer, 2012). This is the more traditional meaning of gratitude, articulated historically by Seneca, who saw this kind of gratitude as intrinsically good, and beneficial within society (Harpham, 2004). If one is helped with their writing by a colleague who voluntarily (at their request) takes time and energy to provide suggestions and alternative understandings, most people see it as moral to thank them through some form of direct response: for example, an email expressing thanks, or some other kind of acknowledgement. From a deontological or other rule-based view (i.e. Confucianism or consequentialism), one should feel a sense of moral duty in such a case of being benefited, to demonstrate gratitude. From a virtue ethics orientation, one should feel a sense of warmth and positive connection through receiving such kindness or generosity, and express it appropriately.

On the other hand is 'generalised' gratitude. According to this approach to gratitude, one can feel gratitude for benefits they have received even if there is no benefactor who directly provides the benefit. There is, thus, no target for their gratitude. This has also been called 'propositional' gratitude (McAleer, 2012; see also Carr, 2015). Here, the cause for gratitude and target of gratitude is not precisely identified or specified, so there is no sense of reciprocity, or positive intentionality towards a specific other. Rather, this is a basic or thin disposition of thankfulness, or sense of appreciation (Watkins, 2014).

This view of generalised gratitude is less traditional and more controversial. Some argue that generalised gratitude should be conceptualised simply as *appreciation*, and seen as a sub-factor of gratitude; others contend it should be seen as separate and isolated from targeted gratitude (Gulliford, Morgan, & Kristjánsson, 2014; Manela, 2016). Psychologists tend to favour and promote this view of gratitude, nonetheless. They defend the view by arguing that it aligns with lay people's perspectives (Lambert et al., 2009). In their research on gratitude, psychologists use both conceptions. They argue with the use of self-report measurements that experiencing either kind of gratitude correlates with greater self-esteem and sense of well-being, more pro-social attitudes and behaviour, and decreased levels of negative and harmful feelings and states, such as depression, anxiety, and stress (Frederickson, 2004; Watkins, 2004; Bartlett & DeSteno, 2006; Emmons & Mishra, 2011; Algoe, 2012; Froh et al., 2014).

Then there are views that appear to fit somewhere between these two framings, or which further nuance the concepts, to approach complicated social situations from a moral view. One of the challenges of gratitude observed by philosophers is that it can introduce a sense of indebtedness in life, leading possibly to a sense of guilt, shame, and embarrassment (Card, 1988; Morgan et al., 2014; Carr, 2015; Morgan, Gulliford, & Carr, 2015). This is one reason why gratitude has not been emphasised in some traditional views of virtue and morality in Western philosophy. For instance, Aristotle writes that a good person does good, but 'is ashamed when he receives it; for doing good is proper to the superior person, and receiving it to the inferior' (cited in Manela, 2015). Kant similarly wrote against the need to owe obligations of gratitude, describing such obligations as sacred duties that can never be discharged (1981). Thus, gratitude can signal problematic social conditions: that one is unable to be adequately self-sufficient as they must accept benefits from others, despite potentially undesirable complications and implications that may arise in the future.

Different perspectives on gratitude and its implications for relationships are also found across cultural communities. Blaire Morgan, Liz Gulliford, and David Carr observe that gratitude is experienced differently across societies, such as the United Kingdom versus the United States and Australia (2015; also Gulliford & Morgan, 2019). In the United Kingdom, shame and indebtedness, and other related negative feelings, are more frequently associated and experienced with gratitude, according to self-report measures. In Chinese philosophy, *renqing reciprocity* reflects that one's gratitude at receiving benefits from others should be a long-term affair (Chen & Caicedo, 2018). As one traditional saying describes it, 'the favour of a drop of water has been rewarded with the gratitude of a fountain of water' (Chi & Hong, 2017). This view reflects that good deeds ripple outward indefinitely. It also seems to echo, but from a more favourable perspective, the deep, nearly infinite sense of obligation related to gratitude also invoked by Aristotle and Kant. In Confucianism, this sense of deep mutual indebtedness is seen as ideal to strengthen connections to others, binding people together, and building social cohesion. Such nuances can indicate differences in deeply held beliefs across groups about the roles of reciprocity, debt, and benevolence in relationships (Wang, 2013).

In relation to the pressures of gratitude in some contexts, Claudia Card (1988) has considered how the cultivation of gratitude can be morally valuable in cases of stark inequality. She notes that in such cases a person may benefit from general (acts of) generosity, not specifically intended by a benefactor to the specific beneficiary. Alternatively, they may benefit from acts they did not desire in the situation, due to their incapacity or disinclination to pay back the sense of debt, emotionally, interpersonally, or otherwise. This alters the sense of the good that has been provided. As Card writes (1988, p. 124), 'generosity can be accompanied by insensitivity to others wishes' [sic] with regard to becoming obligated ... Genuine benevolence is incompatible with disregarding others' willingness to be obligated.' This situation can be difficult to bear in contexts of extreme inequality, such as when a wealthy person gives to a person living in poverty. Such a situation can enable a sense of subservience that can be harmful for one's sense of self-respect and personal autonomy.

Thus, Card argues that one can be grateful for a generous benefactor's acts or existence, without having or expressing gratitude towards the benefactor directly. They can feel a kind of appreciation for benefits received, but should not necessarily feel or express gratitude towards a generous or wealthy benefactor, as it may cause problematic future social relations, or a sense of subservience. This approach seems to transform targeted gratitude to generalised gratitude, to maintain gratitude as moral in the particular context.

Nussbaum (2013) also suggests gratitude can be generalised, to be extracted out of complicated interpersonal relationships. Here, Nussbaum describes a hypothetical case of a professor 'Louise', who is happy to receive feedback on her work, although it is from a colleague she regards with reasonable dislike and suspicion. Like Card, Nussbaum wants to preserve a positive place for gratitude here, despite the interpersonal complications of the situation. In the case of Louise feeling gratitude in this situation, Nussbaum writes,

> we could read Louise's relation critically and uncharitably, saying that her gratitude betrays unwise and inappropriate dependency on ... undependable people. But why not just allow her to enjoy the surprise, uncriticized, and feel an emotion wishing them well? So long as she doesn't alter her basic strategy of prudent caution, why can't she

> simply enjoy the windfall? ... why not feel a limited sort of gratitude, and why not wish that person a limited sort of reciprocal benefit? ... When gratitude comes as a windfall, too much censorious questioning betrays an ungenerous disposition.   (2013, p. 163)

Here, Nussbaum emphasises the risk of being uncharitable in failing to appreciate others' generous behaviour. She therefore encourages that in such a context one can still develop a positive and pro-social view.

Saul Smilansky (1997) broadens possibilities for gratitude further, by generalising what counts as benefits one can be grateful for. Like Nussbaum, he regards gratitude as a positive emotion that should be enabled as much as possible. As he writes, gratitude 'creates good feelings [and] introduces an unforced element of mutual respect into human interaction' (Smilansky, 1997, p. 594). Yet he also observes nonetheless that the personal and social benefits of gratitude may not be evenly accessible to all, given the extreme inequality in society. Not all people are equally benefited by others. Nor are all people equally capable of providing benefits to others. In this case, Smilansky considers how all people can enjoy the benefits of gratitude in a world marked by scarcity, inequality, and social tension. He thus argues that people ought to have more gratitude than they normally do for others *not harming* them, expanding the notion of intentional beneficence to include intentional non-maleficence.

Non-maleficence, Smilansky contends, requires effort, at least a choice to not harm, as one has opportunities and reasons to ignore others' ends. As he writes, 'not harming regularly requires concern and effort, and is clearly beneficial to people. To be ungrateful for such beneficial efforts is often not different in kind from ingratitude towards our (positive) beneficiaries, one of the most morally distasteful and socially harmful traits' (Smilansky, 1997, p. 593). Smilansky promotes this model to enlarge the group of people who can be counted as beneficiaries and benefactors of gratitude.

With this move Smilansky observes that gratitude can be felt in relation to 'a multitude of unknown people' (1997, p. 596). Simmel similarly argues for people feeling an abstract sense of gratitude, as 'the artist or poet who does not even know us ... creates innumerable connections' while society 'would break apart' without the social linkages provided by gratitude (1950, p. 389). Others argue that one can feel gratitude towards a state that benefits (or at least does not harm) them, among other institutions, such as schools and universities, that benefit themselves and others in society (Walker, 1988; McConnell, 1993; Manela, 2015).

Fitzgerald (1998) defends the most extreme view of situations enabling gratitude. He contends that just about anything can have a potentially positive benefit to an individual, from political oppression to physical abuse. He thus argues that (1) being harmed and (2) helping others (giving) can be situations meriting gratitude. The cause or benefactor for gratitude in a case of harm is not the author of the harm, but the educational benefit of the harmful event, which the author of harm may not intend. Fitzgerald contends that this type of gratitude is 'a common ideal within Buddhism. The Dalai Lama often repeats this Buddhist teaching by telling his audiences that he is grateful to the Chinese for giving him the opportunity to practice love for this enemies [and for] training in patience and helping his development as a person' (1998, p. 124). According to Fitzgerald, having gratitude in cases of harm can help prevent further harm, promote or preserve interpersonal and communal relationships, and 'aid in the development of virtues or help prevent the formation of vices' (1998, p. 130). Psychological studies partly back up this view, suggesting that in times of hardship, gratitude (or happiness stemming from gratitude) can still lead to pro-social behaviour, compassion, and altruism (Emmons & McCullough, 2003; Froh, Sefick, & Emmons, 2008).

In discussing gratitude for giving, Fitzgerald likens his reader to Card's wealthy benefactor, who feels unable to respond to the expressed needs and desires of a less advantaged person while wanting to be generous. This benefactor can learn from the experience of being generous, despite the inappropriate demands gratitude might make on the beneficiary, in cases of extreme inequality. As Fitzgerald imagines the case, '"If it weren't for you," the benefactor might say to the beneficiary, "I would be miserably self-absorbed"' (1998, pp. 133–134). As there are cases where a person cannot face an obligation of gratitude, experiencing gratitude in giving is essential, Fitzgerald argues. A person then would have gratitude for their opportunity to develop sympathy and compassion towards others (Jackson, 2016).

Given all the possible conditions for experiencing gratitude and appreciation, and its many recognised benefits across a wide range of circumstances, most philosophers, educators, and psychologists tend to emphasise the value of learning about the benefits of gratitude in schools. They also tend to do away with the details of justifications for gratitude, given the wide variety of contexts in which gratitude can be cultivated, resting assured that many experiences can be opportunities to develop gratitude. It is therefore common practice, and not held as controversial, that parents and educators encourage children to regularly feel, express, and reflect on opportunities for gratitude (McCullough et al., 2001; Carr, 2015; Carr, Morgan, & Gulliford, 2015). An early lesson in targeted gratitude is being guided to say thank you, and write letters to benefactors, such as grandparents for toys, or guests who visit class.

Internalisation, not just of rational duty but of affective and emotional training, is usually meant to take place here, as the concept may be foreign to a toddler but develops within a context as a deeply felt personal commitment (Graham & Taylor, 2014).

The Jubilee Centre is active in working to cultivate gratitude in Great Britain, based on findings that '80% believe there is a lack of gratitude in society', and 'would like to see more effort spent on promoting gratitude, particularly in educational and workplace contexts' (Arthur et al., 2015, p. 5). In relation, the study's authors write that 'there is a growing consensus in Britain that virtues such as … gratitude … are part of the solution to many of the challenges facing society today' (Arthur et al., 2015, p. 5). A Jubilee-produced handbook provides a 5-week intervention for students. The intervention requires that students indicate things they are grateful for in various ways (i.e. through writing and speaking), create journals recalling grateful experiences, write and send thank-you letters, reflect on experiences of sharing thanks with benefactors, and explore how they benefit from difficult experiences and can therefore be grateful for challenges (Kristjánsson et al., 2017).

Such practices are supported by psychological research on gratitude. In one study, one group of students received two weeks of daily interventions, in which they were asked to list five things they were grateful for. Another group of students received alternative interventions, in which they were asked to list five 'hassles', defined as 'irritants – things that annoy or bother you' (Froh et al., 2008, p. 220). Both groups of students were asked at the same time about their sense of well-being and whether they had helped anyone with a problem recently. Three weeks after the interventions, the students were given a more extensive survey of their feelings and experiences. The study found that 'counting blessings', in the experience of the first group of students, was associated with more self-reported gratitude, optimism, life satisfaction, and satisfaction with school (Froh et al., 2008). Based on such findings, psychologists thus encourage implementing classroom practices of gratitude chronicling and journaling, and positive reframing (seeing 'silver linings' across a range of situations; see Froh et al., 2014; Morgan et al., 2015). Nonetheless, there are reasons to remain wary of gratitude, and more cautious with regard to its cultivation.

6.2   Problems

Teaching gratitude, be it targeted or generalised, is regarded as moral for educators to do in two senses. First, it aligns with benefiting students as members of society and as individuals, to enhance their well-being and cultivate their character or virtue. Second, it is in line with relatively uncontroversial, widely-held moral values, and may help to socialise students to function well and positively in society. However, there are reasons for caution when it comes to promoting gratitude in education and society.

First, the way gratitude is understood, and the pro-social and related justifications undergirding rationales for gratitude, are culturally bounded. As mentioned previously, gratitude is experienced differently across societies, such as the United Kingdom, the United States, Australia, and China (Wang, 2013; Morgan et al., 2015). From a broader perspective, as gratitude is tied up with particularities of social relationships and customs of gift giving, gratitude is culturally framed within particular cultural and situational contexts. Understandings of gratitude are also influenced by subculture, religion, and class. For instance, James Arthur and his colleagues (2015) observe that Christians express valuing gratitude more than non-Christians in the British context (p. 15). This does not mean that gratitude cannot be a universal phenomenon. However, this indicates that gratitude is understood, experienced, and expressed in specific, non-universal ways, within particular moral and cultural contexts. Thus, one should avoid a simplistic endorsement of particular experiences or expressions of gratitude as a good in education, as norms in relationships and cultural communities also impact views about and feelings of gratitude.

In relation, within cultural groups, expectations of gratitude (and related 'feeling rules') can be uneven across gender, among other traits. In the aforementioned study (Arthur et al., 2015), participants in Britain were asked to rank how often seven values guided their behaviour: courage, honesty, kindness, fairness, gratitude, self-control, and humility. Men ranked gratitude last out of the seven, while women ranked it fourth (p. 15). As values (such as gratitude) are learned in social settings, this suggests that women may have been taught to express and be guided by gratitude to a far greater extent than men. Women's gratitude may be valued over their courage, for instance, in schools and in society. On the other hand, for men, gratitude is associated more with a sense of obligation and burden (Kashdan et al., 2009). This is particularly found among older and United States men, and is likely to decrease their capacity for benefiting from gratitude (Allen, 2018). It is plausible in this case that boys are implicitly taught that receiving benefits from others is a sign of weakness. They therefore may face greater challenges in effectively receiving and positively responding to gratitude curricula.

Additionally, such unequal feeling rules in this case can also reflect a societal-level sense that men are entitled to things women should be grateful for. Thus, gratitude may be unevenly expected (e.g. in a classroom) based on bias related to identities and appearances, rather than universal conditions for gratitude involved in philosophical analyses. For example, a girl may be regarded as naughty, selfish, or thoughtless (or uncaring) for not expressing gratitude, while a boy's ingratitude may not be seen as noteworthy. Such a situation can be enabled if curricula are highly individualised, encouraging students to imagine gratitude as an individual affair, as the possession of an emotional virtue, rather than it being of value within and for social relations.

Examples of the individualisation of gratitude can be found in curricula on gratitude by Character First Education, a United States-based character and leadership programme provided by Strata Leadership, a private organisational development firm. Character First Education disseminates guides for children to learn emotional virtues. For each virtue, a small and simple story, usually from history, is provided, as well as activities and tasks for students to complete. In a Character First lesson on gratitude (2019a), students are asked to describe what a grateful person does, and to indicate that they will as individuals feel and express gratitude ('I will appreciate the people in my life.' 'I will write thank you notes.'). An included 'Gratefulness Story' describes how Abraham Lincoln had gratitude despite the many hardships of his life, such as his sister dying (Character First, 2019b). An older version of Character First curriculum for gratitude (1997) asks students to wear blindfolds and then try to make a simple drawing, to 'point out the benefit of eyesight' (p. 9).

Most of these examples focus on an individual with gratitude. That Lincoln's gratitude benefits others, and that gratitude exists in relations, is not reflected in these examples. In the latter case (about vision), the students could be encouraged to be grateful for friends who might help them make their drawing. Instead, these tasks and stories only reflect on individual development. In contrast, Jubilee materials on gratitude encourage student reflection regarding its social nature, considering how gratitude may be received by recipients of thank-you letters, and making group projects (films and artwork) exploring reasons for and benefits of gratitude, in addition to more individual gratitude journaling (Kristjánsson et al., 2017).

More generally, gratitude should not be regarded as always good in education, in the case that it conflicts with other moral principles, such as justice or non-maleficence. As Carr argues (2015), 'just as promotion of or habituation in courage and temperance has produced brave and self-controlled villains and crooks, it could be that sincere, heartfelt and well-judged gratitude might be inculcated or promoted to ends that are quite corrupt or self-serving'. A person should not have gratitude if someone murders her sports rival, for example (Carr et al., 2015). This may seem to be an obvious point, but it is often neglected in educational materials that treat different virtues and principles individually, without reflecting on the need for practical judgement, thereby failing to consider that not all occasions demand all emotional virtues. That gratitude can be immoral also points to a pathology of gratitude, as psychopaths and narcissists may have gratitude for things that are harmful to others, or for undeserved privileged, and may effectively bolster their negative social tendencies if exposed to simplistic discourses on the goodness of gratitude (Watkins, 2019).

Thus, gratitude can take darker forms, of self-satisfaction and joy at others' misery, which are clearly undesirable traits in education (Jackson, 2017c). Returning to the example of gratitude for good vision, differences in ability, which create divergent and inequitable experiences for people in society, should be considered thoughtfully by students, in the course of their education for moral development and social justice. That one has an advantage over others should not be exploited as a means for them to develop emotional virtues at an individual level (Jackson, 2016, 2017c; McConnell, 2019).

In the context of such real-world complexity, Gulliford (2018) provides a more effective resource for children to learn about gratitude that can help them reflectively explore how expectations for gratitude can rub against other moral principles and virtues. Her text *Can I Tell You About Gratitude?* tells the story of a girl Maya who is considering whether she should be grateful when her friend Laura gives her a pair of earrings but later asks if she can copy Maya's schoolwork. Such difficulties with gratitude as potentially enabling indebtedness go unseen in more simple lessons. Additionally, this story reveals the difficulties in deciphering people's motives, a practical challenge for students and educators that is often neglected in theoretical analyses of the intentions of benefactors, in relation to the requirements for gratitude.

Thinking more about gratitude and education for social justice, many examples given in gratitude chronicling reference privileges, like being given earrings, or having a comfortable home to live in. Such gratitude, for being given earrings or for having a comfortable home, may aid social cohesion and psychological well-being, but it remains morally problematic to in effect be happy for advantages and privileges over others, in relation to unjust systems and status quos. Psychological considerations can thus be at odds with moral ones, if a person has gratitude for wealthy parents' generosity (or their socio-economic status) in a highly unequal society with limited social mobility.

People promote generalised gratitude or appreciation, in part because it can help a person move away from these sorts of challenges related to interpersonal comparison with others. Yet there are also problems with endorsing generalised gratitude or appreciation, in relation to social and political conditions and situations. Smilansky suggests that disadvantaged people should be grateful to not being harmed, so they can cultivate gratitude and pro-social connections. However, this solution seems to risk encouraging toleration of injustice and inequity, because most societies still hardly benefit people equally, but simultaneously harm some for the advantage of others, albeit in rather hidden and indirect ways. Smilansky claims that 'not harming regularly requires concern and effort', but he overlooks the ways that social institutions can and often do perpetuate system-level injustice without anyone in particular actively and visibly engaging in wrongdoing or harming particular others.

For example, schools disproportionately benefit children with more resources at home. For schools to operate otherwise would require a redistribution of educational resources, from wealthy to impoverished children and families in society. Such educational equity is not forthcoming, because it is not regarded as a duty or responsibility to use personal wealth (or to be significantly taxed from income) to substantially benefit other people's children (Merry, 2013). In this case, no one is 'harming' anyone. Yet some benefit a great deal from a system, while others benefit very little, as the system does not provide equal opportunity for all children. To regard gratitude for societies and schools as praiseworthy or expected in this context is therefore not quite the same thing as asking people to be thankful for a lack of harm. Furthermore, for a disadvantaged student to have gratitude in this case can enable those in more privileged positions to continue to exploit their unfair advantages, rather than critically explore their capacity towards enhancing equity. Smilansky seems to be suggesting that a homeless man should be grateful whenever nobody is kicking him, and that students in an unjust schooling system be grateful for the same. But they are being kicked, just not in an obvious way. Smilansky seems to want these people to be optimistic. Yet these people's need for self-respect and their rights to equal opportunities and personal autonomy are ignored in this overly narrow framing of gratitude.

Likewise, promoting gratitude in cases of harm has troubling implications in real-life contexts such as schools. While one can theorise about how such gratitude could be beneficial to a person, to teach people to develop gratitude in such cases is another matter. While it may be possible to benefit from gratitude by learning from experiences of harm, abuse, and oppression, promoting gratitude over other responses in such contexts can effectively amount to encouraging people to accept and tolerate servility, injustice, and mistreatment, neglecting their needs to not be harmed, and for self-respect (Wood et al., 2016).

Fitzgerald (1998) concedes this case in part, noting that a 'reason we might think that such gratitude is wrong is that it demonstrates a lack of self-respect or makes us servile. . . . Shouldn't we try to dissuade victims of abuse from being grateful to their abusers?' (p. 140). Here, Fitzgerald specifies that one must have self-respect to cultivate gratitude from learning from cases of harm. Here, he relates a fictional woman, Faye, who:

> thrived after she severed ties with her abusive father. She had no fear of other adversities in her life since they looked so small in comparison to the ones she had already survived. She became very compassionate because her own pain gave her insight into the suffering of others. She developed an unwavering passion to fight the kinds of abuse to which she had been subjected. As she looks back on her life, she sees her father both as the cause of her suffering and as a catalyst to the person she has become. Because she values her life so highly she finds herself feeling grateful for the role her father played. This gratitude does not express itself in acts of servility. (1998, p. 143)

Fitzgerald argues that Faye can have gratitude for learning from an experience of harm, as the learning and the person who facilitated that learning made her a better person. He goes on that Faye could try to forgive, or to forget, and that these may also be worthwhile (praise-worthy) ways forward. However, his main concern is that people over-come any sense of anger related to harm, which he regards as never justified. He concludes: 'Some readers may want to reject the . . . analysis, while allowing for cases where anger is justified. They will see the role of gratitude in our moral lives as more restricted than I do' (1998, p. 144).

I discuss anger more in Chapter 9, and its potential value for communicating about and halting harm and injustice. Here, it seems worth mentioning that in Fitzgerald's delineation of conditions warranting gratitude, the outcome – that Faye is emotionally well, perseverant, and just – is not clearly caused by harm, or her father. She has these characteristics despite the harm, arguably. Women who are abused by their fathers do not necessarily (or usually) develop like Faye. Meanwhile, Fitzgerald does not advocate gratitude for harm in cases where one is not emotionally well, including cases where one allows harm to be ongoing. This is not precisely gratitude for harm, then, as the harm should have ended. This is not gratitude for harm, but for harm specifically in the past. This is gratitude for learning from a harmful experience.

In the case of the Dalai Lama, Fitzgerald seems to treat ongoing harm as acceptable, as a good response to the situation of political oppression. Fitzgerald sees the Dalai Lama as having self-respect, as he opposes the Chinese government's oppression of Tibet, but not in an angry or servile way. Yet if such harms are beneficial, why should a person work to stop them? A slave morality, wherein one effectively expresses toleration of undue harm and suffering, seems enabled in promoting gratitude for harm in such cases.

Fitzgerald describes gratitude for harm as 'a common ideal in Buddhism'. However, in contrast to Fitzgerald's example, the 'arising of normal anger is important to many Buddhist thinkers' in cases of harm and oppression, who also emphasise and express concern about the harms suppressed by the tendency for self-deception (McRae, 2015, p. 119). Dharmaraksita emphasises 'metabolised' anger, 'a virtuous channelling of the power and fierce energy of anger without the desire to harm or seek vengeance. It is grounded in and energized by – but not reducible to – an active, engaged compassion' (McRae, 2015, p. 115). This view of anger is advocated for in cases of oppression by some Buddhists, who see the risks of suppressing anger, in contrast to the value of responding in a more active way, to make positive change.

It is difficult in a situation to judge whether and how someone is dealing with harms and challenges in an appropriately grateful, rather than ungrateful or servile manner. Fitzgerald attempts to describe ways to make these identifications, by discussing different fictional women who have been abused by their fathers, and the ways they handle it. He describes a woman, Gail, who tries to ignore or deny the harms she experienced, in contrast with Faye, who acknowledges the harms effectively and moves beyond them. However, in real life, different psychologists may give different diagnoses about effective acknowledgement of harms versus ignorance or denial about them.

From a psychological viewpoint, promoting gratitude may benefit disadvantaged people, people who have faced abuse, or children in bad family or school situations. However, this is not necessarily going to be the case. People may appear to be beyond anger, and appropriately grateful. But they may be denying their anger, in hope that this can help them change their conditions, given their lack of control over the situation. Or they may be in denial and suppressing their rage. On the other hand, even if they are feeling gratitude, this could lead to minimisation of problems, which can also be unhealthy in cases of harm (Wood et al., 2016).

In this context, psychologists face challenges in productively developing gratitude among people who suffer from relationship and childhood abuse and related experiences, as well as others who lack a strong sense of self and self-control. Those in the former group are likely to resist experiences where they would normally be expected to have gratitude, due to fear of close relationships which they fear may become exploitive and harmful to them (Freund, 2019). In this case, experiencing gratitude can be associated not simply with 'mixed' emotions of guilt and shame, but can bring with it intense fear, anxiety, and dread, and urges to escape the situation or relationship. Knowing that gratitude is supposed to feel good and be pro-social, expectations and promotions of gratitude can confront these people as coercive and harmful feeling rules, and bring with them confusion, shame, and embarrassment. Psychologists would not recommend such people to focus on cultivating gratitude before dealing with these other challenges (Jackson, 2019e).

For those with a lack of sense of self-control, gratitude can be easy to feel, but can increase a harmful sense of lack of empowerment, fuelling self-narratives of lack of control, helplessness, and uselessness (Freund, 2019; Manela, 2019). Again, cultivating gratitude would not particularly be recommended by psychologists and therapists here. While such people may have been pressured in religious or other cultural contexts to have deep subservient gratitude and thank others for everything around them, they need to learn how to develop their self-confidence, by not giving gratitude in relation to every good thing in their lives, and develop an appropriate sense of personal agency (Wood et al., 2016).

Such challenges to cultivating healthy gratitude are not simple to rectify, even by expert therapists and counsellors working interpersonally with clients over long periods of time (Wood et al., 2016). Thinking again of education, it is not unlikely that the typical classroom would include one or more young people facing risks and challenges related to gratitude being painful or otherwise unhelpful as a deep emotional experience, rather than beneficial. After all, even in the best of cases gratitude is accompanied by mixed feelings for many people (Jackson, 2019e). The likelihood of this possibility should give pause to educators before making blanket endorsements of gratitude as an ultimate priority to cultivate, in the case that they are unwittingly creating conditions for more harm for some young people, rather than simply spreading optimism and sociality, as they may hope to do.

Jubilee guidelines for cultivating gratitude in schools encourage gratitude in case of challenges (2017). In this context, teachers are recommended to write prompts on the board for students to respond to, such as 'sometimes you go through a difficult path . . . ', 'Looking back it wasn't all bad . . . ', 'There were some good things to come out of the experience . . . ', and 'In some ways I'm thankful/grateful for what happened because . . . ' (p. 13). The guide also notes, however, that 'some people in the class may have endured particularly distressing events in their relatively short lives and that it is possible this will come to mind. Any children for whom this task becomes upsetting can instead write an entry in their gratitude journal . . . or create a front cover for their gratitude journal' (Jubilee, 2017, p. 12). This approach is better than some others, as it reflects acceptance and awareness that children (among others) do suffer from serious challenges, and that this should not necessarily be treated lightly, or framed positively at the outset. On the other hand, such learners and situations remain cast as deviant and seem to be somewhat stigmatised in this framing, while a general message is still given that one should respond to challenges with gratitude, rather than other kinds of action or perception.

Finally, from a psychological view a grateful society may be ideal. However, it may not be morally ideal to cultivate gratitude across society if the society is unjust, with many innocent people suffering from harm and inequity. In this case, as in cases where people are experiencing harm and other treatment that should not be tolerated or accepted, a lack of gratitude, which some may regard as 'ingratitude', may be a more moral response. While Christianity today is often associated with greater experiences of gratitude, Peter Leithart (2014) observes this has not always been the case. While Greco-Roman society required deep expressions of gratitude among people which implicated them in hierarchical, inequitable, oppressive socioeconomic relations, Leithart argues that 'Jesus was the first great ingrate in Western history, and he set the pattern for later ingrates. With Jesus and Paul, a seed of ingratitude was planted ... which grew to be one of our civilization's most important and enduring features' (2014, p. 77). Leithart goes on that 'Jesus and Paul look like ingrates ... because their gratitude ... confused and destroyed normal expectations about giving and receiving' in society (2014, p. 77). Some calls for gratitude in society can be morally suspect, and manipulated to support unjust relations. Such possibilities serve to justify instances of ingratitude as responses to injustice, corruption, and efforts at immoral manipulation.

Returning to empirical matters, whether educating gratitude leads to positive benefits to individuals and communities over time has also not been effectively evaluated. In psychological research, as discussed previously, benefits are deduced based on perceived rises in people's positive emotional experiences and attitudes and pro-social behaviour, mostly gleaned from self-report. As studies tend to be short term – measuring beneficial impacts in the course of a few weeks – it is impossible to know in such cases whether interventions have a lasting impact. Meanwhile, self-report measures can indicate desirability responses, as students are guided by teachers or other authorities to express gratitude as a good thing, before being surveyed on whether they feel and enjoy gratitude. Thus, the benefits of interventions for gratitude may amount to simple training.

In one study that aimed to demonstrate that developing gratitude leads to greater civic-mindedness, students were surveyed and interviewed after a gratitude intervention regarding their interests in community service. Of the 40 percent of students who underwent the intervention and participated in the survey, just over half indicated 'they would help an individual less fortunate than themselves', while others answered that they would 'possibly' do so (Rogerson, 2015, p. 18). The study's author concludes that 'gratitude is a strong motivator to civil service' when 'connections are made' amongst 'making the world a "better place"', 'being willing to help unfortunate individuals', and '"giving back" to the wider local community' (Rogerson, 2015, pp. 18–19). Yet most students refused to even take the survey, while it remains unclear whether those who answered positively did go on to engage in community service.

In summary, while benefits of gratitude may be clear and intuitive in many cases, there are risks to promoting gratitude in education across diverse situations and circumstances that have not been well reflected upon. The blanket endorsement of gratitude in educational spaces can be taken up in a number of unhelpful ways. It can encourage people to be inattentive to harms and challenges they are facing, alongside others in society, while no necessary link has been established between being grateful, having empathy, and being altruistic, despite self-reported links in surveys with highly limited scope. Simple endorsements of gratitude can lead to feeling rules which can be discriminatory and biased, and met with mixed emotions across cultures, even in Western societies. Asking people to be grateful more generally puts the impetus of action on individuals in society to have a good attitude, despite social problems and challenges. Then, there are cases where people experience feeling rules for gratitude in ways that can exacerbate harm, which may be complicated for teachers to evaluate and understand in the context of education.

In place of simplistic endorsements of gratitude and positive reframing, a more critical focus on teaching for and about gratitude can help students 'appreciate the complex grammar of gratitude discourse' in a morally complicated world (Morgan at al., 2015, p. 12). Caution should be exercised in encouraging children's gratitude at every turn, by parents, schools and institutions, and society, lest gratitude be thereby used to turn away from challenges and problems, injustices and harm, in place of sunny ignorance. As an alternative to cultivating gratitude, teachers can facilitate student consideration of whether and how gratitude may or may not be warranted, such as in cases of self-interest, for example, and how in some cases expecting gratitude may be unreasonable, such as when people face hardships. In relation, Gulliford's (2018) book on gratitude for young people is promising, for it indicates, in the place of certainty and simplification, some of the complexity of real-life experiences of gratitude, and the challenges of making good judgements about its role in one's life and relationships. Instead of teaching gratitude moralism, educators should question with students when and how gratitude can be good or bad, based on morally relevant features of the situation (Gulliford & Morgan, 2019).

6.3   Concluding Thoughts

Gratitude is often psychologically productive for individuals and socially beneficial, and it can be cultivated even in unjust and harmful conditions. However, educating for gratitude, particularly in light of harm and unjust conditions, and given the imperfections of the real world, is another matter. Gratitude for general non-malevolence or good luck in the context of injustice and harm can be instrumentally self-serving. Such may benefit the individual, but possibly at the cost of developing a more just community, particularly if one is lulled into inaction, given the ease of gratitude reframing, in contrast with the complexity of injustice in the world. Thus, there is a possibility that gratitude reframing or other activities in the classroom for gratitude could preclude a critical understanding of societal ills and one's position, active or passive, in relation to them. Students could learn that they are better off than youth in another part of the world without grappling with the challenges faced, or developing an effectively compassionate or altruistic spirit. Young people may effectively learn to just serve themselves by focusing on their own luck, not recognising that social structures of luck also have a dark side for disadvantaged members of society (Warren & Hytten, 2004).

On the other hand, for some children, developing favourable comparisons of one's experience alongside those of others can be traumatising, even in cases where moral lessons are learned (as discussed in the last chapter). Gratitude can also lead to negative experiences of guilt. Some may feel angry to discover injustice for the first time. Thus, an educator's good intentions will not necessarily have the desired impacts. Students might in this case feel outrage, not appreciation, as a morally justified response.

Relatedly, the emphasis on gratitude in education can have paternalistic overtones, as those in authority risk expressing through gratitude promotion that they know more than students do about what is best for them and how they ought to feel. As misplaced gratitude can harm self-respect, educators cannot know when whole-hearted expressions of gratitude are warranted among their students, as they do not necessarily know about their students' lives beyond school gates. Given educator authority, students may feel obliged to express appreciation in relation to the harms they face. This can lead to a neglect of self-respect needs, if gratitude is praised above and beyond all else. More generally, teachers promoting gratitude across diverse scenarios and contexts may risk suggesting to students that servility is warranted among disadvantaged people and groups, and that a focus on social problems is morally distasteful, or psychologically unhealthy. Such simplistic and superficial 'lessons' can and should be avoided.

Instead, educators should reflect more critically alongside their students on the morality of gratitude in diverse settings. By regarding gratitude as simply and always good, an educator can send a message that students' and others' challenges in life are not important. Yet children can face challenges and compromises to their self-respect and development (as all people do) that may limit their capacity for self-respecting gratitude. Some argue that gratitude can be a blessing, given all the struggles people face in the world. However, in a world where social injustice is rife, there are certainly worse moral crimes than ingratitude, even within instances where gratitude may conceivably be beneficial. Thus, a lack of gratitude should not be simply regarded as problematic, or as a kind of moral crime. Ingratitude can also be righteous and just in certain circumstances. When it comes to gratitude, discussing moral decision-making reflectively and critically, rather than emphasising the psychological priority of gratitude, can encourage a more effective moral education for social justice. Students can learn that gratitude can be difficult to strive towards in some instances, and that lack of gratitude is not always morally problematic, while also learning of gratitude's merits and value from different philosophical and societal perspectives.

CHAPTER 7

Resilience and Mindfulness

In recent decades, resilience and mindfulness have become highly sought qualities in education and society. In contrast with some of the emotional virtues discussed here, these traits are not primary in virtue ethics. They are not even normally described as emotions. Rather, they are capacities which invoke particular emotional states, as prerequisites and as outcomes. Resilience is not closely related to Aristotelian virtues, and its contemporary conceptualisation has no firm grounding in moral philosophy. Rather, it is a trait or disposition enabling adaptability, as seen in human and social resilience scholarship. In such research, the focus has been on psychological interventions, such as cognitive behavioural therapy, to make challenging circumstances manageable. With resilience, strong emotional reactions to challenges are evaded through changing oneself to stay calm and rational when faced with obstacles, rather than focusing on the wider world. Calls for resilience may encourage people to be more stoic, in a sense (Robertson, 2014). Mindfulness is also partly aligned with a stoic sensibility, as it involves developing a similarly peaceful and calm emotional state (Gill, 2018), although it is more closely associated with Buddhist and related traditions of meditative practice, wherein one focuses on oneself and one's internal experience.

In education and society, resilience and mindfulness are valued more for their instrumental benefits than for their moral value. They both assist specifically with the evasion of what are seen as negative and harmful emotions, and with the related development of positive emotions and behaviours, for functioning in schools and in society. Yet while resilience and mindfulness are regarded as educational assets today, there are also problematic aspects of their promotion and cultivation in schools and society. Additionally, these qualities can be cultivated for good or ill use, as with other emotional virtues explored here. This chapter examines each of these traits in turn, tracing from philosophical, psychological, and political perspectives how they can constitute and intersect with other emotional virtues and how they are approached within education and society. As with the emotional virtues explored here thus far, resilience and mindfulness may be useful for the emotional development of young people, but there are also limitations to promoting them, particularly in relation to education for social justice.

7.1   Resilience

Resilience is not only, or primarily, discussed as a good virtue or quality of people, but is understood firstly as a means or state of enlarging capacity and ameliorating or diminishing vulnerability (another interesting concept, which will be discussed in depth in the next chapter). In this sense, the word is used to describe all sorts of systems, such as environments, theoretical arguments, organisations, and individual humans, and to evaluate whether and how they can continue to function in the face of systemic threats, changes, and challenges. When it comes to human resilience, psychological research focuses on how humans can adapt to situations from a cognitive and socio-emotional view, so that one's academic or work performance or other personal functioning does not suffer due to negative emotions and experiences, possibly related to external or interpersonal challenges faced. Thus, it is in the context of anticipated challenges to mental and emotional health and well-being that resilience is valued.

In schooling, resilience is promoted where education is framed as inherently challenging, as it is at the start of one essay on emotion, resilience, and education:

> Learning in school is hard work. It requires effort, determination, and persistence in the face of challenges and setbacks. In order to learn, students must focus their attention, listen to their teachers, and expend mental energy participating constructively in academic tasks. In fact, this kind of wholehearted (and whole-headed) participation in academic work is considered by many educators and researchers to be a necessary condition for learning and a precondition for students' long-term success in school.   (Skinner, Pitzer, & Brule, 2014, p. 331)

To be cognitively and emotionally resilient in this context, a number of emotional needs must be met, from a psychological view. This includes experiencing and maintaining feelings of competence, relatedness, and autonomy, in accordance with self-determination theory. Emotional 'buoyancy' is part of the equation as well, so that 'students can cope in ways that allow them to keep going despite worry or frustration ... or that allow them to regain enthusiasm for challenging tasks' (Skinner et al., 2014, p. 337). When students are vulnerable to so-called negative emotions, like frustration, anxiety, and boredom, a greater focus on purpose is also seen as useful, to keep them moving forward, staying in action, and positive and motivated.

Yet one of the first challenges in understanding the value of resilience in education is that it is not clear across literature what resilience *is*. It can be defined broadly as the capacity to face adversity, but what this consists of varies based on the context. Thus, in research on resilience, lists of traits and requirements are found in place of definitions. In relation, while 'there is an intuitive appreciation for the "meaning" of resilience and what it infers (about the individual), consensus in defining psychological resilience, both conceptually and operationally as a measurable construct, has yet to be reached' (Cassidy, 2015). It may refer to 'hardiness, toughness, and resistance, along with – somewhat paradoxically – elasticity and flexibility' (Cassidy, 2015; also Friedland, 2005); 'a set of qualities that help a person to withstand the negative effects of adversity' (Gilligan, 2001); 'inner strength, competence, optimism, flexibility ... optimism ... and active coping' (Abiola & Udofia, 2011); 'an increased likelihood of (academic) success despite environmental adversities' (Cassidy, 2015; also Wang, Haertel, & Walberg, 1994); or 'a multifaceted process by which individuals or groups exhibit the ability to draw the best from the environment in which they find themselves' (Freiberg, 1993).

In this case, the existence and relevance of a global concept of resilience is debatable, as context makes a difference to what are perceived as challenges and the related requirements of resilience. To be resilient will require different qualities and strategies when attending a rock concert, in comparison to taking an academic examination, or going through a divorce. This makes the idea of an intervention for resilience as a global approach problematic. As proponents of resilience as an emotional virtue in education relatedly note, 'there are no universal protective factors' (Roberts, 2009, p. 39). Resilience in education generally seems to be understood as a disposition, emotional and cognitive, to respond effectively and functionally to typical challenges faced. Thus, it is a not a single feeling or experience, but a manner of emotionally being in the world, characterised by a lack of expression of 'negative' emotions in challenging situations. 'Negative' here connotes detrimental, risky, or potentially obstructive, rather than helpful feelings, again to be framed within a particular situation.

Conceptual challenges in defining resilience notwithstanding, strong claims are made regarding the efficacy of interventions and related teaching for emotional resilience. The most well-known programme for enhancing resilience is the Penn Resiliency Program, which has been used across fields, from education to government and military, and was developed by Seligman (Suissa, 2015). According to the Program, 'decades of empirical studies indicate that the program: increases well-being and optimism, reduces and prevents depression, anxiety, and conduct problems, results in fewer substance abuse and mental health diagnoses, and improves physical health' (2019). No straightforward definition of resilience is provided here. Instead, the Program claims to focus on twenty-one specific skills within six competencies which are to be catered to and prioritised in relation to a particular client group, and their needs and context. Included in the core six competencies are self-awareness, and the ability to change one's emotions, making resilience then similar, in a sense, to EQ or EI.

In terms of techniques and strategies, cognitive behavioural therapy is widely used in programmes and interventions for enhancing resilience. Cognitive behavioural therapy is a kind of training to, according to proponents, enhance optimism, see the brighter side of things, 'generate alternatives to the initial, explanatory style-driven thoughts', avoid 'catastrophizing' and wasting 'critical energy ruminating', practise assertion techniques as well as physical and psychological relaxation techniques, and distract oneself from problematic and upsetting foci (Penn Program, 2019; also Kranzler et al., 2014). It can thus be seen as a kind of extensive coping mechanism technique, focused on developing and maintaining an optimistic and happy outlook. The Penn Program caters to education by offering interventions 'for adolescents that teaches them gradually to change the beliefs that are fuelling their maladaptive emotions ... to keep a sense of perspective; to "think outside the box" and more flexibly about the multiple and varied causes of problems ("self-disputing") and to restrict the tendency to "catastrophise" that fuels negative thoughts' (Roberts, 2009, pp. 20–21).

Another programme for young people to develop resilience is the Resilience Framework, an online app where young people can enter their progress on having their needs fulfilled, which are categorised as 'basic,' 'belonging', 'learning', 'coping', 'core self', and 'noble truths' (Merseyside Youth Association, 2019). Basic resilience needs here include being safe, with 'good enough housing', and 'enough money to live'. 'Accepting' is one of the 'noble truths'. Here, a scale of acceptance is provided for students to succeed by 'concentrating on what needs to happen and getting on with it, rather than complaining about how we wish things were different' (Merseyside Youth Association, 2019).

Resilience is also held up as something educators and schools as systems can more generally work to cultivate. The resilience of educators is also an emerging research area, given that teachers suffer from stress and burnout (Beltman, Mansfield, & Price, 2011). Similar interventions are encouraged for teachers in this case, in order to 'react with adaptive coping – such as problem solving, searching for more information, or seeking social support' when facing challenges (Skinner et al., 2014, p. 344). More specific recommendations to bolster educator resilience include developing skills to manage personal stress and developing emotional self-regulation, within teacher education and related interventions. That schools play a role in the resilience of students and teachers has also been recognised in research, which indicates that schools can strengthen student resilience by enabling positive relationships across students and staff, reducing student–teacher ratios, focusing on culturally relevant lessons, and training educators and staff to be encouraging and empowering towards students (Johnson, 1997; McGee & Stovall, 2015).

Despite its conceptual fuzziness, a great deal of attention is paid to resilience in relation to emotional well-being, particularly of students, in education. This is because it is seen as a means to help deprived and disadvantaged youth to achieve academically, despite challenging conditions (Cigman, 2012; Ecclestone, 2012). Measures of resilience such as personal and social competence and 'personal structure' (meaning the ability to maintain routines, and plan and organise one's schedule) are observed to correlate with academic success in psychological research (Friborg et al., 2003; Munro & Pooley, 2009). Meanwhile, programmes fostering positive self-perceptions and self-esteem are also seen to bolster resilience, and thereby are also said to particularly support the success of disadvantaged children (Kanevsky, Cork, & Frangkiser, 2008).

Nonetheless, independent and non-sponsored research on the Penn Program and other similar interventions shows that immediate positive results observed tend to fade away over time. In a study of dozens of secondary schools in the United Kingdom where the Penn Program was implemented, researchers found short-term improvements in depression symptom scores, attendance, and English achievement, particularly among students who were weaker in those areas in the first place. However, the impacts were short-lived, and 'had little to no traces in the next academic year' (Challen et al., 2010, p. 4). Participant teachers also had mixed feelings about the programme. Some found that it invited difficult classroom discussions, such as students confessing to home violence, disturbing other students and the teachers. Some teachers described it as scary and uncomfortable, too 'touchy-feely', and 'too American', not connected with the communication styles and related values and norms of British students and other school expectations (Challen et al., 2010). Other research indicates that resilience interventions can be effective in reducing rates of depression among vulnerable students. Still, effects have been small and inconsistent, overall (Gillham et al., 2006; Kristjánsson, 2013b).

Given the slippery definitions of resilience and its context-specific focus, the concept may be used pragmatically in some cases, to diminish outward signs of negative responses to educational situations that are regarded by teachers as distracting, challenging, or disturbing (Ecclestone, 2012). For instance, research on educator resilience shows that 'expressions of negative affect can make teachers feel as if students do not like them … interrupting the flow of a class and forcing teachers into confrontations they would prefer to avoid' (Skinner et al., 2014, p. 343). In this context, resilience can be framed as a cure for classroom apathy, bad attitudes, or disturbing or annoying emotional or social problems of students (Skinner et al., 2014). Resilience discourse can thus be used to encourage students to 'get on with it', as in the Resilience Framework. Here, one can imagine a teacher responding to everyday classroom distracting behaviour by claiming students need more resilience (Ecclestone, 2012), given that most interventions focus on student behavioural (including communicative) changes, rather than teacher or school changes.

Others question the philosophical and moral foundations and lack thereof for resilience programmes. Some proponents of cognitive behavioural therapy for developing resilience reference Stoic philosophy as foundational to their approach (Kristjánsson, 2013b). Stoicism encourages, among other things, the diminishment of negative emotions, in order to be rational, adaptive, calm, and more (if not entirely) indifferent in the face of challenges. In the framework of cognitive behavioural therapy, 'what disturbs us are not external things, but merely our "attitudes" toward them', while events in themselves are not judged critically (Kristjánsson, 2013b, p. 209). This is in contrast with any more specifically moral framework, such as virtue ethics, as 'negative emotions' are to be eliminated, in favour of 'going with the flow'. In other words, there is no foundation for seeing resilience as a particularly moral emotional virtue or disposition (see also Robertson, 2014; Gill, 2018). A criminal could become a more resilient criminal, which may make them more effective but not a better person.

In relation, interventions focused on resilience 'avoid moral and political debate about the material conditions, knowledge and experiences that maximise opportunities for a broad balanced cultured life, the capacity for deep reflection and the ability to allow unhappiness (or to acknowledge the importance of pessimism)' (Ecclestone, 2012, p. 476). As discussed in Chapter 4, happiness is not always a good thing, and sometimes unhappiness can be a more sensible response and appraisal in observing some real-world challenges. In this case, when it is known that poverty and other personal and family factors (and school factors) play a larger role in achievement or lack thereof in schools than student attitudes and feelings, it seems disingenuous to suggest that individuals can tackle inequity by 'self-disputing' their problems, or locating the onus of responsibility in cases of crisis to personal 'catastrophising', while possibly turning away from real threats in the environment.

Kristjánsson (2013b, p. 65) nonetheless defends resilience programmes against charges that they individualise societal issues in problematic ways, given that they still can help people. As he writes,

> there are good pragmatic reasons for starting at the individual level . . . Giving extra punch to this strategy is the suggestion that by insisting nothing can be done to improve people's lives unless their social

conditions have been radically overhauled – and by implying that 'people in Rwanda and Calcutta' are concerned only with the society in which they live and not with their own personal character traits – the self-proclaimed radicals from the left become true reactionaries.

It may seem pragmatic to intervene on individuals and 'reactionary' to suggest that systems should also be changed, although it is not clear (or clearly relevant here) who suggests that Rwandans have no interest in personal development. However, some research indicates that resilience interventions aimed at benefiting disadvantaged and vulnerable students can sometimes exacerbate their challenges, particularly when they enable rejection or dismissal of challenges and suffering they face. Ebony McGee and David Stovall (2015) observe that within resilience interventions, so-called successfully resilient students produce more stress hormones, in such a way that these students may 'compromise their mental and physical well-being by being resilient, where the cumulative burden of lifetime adversities actually predicts mental health symptoms' (p. 502). Relatedly, resilience education can lead to an enhanced rather than a diminished sense of vulnerability among target students, who are identified in the process of intervention as potential victims and as deficient at the start (Furedi, 2004). Given that observed positive impacts of resilience interventions in education are short term, it thus is worth considering that cultivating resilience in the face of challenges does not necessarily help people in the long term, without other kinds of interventions in the environment.

Finally, there are cases where the value of cultivating resilience is used to explicitly justify providing less effective (and less expensive) education for students. In 2019, the Ontario Education Minister Lisa Thompson defended changes to cut teachers and increase class sizes (from 22 to 28 students per class) across secondary schools in the province, on the basis that doing so would bolster student resilience, 'preparing them for the reality of post-secondary as well as the world of work' (Draaisma, 2019). In this instance, resilience discourse is used not only to justify maintaining a challenging environment – despite the fact that the environment is causally related to the identified need for resilience – but it is actually being used to rationalise making the environment more challenging. In this situation, the value of resilience is promoted to support providing lower-quality education: education which is more challenging, as students subject to it need more resilience. Resilience discourse thus has its uses and abuses in relation to education as a just and moral practice.

Zooming out from this context, when resilience is not seen from a political perspective, students are discouraged from asking moral and political questions about whether they should be resilient, and in what regard, in relation to problematic political and social trends. As Suissa notes (2015), students labelled as vulnerable and in need of resilience today were in the past described as 'maladjusted'. King attacked this language in a 1967 speech to the American Psychological Association, where he noted (cited in Suissa, 2015, p. 111):

> Certainly, we all want to avoid the maladjusted life. In order to have real adjustment within our personalities, we all want the well-adjusted life in order to avoid neurosis, schizophrenic personalities. But ... there are certain things in our nation and in the world which I am proud to be maladjusted .... I never intend to become adjusted to segregation and discrimination. I never intend to become adjusted to religious bigotry. I never intend to adjust myself to economic conditions that will take necessities from the many to give luxuries to the few.

Thus, students are being asked to be resilient to situations, in the classroom and outside of it, that they may, from a political and moral view, have reason to question, and not be resilient about, by 'accepting and getting on with it'. As Suissa argues (2015, pp. 115–116):

> ... if one genuinely believes that radical social change is necessary to overcome urgent social problems of injustice, inequality and oppression, then surely an essential part of such an approach is convincing people that such change is both possible and necessary .... An educational approach that puts all pedagogical emphasis on individuals and their character traits mitigates against this, both reflecting and reinforcing the dominant policy discourse that views the system as here to stay and individuals as to blame for social problems.

Research on best practices to bolster student resilience for their well-being suggests that enhancing the environment and educators' skills and experiences (to help students) is an important part of the equation. However, resilience discourses in education tend to remain student-based and individualistic. When 'getting on with' the status quo is encouraged in this way, victims of unfortunate social and educational situations seem to be blamed for their negative feelings and reactions, as if they are accountable for external challenges they face, and as if the external situation is good and worth preserving, and not worth more critically considering. As a result, a deficit among individuals is invoked in these strategies, while the status quo is treated as worthy of being preserved and tolerated. When students are typically targeted for programmes due to identity factors signalling societal disadvantages, the interventions suggest their challenges are caused by their personal characteristics, as they are not encouraged to see their environment and situation in a critical way. Yet societal structures not isolated individual choices or traits are the bases of disadvantaged youth's problems, while stigmatising disadvantaged youth hardly helps them. Related trends are seen in educational promotions of mindfulness.

7.2   Mindfulness

Mindfulness is a personal cognitive and emotional state oriented towards momentary awareness, with relative detachment from worldly and inter-personal relations, and other external events and conditions. Mindfulness as an emotional virtue has direct bases in Buddhist meditative philoso-phy and practice. Meditation is one practice encouraged here, while related exercises that bolster or spark mindfulness and other related positive mental and physical states include yoga and Tai chi. Engaging in these practices in pursuit of mindfulness can help enhance general focus and mental health, and relieve stress. Such practices and the culti-vation of mindfulness are thereby recommended for youth and others across societies by practitioners and increasing numbers of educational researchers. Like resilience, mindfulness is seen as instrumentally valu-able among psychologists and educational psychologists, enabling one to achieve more in the context of anticipated external challenges (Schwimmer & McDonough, 2018). Mindfulness is also seen as useful to bolstering resilience.

Mindfulness practices, including meditation, yoga, and other techni-ques, aim to sustain cognitive focus on one's mind or body, 'on mental contents of particular objects, such as the breath, a sound, or a visual percept' (Greenberg & Harris, 2011). This can take place in structured physical exercise, as in yoga, or through sitting or walking. The goal is to deeply, actively experience one's consciousness in an open and accepting way, which may include recognising emotional feelings and impulses and other bodily affects, while observing the thoughts which arise spon-taneously. This experience invites self-knowledge and focus, and is believed to make one less reactive and sensitive to challenges, physical, social, or emotional. Meditation can also have other, more specific goals. As mentioned in Chapter 5, mindfulness meditation can be used to develop compassion or empathy, as in practices that encourage a person to imagine directing love and warmth from oneself to others, who may be distant acquaintances, or even people disliked.

Thich Nhat Hanh emphasises meditation's 'attention to the present moment' that is 'inclusive and loving', and that 'accepts everything with-out judging or reacting' (1999). In addition to non-judgemental practice, mindfulness enlists patience, an open mind, a sense of trust in oneself, acceptance, and a letting go of challenging thoughts and related desires. It is therefore similar to resilience, in inviting an accepting attitude towards external events and challenges. In relation, cultivating mindfulness encourages one to shift away from a passionate state of striving for things external to their body or mind (Hyland, 2009). Some thus view Buddhism as fatalistic, as the 'ultimate goal of mindful meditation, as practiced along Buddhist lines, is to develop non-judgemental equanimity in the face of both positive and negative emotions' (Kristjánsson, 2013b, p. 210). This interpretation aligns with Zen Buddhist Daisetz Teitaro Suzuki's view, that 'the essence of Buddhism really has nothing to do with morality', similar to resilience discourse (cited in Harrington & Dunne, 2015).

In Western societies, meditation and yoga have become very popular, in everyday life and schooling practices (Jackson, 2019d). To develop the capacity to meditate, people may take classes or use online programmes. Among such programmes, Headspace is one of the most popular. A commercial enterprise founded by an ordained Buddhist monk, Headspace has more than 16 million worldwide subscribers, who pay (on a monthly or yearly basis) for access to audio recordings that can be streamed from the Internet or downloaded to computers or phones. (Such recordings have also been found on commercial airplane media systems in recent years.) These audio (and sometimes video) recordings modernise traditional Buddhist techniques in a personalised way, catered to Western audiences, with programmes featuring series of meditation sessions dedicated to particular personal issues and goals, such as seeking happiness, compassion, or focus, or avoiding unhealthy diet, stress, anxiety, or relationship difficulties. Headspace also produces and offers recordings for children, in case parents or teachers wish to engage their children in meditation.

Practices for mindfulness have also found their way into classrooms. Montessori schools emphasise mindfulness, to develop 'concentration skills, independence, and intrinsic motivation' (Montessori, 2017). Children engage in a walking meditation called 'walk the line' in Montessori curricula, where they focus on 'shifting their weight from one foot to the other, balancing, and being supported by the floor beneath them' (Montessori, 2017). Other activities encouraged by Montessori schools include practising silence and becoming more aware of one's surroundings. The Jubilee Centre encourages mindfulness practices, with lessons on how to use mindfulness meditation for compassion in schools, as discussed in Chapter 5. In higher education, meditation has also become a popular field of study and practice, linked to academic achievement and relieving academic and other forms of personal stress (Bush, 2011; Williams & Kabat-Zinn, 2011).

Yoga's use and definition have also evolved over time. From an early focus in Indian texts on achieving 'an extraordinary state of consciousness' (Godrej, 2016, p. 3), yoga is now increasingly regarded as a physical practice, of moving the body into particular challenging postures, influenced by a 'hotchpotch of Buddhism, Saivism, Vaisnavism, with even Islamic influence and non-Hindu tribal asceticism' (Liberman, 2008, p. 104). While students practise postures, yoga instructors tend to encourage students to retain mindfulness, not letting their thoughts take them from focused practice. They may give short lectures on the need to accept oneself and their surroundings, the body and its limitations, and the impossibility of ever achieving perfection, given highly challenging yoga postures (such as those that require a high degree of flexibility). Indian models and approaches to yoga vary, while Western-based adaptations have proliferated in recent decades. There are classes for 'aerial or flying yoga … acro-yoga … Stand-Up Paddleboard (SUP) yoga … "rock-n-roll yoga" … "yogalates" … "hot yoga"', and more (Godrej, 2016, p. 5). Despite this variety of yoga experiences, at the core of most yoga is an emphasis on repeating movements to perfect postures and increase flexibility and strength, a theme of pre-modern Indic texts on yoga, as well (Godrej, 2016, p. 10).

Educators and positive psychologists encouraging mindfulness characterise it as non-judgemental awareness and present-minded inner focus (Dreyfus, 2011). This view is also linked to a therapeutic approach to mindfulness, as a means to decrease and adapt to or cope with negative emotions, to enhance well-being. Mindfulness is thus particularly recommended to support youth well-being, with studies reporting its benefits for reducing social-emotional and behavioural problems, decreasing 'negative emotions' of anxiety, anger, stress, confusion, and neuroticism; and increasing memory, optimism, social skills, emotional regulation, and contentment (Greenberg & Harris, 2011; Meiklejohn et al., 2012). Strong claims are made about the benefits of mindfulness, for instance: 'Research on the neurobiology of mindfulness in adults suggests that sustained mindfulness practice can enhance attentional and emotional self-regulation and promote flexibility, pointing toward significant potential benefits for both teachers and students' (Meiklejohn et al., 2012, p. 291).

Similar benefits are observed of incorporating yoga in education. Studies in schools describe its potential to improve student emotional experiences and psychosocial quality of life, reduce stress and cognitive disturbances, decrease anxiety and negative behaviour and impulsivity, enhance self- and social confidence and emotional balance, and improve communication, classroom contributions, attention, and concentration (Bazzano et al., 2018). Such benefits are emphasised as possible for both well-functioning children and children with mental and emotional challenges (Serwacki & Cook-Cottone, 2012). Studies also indicate benefits particularly for disadvantaged 'urban' students (in the United States), in programmes focused on 'helping students focus on their work and develop the ability to respond appropriately to challenging situations' (Wang & Hagins, 2016, p. 2).

However, most studies of mindfulness and yoga have not been conducted in rigorous settings. Reports on experimental studies on mindfulness interventions in schools often fail to describe key aspects of their methodology (Greenberg & Harris, 2011). Long-term follow up is generally lacking, as are clear comparison procedures and descriptions of interventions (Greenberg & Harris, 2011; Meiklejohn et al., 2012). Additionally, some of the findings related to educational achievement and mindfulness are less encouraging. Meditation's relationship to focusing on achievement is often found to be negative. In this case, the direction of causation is not clear: less outward-oriented people may prefer to meditate more, for example, in contrast with more achievement-oriented people (van den Hurk et al., 2011). At the same time, a focus on oneself and the value of relaxation and contentment apart from situations could lead a person to ignore external situations and decrease energy used for achieving goals (Parrott, 2014). Studies on yoga in education are particularly wanting and inconclusive, due to 'lack of methodological and statistical rigor, small sample sizes, absence of systematic randomization, and a high degree of variability between intervention methods' (Serwacki & Cook-Cottone, 2012, p. 106).

Other critiques of mindfulness education and related practices question their moral value (Ergas, 2019). Given the orientation in mindfulness exercises towards working on oneself, rather than scrutinising the outside world, many view the use of mindfulness techniques in education as therapeutic and non-moral (Schwimmer & McDonough, 2018; Jackson, 2019d). Changing the world around oneself seems to be the opposite goal of mindfulness meditation. Thus, contemporary Western mindfulness practice has been described as 'a banal, therapeutic, self-help technique' (Purser & Loy, 2013). Others question the moral image of yoga, given problematic political projects associated with yoga within and beyond Western societies.

First, the emphasis on individual choice and responsibility found in yoga discourse can complement neoliberal socio-economic and political perspectives, which dismiss the value of welfare and social equity, as one is regarded as accountable for their own well-being (Godrej, 2016). In this context, some yogis endorse ethical egoism, describing and justifying yoga as selfish (Jackson, 2019d).

> In my opinion, rationale egoism is the proper moral code for a yogi. I practice to achieve the integration of MY mind and body. I seek to control MY breath. I cherish MY right to life, liberty, and the pursuit of

MY Happiness. In self pursuit, I hope to achieve MY inner peace, and with it, the realization that all human beings have the right and capacity to achieve THEIR happiness ...

(McGee, 2014, p. 12, emphasis in the original)

Other yoga instructors similarly promote a kind of ethical egoism, stating or implying, for instance, that 'if everyone loves themselves, then the world will be loved' (Godwin, 2017). Yoga teachers 'gently exhort the students with slogans such as "this is *your* time"', while the variety of classes and modifications for postures further encourages people to focus on the individualisation of their needs (Godrej, 2016, p. 10). Seen as 'self-care', such yoga practice is also used 'to enhance one's own esteem and future value, whether understood in terms of stress reduction and overall good health, or attracting future "investors" such as significant others' (Godrej, 2016, p. 12). Relational and societal care are unimportant in these views.

Yoga practices also serve, as discussed by many yoga teachers, to ameliorate the damages of living a relatively sedentary lifestyle, always online and connected, at desks in front of screens. Teachers often focus particularly on neck and shoulder stretches, reminding students during exercises how essential they are for continued good health for desk workers. Thus, yoga is framed as a way to 'allow subjects to continue coping with the stresses of the post-Fordist workplace, while keeping the body healthy, useful, flexible, and productive enough to work all hours' (Godrej, 2016, p. 13), reflecting the position that societies and employers owe individuals little apart from monetary pay for their labour. Farah Godrej summarises the implications of this approach as follows:

... contemporary yogis may become perfect neoliberal subjects, as the practice of yoga may inadvertently reinscribe a consumerist, politically passive, undemocratic, and anti-egalitarian orientation. Responsibilizing yogic subjects for ... 'consumption' of yogic opportunities ... may imply that poor, heavy, unhealthy, or unemployed others have only themselves to blame. Inequities ... can be legitimated and depoliticized by being relegated to the realm of 'personal' choice and a failure of disciplined self-optimization .... In pursuing yoga, many may see themselves as making a lifestyle 'choice' that seems to supply a seemingly benevolent ethical content. Practitioners of yoga may imagine that they have discovered a broadly palatable ethics that feels exotic and countercultural. But in actuality, this choice may function to displace politics, by pacifying. ... It may provide the illusion that one is taking a drastic step away from the dominant system, while simultaneously consuming the resources and effort required to explore truly radical alternatives. (2016, pp. 14–15)

Yoga practice can also be seen to intersect with other politically problematic projects beyond Western societies. Yoga is promoted in India at a national level to enhance a Hindu majoritarian identity, and a related view of India as a Hindu nation that non-Hindus must assimilate to (McCartney, 2017). In this context, Hindu nationalists introduce Hindu spiritual and religious teachings associated with yoga into secular spaces, bolstered by a sense that yoga is simply best practice, with medical benefits. Leaving aside ongoing debate over whether yoga is physically healthy for diverse individuals, many Western yoga practitioners see their engagement as secular, just, and cosmopolitan. Yet their enthusiasm for yoga can nonetheless help 'facilitate the assimilationist processes of an expansionist, Hindu agenda, which directly incorporates the soft power of yoga into broadening the sphere of cultural, political and economic influence of the Indian state [through] uncritical consumption of a homogenised cultural practice' (McCartney, 2017, p. 12). Western practitioners may tour India to learn yoga in an 'authentic way', while their funds partly help sponsor Hindu nationalist projects. Such politics may go unnoticed by these yogis, who are encouraged by tour organisations to see themselves as contributing to global peace and harmony through their choices. Likewise, young people exposed to yoga in schools hardly learn of yoga's history and global significance.

In relation, Western fascination with yoga can also be culturally appropriative. Westerners regarded Indians as uncivilised and irrational in the colonial era, mocking practices such as yoga. In this context, Western-based yogis have taken something from India and transformed it to be palatable to Western consumers, without considering the historical relations of India and Western societies. In Western societies, people of Indian descent practising yoga experience being treated more negatively than white women, as yogis (Berila, 2016). Thin white women are often regarded as ideal practitioners, while people who are larger or who have mobility and ability challenges face inequitable treatment in many studios.

Finally, yoga's profitability in Western societies has led to horrendous corruptions, which further indicate how yogis are not necessarily models of justice, or peace and harmony (Jackson, 2019d). Bikram Choudhuri, who made 75 million dollars certifying hot yoga teachers, is known for making homophobic, racist, misogynist rants while teaching in the United States. He shunned overweight students from his classes, and is alleged to have raped and molested several students (Godwin, 2017). Other sexual scandals involving yoga teachers assaulting students have emerged (Chatel, 2015; Grant, 2015; Priest, 2017). In some cases, women students noted how yoga discourse (and the words and authority of their teachers) influenced them to accept abuse, by encouraging them to focus on their practice rather than on their instructors harming them. The founder of Lululemon, one of the most popular yoga apparel companies, has publicly disparaged and mocked Japanese people, publicly saying that he chose the name 'Lululemon' to make it difficult for Japanese people to pronounce (Peterson, 2013). He has mocked the use of child labour in his company, and implied that overweight women are too large for yoga. Thus, while Western people may be attracted to an 'exotic ethics' of yoga, there is nothing essentially ethical about Western yoga practice.

Mindfulness more generally has also been used for questionable ends. As Terry Hyland notes, 'the inclusion of mindfulness in US army training regimes and by Google in staff development programmes clearly raises issues about the misuse and, in some cases, outright abuse ... foundational mindfulness values such as right livelihood, loving-kindness, compassion and non-materialism are self-evidently and fundamentally at odds with aspects of the core business of corporations and the military' (2015, p. 181). In this context, critics of Western discourses on mindfulness note their philosophical departure from Buddhist orientations that are not merely present-centred and non-judgemental.

> By over-emphasizing the non-judgmental nature of mindfulness and arguing that our problems stem from conceptuality, contemporary authors are in danger of leading to a one-sided understanding of mindfulness as a form of therapeutically helpful spacious quietness. I think that it is important not to lose sight that mindfulness is not just a therapeutic technique but is a natural capacity that plays a central role in the cognitive process. It is this aspect that seems to be ignored when mindfulness is reduced to a form of non-judgmental present-centred awareness of one's experiences.   (Dreyfus, 2011, p. 52)

Despite some associations of mindfulness and Buddhism with fatalism and being non-judgemental, others emphasise the connection between mindfulness and good action in some Buddhist philosophies and practices. As discussed in previous chapters, Buddhism has a reputation among Western thinkers for being passive, but this is not essential to Buddhism. In contrast to practices which solely emphasise being accepting, forgiving, and non-judgemental, socially engaged Buddhism may embrace anger and other 'negative emotions', as it is oriented towards alleviating suffering of oneself and others, through compassion and being in tune with the world (e.g. McRae, 2012, 2015). Thus, only a limited, amoral form of Buddhist mindfulness has been embraced in mainstream Western societies and schools.

In addition, some argue that mindfulness need not be seen as an individual capacity, but can also be conceptualised as an attribute of a community, such as a school. Wayne Hoy (2003) describes mindful school structures as those that encourage participants to cultivate mindful views. Hoy notes that most institutions discourage mindfulness, by encouraging a focus on outcomes rather than processes, optimistic negligence of complexity in perspectives and possibilities, and the dismissal of expertise in light of rigid structures (2003). Instead, Hoy recommends that institutional leaders facilitate organisations to become mindful, through developing flexible rule structures, being open-minded to problems, negativity, and new perspectives, and cultivating humility about achievements. In this way, teachers and students can be empowered to be morally mindful, in working to fulfil goals held across the school.

Likewise, some urge a reinterpretation of yoga's philosophy in the Western world, to better align it with social justice values. Beth Berila (2016) argues that yoga and mindfulness can be the cornerstone of anti-oppressive pedagogy. Godrej also provides a 'counter-neoliberal reading' of yogic philosophy (2016). In relation, she points to some yoga communities where participants question consumer culture in their practice, and engage at the same time in political and justice work. Thus, while some yogis encourage indifference to or withdrawal from worldly concerns, others emphasise moral and political engagement (Schwimmer & McDonough, 2018). Diverse interpretations of mindfulness, yoga, and meditation are possible.

7.3   Conclusion

This chapter has considered some less traditional emotional virtues which have become popular across societies and their educational systems in recent decades. Resilience and mindfulness are both dispositions with regard to one's emotions and experiences of the world, increasingly held as key in educational discourse to developing focus and purpose, and moving through challenging worldly circumstances in clear-headed ways. Resilience as a concept suffers from theoretical incoherence, however. It seems to be used as a place header to solve a variety of problems, which are particularly faced by disadvantaged youth. Yet while resilience is encouraged and promoted to increase equity for vulnerable young people, it has no clear moral foundation or moral status: one can be resiliently good or resiliently unjust. In relation, what interventions for resilience achieve is not clear. If resilience is used to enable positive student attitudes, interventions may show students performing as required in the short term, but long-term possible benefits for students may be unlikely. In worse cases, calls for resilience can result in students suffering silently, as some so-called resilient students may develop a worse sense of self after interventions, or develop unhealthy states, related to tolerating problematic conditions around them. Ultimately, resilience is a morally questionable concept. It should not be taken for granted as a means to fix challenges faced by students and educators.

Mindfulness similarly encourages an inward focus to resolve people's challenges, in education and society, through meditation, yoga, or other practices which redirect attention from the outside world to the experiences of the body and mind. While many claim to benefit from mindfulness practices, as in the case of resilience, such practices are not moral, in and of themselves. People can become more mindful while being selfish or harmful to others, such as in the cases of mindful military bombers and abusive yogis. Interventions may or may not be useful at the individual level for enhancing educational and other success, as practices which are inward-oriented do not particularly drive achievement. On the other hand, more moral and politically informed orientations to mindfulness are possible. Here, 'exotic' practices from India and Buddhist traditions are embraced in Western societies as aiding productivity and student achievement, yet their more morally and politically aware variants and other political considerations in utilising them have largely been neglected. In sum, mindfulness and resilience can both be promoted in moral and just ways, or in harmful, unjust ways.

Behind many calls for resilience and mindfulness in education is concern with youth *vulnerability*. To combat young people's vulnerability to failure, low self-esteem, and other challenges, resilience and mindfulness interventions or other programmes which are aimed at bolstering their courage or grit may be encouraged. The next chapter describes how vulnerability, courage, and grit are conceived in society and education, continuing this discussion about approaches to students facing emotional challenges to well-being.

CHAPTER 8

Vulnerability, Courage, and Grit

Vulnerability, courage, and grit may not initially appear to have much in common. However, as emotional virtues (as defined broadly here), they intersect in significant ways. In contrast with the emotional virtues discussed thus far, vulnerability and courage are less frequently prized in educational settings. Vulnerability is often seen as a negative quality of people generally, and for youth in the context of education. To be vulnerable is in everyday language associated with being prone to challenges and obstacles, and being weak. As Chapter 7 discussed, promotions of resilience and mindfulness in education are often responses to vulnerability (in part), and recommended to make vulnerable or at-risk youth less vulnerable, to mental or emotional disturbance, poor academic achievement, drop out, and related concerns. Yet, as this chapter argues, there is also a bright side to vulnerability, and good reason to question common conflations of it with entirely negative experiences and feelings. There can be a positive role for particular kinds of experiences of vulnerability, generally within communities, and particularly in education.

On the other hand, courage is normally prized in society, and it has been promoted in education, although it is not normally held in psychological or educational discourse as a primary or core emotional virtue. Courage is also encouraged in moral philosophy, where it is typically emphasised as a mean-state virtue. To be understood as a virtue, courage must be tempered, so that it is not reckless, careless, or brash. The value of courage also hinges on its appropriateness within situations. It is therefore not conceptualised upon reflection as an absolute good. It is also possible to think of vulnerability and courage as describing similar emotional and cognitive dispositions, as will be discussed here.

Courage can also be considered as a core value underlying the quality of grit. Grit, as defined by its lead proponent Angela Duckworth (2016), is a combination of passion and perseverance. Grit as an emotional virtue is a relatively new concept. As such it does not have a clear moral or philosophical foundation. As an underlying aspect of grit, passion is typically seen as a quality to avoid, across many philosophical traditions. Meanwhile perseverance, like resilience, mindfulness, and courage, can be recommended and used in moral and non-moral ways. This chapter thus explores vulnerability, courage, and grit in turn, considering their relationship to one another, and the task of educating for emotional virtues and for social justice.

8.1   Vulnerability

People tend to presume that vulnerability is a bad thing. This can be seen in discourse that describes 'vulnerable populations'. The assumption and connotation in many uses of the term as an adjective is that to be vulnerable is to be susceptible to risks and challenges: to be vulnerable to such things as anxiety, mental health problems, underachievement, and failure (Jackson, 2018b). In psychology, one is said to be vulnerable to depression or anxiety. In sociology, a student may be vulnerable to bullying or academic failure. Medically, some people may be vulnerable to cancer and diseases. According to this view, vulnerability is akin to weakness, and 'at-risk' status. From this framing, it seems reasonable to argue that a person or social institution should work to decrease vulnerability, or at least not be 'too vulnerable', but aim rather to be secure from risk, challenges, and problems (Fineman, 2008).

This negative, deficit view of vulnerability is also seen in research literature in education (Engers & Teichler, 1997; Williams, 2008). Psychological assessments of vulnerability in education focus on the individual level of risk, and proneness or susceptibility to challenges of a mental, emotional, or cognitive nature. Vulnerability can also be understood as a lack of resilience, as discussed in Chapter 7. If one is vulnerable, they may face a downward spiral of mental, emotional, and physical and biological challenges from a systems view. When faced with a major change, one should therefore bolster their resilience, to meet their challenges with a sense of buoyancy, and not create a negative chain reaction of further challenges.

Assessments of vulnerability in society contribute to a discourse of widespread crisis related to mental health, as categorisations of vulnerability are expanded over time to include more people. For instance, in one estimate, one quarter of Britons are vulnerable to emotional distress (Ecclestone, 2012). At the same time, the discourse of rising youth vulnerability can be seen to 'accompany apocryphal claims . . . A commonplace assertion is that children diagnosed at five with single or multiple conduct disorders are significantly more likely to commit crimes, be unemployed, experience marital breakdown and have drug or alcohol problems' (Ecclestone, 2012, p. 466).

The means to predict and meaningfully quantify the impact of youth vulnerability are not altogether clear, however. People who make apocryphal claims about vulnerability often do so at the same time that they are pushing for particular kinds of intervention, while others may challenge the bases for these predictions. At the same time, this discourse has a psychological educative impact. Students can learn to see themselves as weak and vulnerable in the course of being subjected to anti-vulnerability interventions, in ways that can decrease their sense of control and efficacy in the world around them (Boler, 1999). If a student is told by an educator or other authority that they are nearly doomed to fail, and if teachers indeed hold such negative expectations, this has a direct impact on the student's sense of self, relationships with teachers and peers, and their future achievement (as discussed in Chapter 2).

Educational psychologists frame vulnerability as an 'ontological characteristic', a dynamic state of being. All are vulnerable, in the sense that they are at risk in relation to various challenges within dynamic, real-world circumstances. However, this particular type of instrumentalist psychological framing tends to slide to the conclusion that people's vulnerability can be fixed, and that all people should therefore 'work on' their vulnerability, as individual risk (Ecclestone, 2012). This can lead to and bolster approaches to societal-level well-being that hold people as individuals accountable for what are arguably systemic problems. As examples, Tessman notes (2005) that people in vulnerable categories, such as women and girls who are regarded as vulnerable to rape and assault, and young black men who are framed as vulnerable to criminal activity, are treated by such individualised discourse as having a personal deficit in relation to these vulnerabilities. Meanwhile, social issues factoring into such vulnerabilities are sometimes ignored (i.e. tolerant attitudes toward violence against women and imprisonment of black men, and correlations between race and greater exposure to crime). In the latter case, a 'culture of poverty' is attributed as a cause of vulnerability, to be resolved by individual actions of self-control and cultivation of good moral character. Thus, vulnerability discourse that individualises the phenomena complements views that welfare is not needed, and that women and girls and black men are to blame for their experiences (Tessman, 2005).

Approaches that individualise vulnerability as personal deficiency also overlook the potential positive value and significance of vulnerability, within relationships and for knowledge generation in communities, if one considers vulnerability instead as an 'existential condition', and an inevitable aspect of life (Ecclestone, 2012). Philosophical defences of vulnerability consider it as an inevitable part of the human condition, not a one-off, peculiar state of being. In this context, some think of vulnerability as of value within interpersonal relationships that are compassionate and loving, where people primarily aim to understand each other and work together. In such cases, without vulnerability, one may be unable to admit that they care about another, that the other matters, and as such that they cannot control the relationship. Judith Butler observes that 'each of us is constituted politically in part by virtue of the social vulnerability of our bodies ... Loss and vulnerability seem to follow from our being socially constituted bodies, attached to others, at risk of losing those attachments, exposed to others, at risk of violence by virtue of that exposure' (2004, p. 20).

From an educational perspective, Erinn Gilson (2014, p. 308) champions 'epistemic vulnerability' as, firstly, an openness 'to not knowing'. She casts this kind of vulnerability as essential to education, as a precondition of learning. This is a disposition to be willing to learn, based on accepting limits to one's knowledge. As she goes on (2014, p. 309): 'Second, it is an openness to being wrong and venturing one's ideas, beliefs, and feelings nonetheless ... Third, epistemic vulnerability entails the ability to put oneself in and learn from situations in which one is the unknowing, foreign, and perhaps uncomfortable party.' Nussbaum (2001) relatedly argues that recognition of vulnerability can enhance compassion, as 'thought about shared vulnerabilities, promotes the selection of principles that raise society's floor' (p. 321). In other words, as in Rawls' (1994) veil of justice, by imagining oneself in the worst situations in society, one is more likely to approach welfare in an equitable way, recognising that anyone can be vulnerable, and anyone can be at the top or bottom of inequitable social hierarchies.

There can thus be something positive about vulnerability from the view of individual and social learning: Vulnerability enables learning. It entails an openness to being proven wrong, or having one's views challenged. If one's beliefs or perspectives are 'invulnerable', they cannot change, learn, or grow. This perspective has different implications, for education and for reforming systems and enhancing environments, than the view that vulnerability is simply bad. Students and other stakeholders, such as teachers who seek positive change at individual or community levels, should not just work against vulnerability from this view. Instead, they should aim to possess, maintain, and even further develop their vulnerability, to be open to new, creative pathways for positive educational and social change and growth.

This view echoes other pedagogical perspectives on learning from mixed emotions, which also tend to be dismissed when vulnerability is presumed to be bad. Jan Meyer and Ray Land (2003) discuss how 'transformative learning' can be 'troublesome for students', as it may entail enduring an uncomfortable emotional state. People can feel anxious or unpleasantly unsettled when faced with uncertainty in understanding and knowledge, and thus may work toward some sense of certainty. As discussed elsewhere here (particularly in relation to existentialism, happiness, and the work of Peter Roberts), this concern with certainty is not necessarily reasonable or helpful, while it is based in desire to ameliorate discomfort and maintain a sense of emotional safety and contentment. In relation, academics (among others) have been observed to erroneously hold on to and defend their prevailing beliefs in new situations, where they may reflect biases, to evade a sense of uncertainty, inexperience, insecurity, or newness in facing novel problems. Misato Matsuoka (2017) argues in relation that people in higher education should more often work toward 'embracing vulnerability', as personal challenges can be venues for growth and development, not merely obstacles.

Such alternative accounts do not indicate that vulnerability is always a good thing. There remain worthwhile rationales to avoid, prevent, and decrease some forms of vulnerability in many situations. Here, a simplistic focus on the benefits of vulnerability might obscure significant differences among forms of vulnerabilities. This can lead to the dismissal of grievances over injustices, and thus exacerbate harmful vulnerabilities (Cole, 2016). A positive view of vulnerability can also work in harmony with neoliberal orientations that cast vulnerability as a personal issue, rather than in terms of systemic and organisational failures. As discussed in the last chapter, the need to cultivate vulnerability could possibly be exploited, like the benefits of cultivating resilience, to justify providing some children with more challenging and less effective educational circumstances, despite the value of equitably providing education in society. Tessman (2005) is also wary of the possible abuse of vulnerability by those with an optimistic view of how it can lead to compassion (like Nussbaum). As she notes, in unequal societies, people do not necessarily recognise their vulnerability as equivalent to that of others, as encouraging in people 'a fear of loss … has variable and not necessarily commendable results' (p. 104).

Having more vulnerability than others to oppression and harm is clearly a bad thing. Yet normalising a place for vulnerability in education can still help to decrease rather than increase harms if thoughtfully managed. Thinking of vulnerability relationally and politically, one can consider the circulation and distribution of vulnerability: that is, who in the group is more and less vulnerable, and in what respects, to which challenges (Jackson, 2018b; Jackson & Muñoz-García, 2019). For example, when some people's perspectives and experiences are normalised, while others are not, those with minority views are vulnerable to misrecognition of their concerns. Thus, if a teacher relates more to some students than others, some students are more vulnerable to having their challenges misrecognised by teachers.

Additionally, locating vulnerability not in particular identity or subject positions, but recognising it as a feature of communities, enables a different outlook on what can be done to enhance the situation of vulnerability in a group (Ecclestone & Goodley, 2016). If vulnerability is seen as a feature of relations of people to each other, then these vulnerable relations can be improved. More specifically, one can examine how vulnerability operates and circulates through relations, and whether there are more equitable ways to distribute and circulate it (Jackson & Muñoz-García, 2019). If vulnerability is not necessarily bad, but problematic in its circulation and distribution, one strategy to enhance it while ameliorating its negative impacts can involve its redistribution.

In such contexts, enhancing some people's epistemic vulnerability can be healthy and helpful to themselves as individuals and in communities, as it can provide conditions for learning and growth, when it exists in a balance with its 'troublesome' emotional aspects (Meyer & Land, 2003). This epistemic vulnerability 'is more appropriately demanded of those who are relatively privileged precisely because they have likely not already found themselves in situations in which they are the unknowing, uncomfortable, and nondominant party' (Gilson, 2014, p. 311). Thus, more privileged people may have insufficient positive vulnerability from an educational view, as they may feel accustomed and entitled to having correct or acceptable perspectives, and to not being questioned, and this may encourage them to maintain their views with a false and unhelpful sense of certainty, and in a stubborn and close-minded way (see Applebaum, 2016, 2017). When those with normalised views who are in more privileged positions develop productive epistemic vulnerability, they can learn from others with less privileged perspectives and identities, so that mutual understanding and social justice can be enhanced. On the other hand, some people, such as those coming from disadvantaged minority groups, may have too much harmful vulnerability, to being challenged, dismissed, and ignored, and become too uncertain about what they know based on experience in relation to diverse others. This will be elaborated on further in Chapter 9, in the context of anger. In this case, some may have responsibilities, in a sense, to develop vulnerability in relation to others.

For instance, in discussing whether racial minorities face ongoing harms to their self-esteem and rights in society due to discrimination and racism, racial minorities in a classroom are more likely to feel significant stress and anxiety, and face a greater emotional and cognitive burden in defending their views, or in discussing views more commonly held among minorities (DeCuir-Gunby & Williams-Johnson, 2014). In contrast, students coming from majority groups do not usually feel (as) emotionally burdened discussing such cases, and often defend normalised, mainstream conceptions, such as that the society is sufficiently just, in certainty, without seeing mainstream majority views as problematic (Jackson, 2014a). Likewise, in discussing the prevalence of sexual harassment or sexism, women experience a burden of proof compared to men, who can claim innocence and lack of experience as justifications for not being aware about, or concerned with the situation (Jackson, 2019b). Many men may feel certain that the issue is not common based on a desire for comfort and certainty, and lacking any burdensome forms of knowledge about the issue. These situations make vulnerability to questions and criticism a burdened virtue, as in these cases victims of harm and injustice have to explain their views to majority people, who may be incredulous, since their own experiences are not as difficult and disturbing.

Confidence, certainty, and a peaceful and clearheaded disposition are often regarded in (Western) intellectual spaces as indicative of preparedness, achievement, correctness, and cleverness. Yet for those with minority views, they face ongoing stress and pressure related to defending alternative perspectives, which makes the conversations more uncomfortable for them. This means that facilitating challenging conversations across difference exacerbates an emotional experience gap across a diverse group, as some students face more anxiety at the threat of being challenged than others. In this context, putting those with mainstream views more 'on edge' emotionally and cognitively can be seen as equalising the playing field and balancing out vulnerabilities, in discussing social justice issues in a classroom, such as racism, sexism, and related issues, where people have divergent experiences and views.

In such contexts, Boler advocates affirmative action pedagogy, where she prizes and positively recognises voices and perspectives which are more marginalised in society in her classroom, over those views and orientations which are less likely to face critical questioning, due to being more predominant and mainstream (2004). This is not to suggest that resources that enhance productivity and well-being among any students should be taken away, or that some views and students should be more positively recognised than others in a classroom, to play an alternative game of identity politics. Rather, this strategy can be seen to respond to the possibility that, from a productive view of vulnerability, some in more privileged social positions have less access to, and less encouragement to access and develop epistemic vulnerability (i.e. to learn in groups), in comparison with others (Applebaum, 2017). Meanwhile, for minorities, mainstream-oriented discussions regularly invoke their epistemic vulnerability, as such discourse often outright rejects and dismisses alternative claims to knowledge. Thus, balancing vulnerability can lead to intergroup relations being more equitable, as with less stubbornness and self-certainty, more privileged people can listen to others with divergent views and experiences in a more open way. It can then be seen as a 'disposition to acknowledge and to respond', and deeply learn from others (Slegers, 2010, p. 241).

Embracing vulnerability in this context does not imply simply admitting weakness, but understanding vulnerability as a potentially positive learning disposition. It is to acknowledge that learning is not always a happy and comfortable process, but may involve 'liminality', in the case that one is unsettled and made insecure, in order to grow and develop (Meyer & Land, 2003). New knowledge is not possible without change and development. Epistemic vulnerability in this context is essential, so that one does not cling to previously held views in order to feel safe and invulnerable. When vulnerability is seen more critically – not as an individual weakness, but as a dynamic feature of people within a community which is differentially distributed – epistemic vulnerability can be embraced as essential to enhancing understanding and positive social processes and practices.

Educators can therefore reframe vulnerability not as deficiency, but as a courageous approach to difference and uncomfortable knowledge: as a virtue of people, as they collaborate in communities to develop and maintain open, broadly inclusive and beneficial, reflective spaces. Teachers can also cultivate vulnerability by admitting to uncertainties, challenges, and deeply felt mixed emotional experiences, of deep hopes, wishes, and fears. By cultivating epistemic vulnerability, they can model and enhance their own positive vulnerability, while at the same time decreasing vulnerabilities of misrecognition, by working to hear others, including those students and colleagues who challenge them or question them, including those with different views, and other diverse students and peers, who they may not immediately or initially understand. Cultivating vulnerability as a leader or authority figure is also more generally of value across professional organisations, to model the trait and to enhance overall relations. This is indicated in research on leadership. For example, as one study describes and commends a vulnerable leader (Fuda & Badham, 2011): 'He could have worked in private to change his behaviour – but instead he stood up at an annual meeting of his top sixty managers, acknowledged his failings, and outlined both his personal and organizational roles. He admitted that he didn't have all of the answers and asked his team for help leading the company.'

Seeing vulnerability as a good, an educator, like a student, can thus aspire toward more productive epistemic vulnerability, for their own moral cultivation and continued education for social justice. As with mindfulness, vulnerability can be valued and modelled by those in leadership, in a school or a classroom, to enhance overall functioning, based on greater awareness of the importance of diverse viewpoints and concerns. By implication, challenges and risks in education related to student (and teacher) vulnerability cannot be resolved only through individualistic prescriptions, such as interventions for resilience or mindfulness (among others). Instead, the circulation of positive forms of vulnerability should be celebrated and enhanced at process and relational levels. Another means to reconceive vulnerability, not as risk but as a kind of possible virtue, is to relate it to courage, which similarly has its potential, as well as its downsides, in everyday circumstances.

8.2 Courage

Some equate the positive kind of vulnerability articulated here with the virtue of courage. This type of courage is like vulnerability, as it requires openness, a confidence against and despite risks and obstacles, and a persevering spirit. Brene Brown (2014) argues that courage and vulnerability are closely related. Defining vulnerability as the experience of uncertainty, risk, and emotional exposure, Brown (2014) argues that vulnerability is scary but worthwhile, and emphasises that it is a myth that people can ever be invulnerable. She further describes vulnerability as a 'catalyst for courage' and courage as necessary for vulnerability, thus seeing them as mutually constituted. In relation, in thought experiments, people often see vulnerability as the same as courage in everyday life. In Brown's study (2014, p. 34), when she asked participants how vulnerability feels, most of their answers connected it to courage: 'going out on a limb – a very, very high limb', 'taking the first step toward what you fear the most', 'terrifying and hopeful', and 'human and alive'.

However, courage has a longer track record than vulnerability as a virtue. It has been described as bravery against obstacles and fear in ancient Greece and Rome, in the Middle Ages, and in Confucian, Hindi, and Islamic texts. It is promoted by Stoics, as well as existentialists, such as Kierkegaard and Sartre (Putman, 2010). It is among Aristotle's cardinal virtues, described as a disposition to fear 'the right things, in the right way' (Roberts, 2017, p. 23).

Many philosophers emphasise that the value of courage is found in situations, rather than in consistent application. There are many situations where courage is not the right thing to cultivate, or particularly relevant: '"Do I dare to eat the cheesecake?" is not the right question', in ordinary circumstances (Curzer, 2017, p. 66). Nietzsche similarly observes that 'Courage as cold valourousness and intrepidity, and courage as hotheaded, half-blind bravery – both are called by the same name!' (1997, p. 277). Courage in wrongdoing is hardly virtuous. Seamus Mulryan emphasises that for Aristotle,

> We do not come to understand courage by mere analytic definition, in the same way we cannot learn to ride a horse by receiving verbal instructions on how to do so. Moreover, exercising courage once rightly does not make for being courageous. Each horse is different, and if we imagine each social situation as a new horse, we never quite ride the same horse twice. Yet with practice, we come better at tuning into the unique attributes of the horse and adjusting accordingly.
>
> (2011, p. 101)

While Aristotle is known for seeing all virtues (including courage) as a singular kind of trait, related to 'passions' (Roberts, 1989), others emphasise courage as an exemplar among emotional virtues that call upon a set of capacity-related components. Roberts (1989) notes that courage is not just a disposition toward fear, but actually requires fear to be enacted. Using the example of Socrates' courage, which was observed in his integrity in the face of his likely execution, Roberts observes that Socrates was undisturbed by, and thereby lacked fear regarding his possible death. Seeing fear as a component part of courage, Roberts thus argues that Socrates 'outgrew the need for courage' (1989, p. 299). Another vital component of courage for Roberts is self-control. Roberts also notes that courage is of value in the context of other virtues, such as compassion, justice, and generosity, pointing out that courage toward evil goals, even if perfectly utilised, is still not virtuous (2013).

Sreenivasan (2020) argues similarly that courage is distinctive among virtues, in that it requires not only simply or primarily exercising self-control over one's fear, but also requires a reasonable assessment of fear in the context of a conflict of desires, wherein one also has an external desire that can be regarded as virtuous, or morally good. Thus, courage requires the ability to act appropriately in relation to this assessment (Sreenivasan, 2020). Such investigations further complicate the picture of courage as a virtue, elaborating on its significance within a complex moral world.

On the other hand, despite its framing in philosophy as a mean-state virtue, courage is often upheld as if it is always obviously good by thinkers outside the field. John F. Kennedy's *Profiles in Courage* (1956) understands courage more simply, as indicating resoluteness, at odds with vulnerability-oriented, more reasoned, conceptions. The popular text among teachers, Parker Palmer's *Courage to Teach* (1997), also praises courage, with an understanding of courage that is more aligned with Brown's view of courage as vulnerability. Palmer states that:

> The word 'courage' comes from a root that means 'heart,' and I like to transpose the words. How can we develop and sustain, in ourselves and each other, the heart for good teaching? Good teaching requires

courage – the courage to explore one's ignorance as well as insight, to yield some control in order to empower the group, to evoke other people's lives as well as reveal one's own. Furthermore, good teaching sometimes goes unvalued by academic institutions, by the students for whom it is done, and even by those teachers who do it. Many of us 'lose heart' in teaching. How shall we recover the courage that good teaching requires?

Palmer's view of courage here emphasises that it may go unseen or unvalued, and its connection to empowerment of all as a duty. Similarly, Tessman (2005) describes courage as a 'burdened virtue', in relation to its significance in striving for greater social justice. This is because courage can be an excessive demand placed on some more than others in some situations. As Tessman highlights, some are called upon to act courageously more than others in daily life, as they face more obstacles. However, those who are effective in managing to develop courageous dispositions as political resisters 'risk sacrificing themselves' (Tessman, 2005, p. 126). One challenge for disadvantaged members of society relates to the practice of socially constructing courage as generally and simply positive, as if it is not inherently related to threat and risk. Tessman continues:

> When resistance movements make heroes of the courageous, they add to the pressure to prioritize courage as a/the praiseworthy character trait of the politically resistant self. In part this is troublesome because the image of courage tends to be based on a masculinist, military model ... which avoids rather than works through a question about what is really more noble: risking oneself in order to achieve victory in a battle against injustice or seeing to it that one returns home consistently, attentively, and safely enough to be able to love and care and be loved and cared for well. With this question obscured, the resistant self is urged to fight and to face the consequences of it: anything from being socially ostracized and harassed and having one's children taunted, to losing one's job or being jailed, or more drastically, to being tortured or killed.   (2005, p. 126)

Given that courage is burdensome, it is disconnected from a person's individual flourishing in cases where people are expected to be courageous above all else. In such cases, a person's own flourishing, and that of those around them, may demand turning a blind eye in part to injustice and how they can fight it, as even appropriate courage is still risky to oneself and others, requiring what may be impossible, and possibly self-sacrificing behaviour. Thus, the philosophical insights, that courage is valuable within particular situations, and that it may imply different behaviours from 'manly' aggression and risk-taking, sometimes get lost in real-life appraisals and expectations for courage, while courage is framed at the same time as always beneficial, despite its disparate risks and demands on different individuals and groups.

Simplistic promotions of courage in education reflect such challenges. Character First Education provides lessons on courage for students and educators. In a short story for students on courage, US past president John Quincy Adams is noted for his 'honorable conduct, devotion to justice, and willingness to speak the truth', for presenting fifteen petitions to end slavery in Congress. He is applauded in the text as 'Old Man Eloquent' and contrasted with those who did not want to end slavery, or listen to his petitions (as the story explains, Congress placed a gag order on Adams's petitions for eight years). The story concludes that 'Adams died in 1848. Seventeen years later and after a terrible civil war, Congress finally ended slavery' (Character First, 2019c). This short story suggests that Adams is commendable for his courage, for speaking out against injustice, which is framed as a factor in ending slavery.

Another Character First Education story, on the theme of flexibility, is also relevant to the promotion of courage, while indicating its potentially burdensome aspects. In this story, black men in Massachusetts choose to fight on the side of the north in the US Civil War, despite hearing that 'the Confederate Congress has said that any black man caught in army uniform will be executed' (Character First, 2019d). While they were apparently to be provided with full discharges in this case, 'Not one of the soldiers had left! The entire 54th Infantry stood ready to serve!' Half of its men are 'lost' in battle, as described in the story. Yet, the text concludes, 'the men ... served their country well and stood firm – for the glory of freedom'. Here, there is clearly a difference between being faced with the likelihood of dying for freedom from oppression and being faced by colleagues being irritated about one's speeches, as courageous moments.

Fear and risk should be evaluated differently across these examples, and inform views of what it means to be courageous. Since fear and vulnerability to risks are so (relatively) slight in the first story, it seems the real meaning of courage is evaded in these texts, while the morality of flexibility remains questionable, as the story does not depict any kind of reckoning with the situation by those involved. In any case, in these stories courage and flexibility are framed as qualities to simply be enacted, without consideration of the significance of inequitable risks and sacrifices recommended by courage (and 'flexibility'), as virtue or as part of character.

Courage is also framed as masculine and militaristic in these examples, as well as in some texts put forward by the Jubilee Centre. Courage is emphasised in one Jubilee Centre curriculum on 'Knightly Virtues', which has been reportedly used in over one hundred schools in Britain

(Arthur et al., 2014). Stories about various heroes are provided in this programme, including Beowulf, Don Quixote, and Joan of Arc. As Suissa notes (2015), in these stories heroes are commended for their individual courage and other virtues, while the social and relational nature of their heroism, and the real risks and sacrifices they faced, are not emphasised.

The Jubilee Centre more emphatically praises (militaristic) courage in a study of British 'Army values' that junior British Army officers are recommended to cultivate (Arthur, Walker, & Thoma, 2018). The authors of this research describe courage as 'an obvious military quality', while stating that there are 'modern reasons for individual retreat from military danger such as psychological illness', neglecting to mention other virtuous reasons not to act on courage (Arthur et al., 2018, p. 9). Cohesion, loyalty, and comradeship are listed as complementary values to courage in the text. The ethics, risks, and complexities of Army and military practices, of knowing when to fight and when not to, are left out of the picture here. As Tessman (2005) observes, calls for courage can lead to questionable, risky choices, to oneself and others. Courage also requires self-control, and a consideration of fear and the likelihood of the success of various choices. To simplify these values as if they are always good overlooks their burdensome nature for many people in the context of social injustice, and the problematic nature of brashness. That courage need not be militaristic is also overlooked in this context.

From an Aristotelian view, rash courage can lead to poor choices, and lack of appreciation for risks, without reflection. Meanwhile, demands for cohesion and loyalty can be regarded as assets in some cases, but are also risk factors for youth in others, when considering the militaristic and aggressive behaviour of gang members or extremists, for instance (Pury & Starkey, 2010). Thus, 'retreat from military danger' is hardly a 'psychological illness', when one's loyalty and courage can also be invoked for morally problematic ends. These complexities and risks related to valuing courage and loyalty are not addressed in many educational encouragements of courage. They require broader, more politically oriented discussions that recognise both the power and the risks of courage and related values and dispositions.

Relatedly, Barbara Stengel (2018) contrasts 'cruel' courage in education, with courage within just and inclusive solidarity movements, to highlight how courage can be a personally oppressive expectation for an individual student or educator, in comparison with a kind of courage which is more akin to courageous, epistemic vulnerability. As Stengel notes (2018), in many educational discourses, teachers' courage is commended, particularly within extreme situations and as individualistic dispositions and actions, such as when teachers risk their jobs or reputations to criticise or resist educational practices they see as ineffective or harmful. This conceptualisation of courage can be seen as cruel (Berlak, 2011), as it bolsters expectations for particular kinds of bold acts that may ultimately be self-defeating or self-harming, which seem to require individual sacrifice, as one single person is framed as battling everyone and everything else in society.

In contrast, what Stengel (2018) describes as solidarity, or collective courage, has a different affect to that of cruel, self-sacrificing courage. This collective courage is more relational, reflective, and oriented toward building positive change in a community, making it akin to epistemic vulnerability. While 'cruel courage' to Stengel (2018) is marked by a resistant, persistent kind of emotional tone, of individual passion and heroism and opposition to others, the type of courage she recommends is not so oppositional and personally self-sacrificing. The oppositional mind-set encouraged as part of cruel courage is also of concern to Stengel, as it again bolsters a view of militaristic fighting as key to virtue, over intelligence, inclusion, and collaboration. In education, courageous teachers and students are not just solo heroes, but members of broader social groups that can be enhanced to be more intelligent, intellectually demanding, inclusive, and democratic (Stengel, 2018). Thus, courage can be seen from a political view, not as a quality of a person fighting the world or serving as an Army officer fighting bad guys, but as an orientation toward social justice and democratic intellectual engagement within society. Stengel also expresses concern in her conception of cruel courage with its conflation with grit, a related problematic emotional virtue which is also often upheld in education and elsewhere today.

Toward educating for a kind of vulnerable courage, in line with views such as those of Brown, Parker, and Stengel, Candace Vogler (2018) notes how a particular kind of virtuous courage is required of students in classroom spaces that is akin to vulnerability, as students can be fearful of looking foolish in discussions. As she observes, this fear can prevent learning, as learning requires that one can be wrong, make mistakes, and not know. As a recommendation, Vogler discusses the use of a 'floating chair', as a technique to develop student courage in this case, to speak in the classroom. On the first day of class, she has everyone design name tags to use in discussion. As a rule for discussion, each student must call on the next student to speak when they finish. As Vogler observes (2018, p. 217), this exercise 'produces a circumstance in which the thing worth protecting and worth taking a small risk for is the educational opportunity afforded by shared discussion'. This exercise thus encourages students to recognise fear as part of their community. In a way, students also author the circulation of fear and vulnerability here, at the same time enabling and empowering each other to be courageous. However, other conceptualisations of fear describe courage as its opposite, and see fear more as a 'negative' emotion to be avoided, in education and elsewhere. I explore fear and anxiety in Chapter 10.

8.3   Grit

Grit is interrelated with courage and resilience, as it is an emotional orientation or disposition to face obstacles in a positive way. However, it is also framed specifically in terms of a passionate drive. Duckworth (2016) defines it as a combination of passion and perseverance in the face of obstacles and challenges. She additionally describes grit as distinct from, but interrelated with, self-control and conscientiousness. Like resilience, courage, and vulnerability, the value of grit is framed as context-specific, as it is viewed as productive particularly within situations that matter to a person, and can fluctuate over time in relation to dynamic situations. Duckworth further describes grit as different from talent, intelligence, or luck, but as a part of character that is essential to success. Her 'Grit Playbook' states that 'grittier students are more likely to graduate from high school, and grittier cadets are more likely to complete their training' (2018, p. 1). Duckworth argues that one should cultivate grit in others by modelling it, celebrating it, and enabling it, with a focus on not giving up on passions and goals.

Duckworth has developed a self-report scale for grit as a psychologically influenced disposition (2016). At the same time, she acknowledges the limitations of such tools. As is the case with other self-report measures, people can fake their scores, and often hold varying standards for self-evaluation, related to their beliefs about the nature of grit and its desirability. Grit can also be evaluated through informant reports. However, this can be resource intensive, and grit can still be hard to assess in this case, as grit is seen as part of a person's dynamic overall psychological and emotional disposition (SRI International, 2018). Sarah Stitzlein (2018) relatedly notes that most research on grit has been conducted with high-achieving populations, 'and Duckworth herself recognises that her grit scores are significantly higher for wealthy students than for poor students' (p. 7). In this case, possessing grit, like resilience, may be a sign of having sufficient external supports through family and school, rather than being particularly shaped by personal will or individual-based interventions.

Grit does not have a strong theoretical or philosophical basis. It is far removed from most philosophical frameworks, from Stoicism to deontology and virtue ethics. Such orientations to emotional virtues and morality tend not to favour passion, or encourage as necessary diligence against setbacks, which can be seen as persisting merely for the sake of persistence. Ariana Gonzalez Stokas's (2015) genealogy of the concept traces the value of grit to tales of cowboys. As Stokas notes, in popular discourse (particularly in the United States) the cowboy has to work in physically strenuous, possibly life-threatening political and geographic conditions. The cowboy is also depicted as an independent, lonely individual, although cowboys usually work in groups in real life. Suffering hardship without complaining is also key in romantic depictions of cowboys. People who 'cowboy up' have a positive disposition, despite discomfort and even physical and emotional suffering.

One can also trace the concept of grit to the more general 'hero's journey', wherein a hero must go on a voyage, usually alone, toward unknown challenges, to learn and grow. Such a story can be found in myths across cultures, reflecting a general imaginary of an individual's overcoming challenges through a personal process over time, where tolerating hardship and embracing adventure is essential to survive and become victorious. As discussed in Chapter 3, experiences of suffering are regarded as an important part of life to some philosophers (Roberts, 2016), and as necessary and in some sense good in some religious traditions. Yet such messages differ from discourse on grit, because the latter encourages a sense of optimism and ultimate overcoming, in relation to such suffering. As Stitzlein notes, grit discourse also 'focuses too much on following a respectable path to success' by 'doing what you are told and not challenging one's conditions ... complying with one's larger circumstances such as poverty and lack of opportunity and persisting to achieve ... in spite of those circumstances' (2018, p. 7). The rebellion of the cowboys is minimalised in contemporary academic and professional discourse about the value of grit. As Stokas also observes:

> The need for grit ... arises when environments lack critical supports for success. It often arises as a way for the individual to cope with suffering and for society to justify social failure through instructing the individual that their condition – poverty, for instance – is related to an intrinsic deficit. It has the potential to indoctrinate the student, through individual metrics such as standardized tests, with the belief that failure is due to an intrinsic lack rather than to systemic inequality.
>
> (2015, p. 522)

Similar to discourse on vulnerability, large-scale social problems are reduced in this approach to personal obstacles to achievement that can apparently be met through grittiness. And like in some discussions of resilience, grit also seems to demand (and positively frame) conditions of suffering and setback as essential for it to be developed (and observed), again failing to emphasise how conditions can also be changed to enhance people's experiences, and instead focusing on changing individual attitudes. For instance, SRI Education, a group funded by the United States

Department of Education (2018), recommends that educators for grit 'frame failure as an act of learning' and treat challenge as 'inevitable for success'. On the one hand, it is true that challenges and failures are inevitable in life. This justifies a positive approach to vulnerability, as previously mentioned. However, promoting an embrace of challenge and failure seems problematic, when they are not always at hand, are not always necessary, and are not evenly experienced across situations and contexts. That there are times when suffering is too great and intolerable should also be explored in education, lest young people receive the message that they should tolerate anything, however horrible, for the opportunity to develop grit.

In relation, McGee and Stovall (2015, p. 499) observe that the focus on grit undermines black students in the United States, by treating racial discrimination as a path to grit, while grit does nothing to challenge racism or other structural injustice.

> Grit is presented as a racially neutral construct that does not impact all demographics equally. The emotional and psychological trauma that African Americans experience in navigating white spaces and their structural foundations is underacknowledged in grit research. There is little attribution of 'grit' as an impact on structures that foster persistent insecurity and a sense of unworthiness in racialized bodies. Moreover, grit framings have yet to respond to racial stereotypes, insults, and assaults that are commonplace in this racially stratified society, which can hamper black students' options for working strenuously toward challenges and maintaining effort despite adversity.

Grit discourse can thus be seen as victim-blaming, especially when it is promoted in contexts of injustice in everyday life, to the exclusion of consideration of the true causes of suffering and vulnerability. Similarly, Merridy Wilson-Strydom observes that 'individualized notions such as grit are insufficient for understanding issues of inequality since the concept locates responsibilities for inequalities of access and admissions at the level of individual students with scant consideration of the complex social, economic and political contexts within which students are embedded' (2017, p. 395).

In relation, some proponents of grit indicate that the promotion of grit is ineffective without a supportive environment, as well as when youth experience 'toxic stress' (SRI International, 2018). Duckworth concedes such points in part, and describes the challenge around knowing whether and how to prioritise individual versus environmental change in relation to such issues as a 'chicken-and-egg problem'. She observes that while the individual and the environment are both important, because educating for grit is possible, it is therefore worthwhile. However, she does not particularly engage with research that emphasises its potential use (or abuse) for enabling and accepting (and possibly even appreciating and preserving) conditions fostering undue obstacles and unnecessary suffering (2016).

Others contend that grit is just what is needed in cases of societal inequality, and that it should be cultivated and drawn upon particularly in these cases. One intervention has used grit as a criterion for a scholarship programme for black students at Vanderbilt and Fisk Universities. In this programme, the grit of applicants was assessed by two interviewers, to recognise student potential, given how higher education entrance examination scores have been seen to systematically downplay the potential of minority students (Powell, 2013). The programme has been reported on as a success, although Duckworth has discussed in relation to this project the need for caution in using grit as a selection criterion, due to measurement challenges (Powell, 2013).

In sum, the 'growth mindset' (Dweck, 2007; Yeager et al., 2019) encouraged in grit may often be helpful, while 'a fixed belief that failure is permanent could prevent students from academic success' (Hochanadel & Finamore, 2015, p. 49). Yet the promotion of grit as an educational feeling and concept should be tempered, within lessons that convey to students 'how to persevere other than through inculcating the belief that they must endure suffering in order to succeed' (Stokas, 2015, p. 527). Suffering may be inevitable in part. However, advocating something like eudemonia, and exploring the potential to change unjust and harmful conditions, seem preferable to simply enabling and promoting suffering in classrooms and other school settings, for the sake of grit. Given the structural nature of injustice and suffering, McGee and Stovall (2015) relatedly recommend that consciousness raising be part of curricular interventions for disadvantaged youth in relation to their developing grit, so that they recognise that their challenges are not isolated to themselves, as 'deficient' individuals. They also recommend that such consciousness raising take place in a safe, non-academic, social space, as academic environments can be experienced as threatening by academically vulnerable youth. Grit may have its uses, but it can also have its abuses, and it should be regarded with caution in education.

8.4   Concluding Thoughts

In Chapter 7 and in this one, some recently popular concepts have been discussed that influence and shape educating emotional virtues across societies. While interconnected, each of these concepts has distinctive features. This chapter focused on vulnerability, courage, and grit. Vulnerability is often conceptualised as a cognitive and emotional 'thing' to be avoided in education, and to be intervened upon, through the cultivation of other traits, such as happiness and well-being, resilience and mindfulness, and courage and grit. Yet, in contrast with an instrumentalist framing of vulnerability as an inherently negative and fixable feature of the human, vulnerability can also be a good thing in education, and in society. Philosophically, vulnerability can encourage open-mindedness and a willingness to confront the possibility that one is wrong or ignorant (i.e. that they do not know). While vulnerability to undue harm is surely to be avoided in education, a relational view of vulnerability reveals that some people (and others around them) may benefit from developing greater epistemic vulnerability, so that diverse people (students and teachers) can learn more from each other, within more inclusive classrooms. Thus, rather than simply being a bad thing, vulnerability has educational potential, to develop students as morally concerned members of society.

Vulnerability is also related to courage. Yet paradoxically courage tends to be overly encouraged in society and education, despite its mean-state status as a virtue in philosophical discourse. Courage can be invoked to increase or decrease vulnerability, but it can also be abused in ways that encourage people to be self-sacrificing in relation to others, for ends that could be seen as good or harmful, for themselves or other people. Thus, a more tempered approach to courage in education is worthwhile in place of blanket endorsements of courage, which could be rash or cruel. Similarly, grit is regarded, like resilience, as a factor disposing one emotionally to persist and persevere through challenges, with passion and confidence. However, grit can also be problematic in education, when it justifies the place of challenges in life, while it can also be used to encourage people to turn away from considering environmental ills, only focusing on having a good attitude. As such, the cultivation of grit is also prone to abuse in education, when it is considered as a moral practice, as promotions of grit can encourage overlooking people's circumstances in possibly harmful ways. Thus, each of these dispositions is more complicated than much of the discourse on interventions for student mental and emotional health implies, when recalling that education is a moral practice.

CHAPTER 9

Anger

Anger is seldom described as something to aspire to. A tendency or disposition toward anger is generally not regarded as a virtue, among lay people, psychologists, or philosophers. Many would agree instead with Nussbaum (2016) about 'the irrationality and stupidity of anger', and the value of working 'to pursue non-anger' in private and public life (pp. 248–249). In education, anger is treated as a negative, undesirable, and distracting emotion for students. Educational psychologists argue that 'anger can relate to various problematic outcomes, such as difficulties at school, alcohol and drug use, as well as health problems' (Pekrun & Buhner, 2014). Thus, anger management and peaceful conflict resolution are often emphasised as part of social and emotional learning.

However, anger is not all bad. Some defend anger. They may follow Aristotle to conceptualise a justified, moral sense of anger, which is articulable in education and in society (Kristjánsson, 2007). Feminist and critical race theorists also defend anger in relation to social injustice, to not accept oppression. In relation, they note double standards, which mark some people as 'too angry' and insist on their non-anger in comparison with others, when observing societal ills and personal harms. This chapter explores competing perspectives and appraisals of anger in society and in education. It highlights the possibility of accepting and productively using moral anger, in contradiction to the prevalent approach of many educational psychologists and philosophers who are basically against anger. The chapter starts with a discussion of views admonishing against anger, from philosophy and psychology, before exploring their limitations, alongside more tolerant approaches to anger. It then considers the potential productive value of exploring anger in education.

9.1   Against Anger

Western (and Eastern) philosophical traditions tend to be against anger, framing anger as a problematic emotion and tendency, harmful to oneself and to others. This may partly be attributed to its association with irrationality (and destruction). The Stoic philosopher Seneca argues that

168

anger is often not well founded. He observed it is often caused by events and things beyond one's control. These things are responded to in an irrational manner when one is angry. He concludes that anger is generally childish, petty, unpleasant, and unhelpful, as it is related to one's sense of vanity. It thus deserves studied scrutiny, not tolerance, in the course of self-evaluation (Nussbaum, 2016).

Plato also associates anger with intemperance and lack of self-control (see Hughes & Warmke, 2017). In many other traditions, it has been regarded as a kind of deadly sin. As Michael A. Peters summarises:

> Anger gets a bad press. By contrast, we never hear of 'happiness management' or 'joy training'. Seneca's negative assessment of anger is echoed by Galen and by most religious-based moral codes: it is one of the seven deadly sins in Catholicism; it is equated with unrequited desire in Hinduism; it is defined as one of the five hindrances in Buddhism; in Judaism anger is considered a negative trait; and in the *Qur'an* anger is attributed to Muhammad's enemies. (2012, p. 239)

On the other hand, from a psychological perspective, anger can have significant adaptive functions. In psychology, anger is associated with appraisals of the blameworthiness of others in the face of challenges. For Lazarus, anger (and other challenging emotions, such as sadness and fear) involves a judgement that a situation is problematic in relation to one's well-being and is incongruous with one's goals (1991). In anger, there is a judgement that a person or their associates has been needlessly or unjustly offended or injured. Thus, 'other-blame' is a key evaluation in experiences of anger (Smith & Lazarus, 1993).

When the appraisal of another's blameworthiness is well founded (and expressed effectively), anger can thus be functional for a person within a social situation. As Novaco notes, 'In the face of adversity, it can mobilize psychological resources, energize behaviors for corrective action, and facilitate perseverance. Anger serves as a guardian to self-esteem, operates as a means of communicating negative sentiment, potentiates the ability to redress grievances, and boosts determination to overcome obstacles to our happiness and aspirations' (2000, p. 170).

Nonetheless, Novaco also stresses the risks and challenges associated with anger, recommending diminishing it rather than cultivating it (2016). When one is angry, rational, cognitive focus is decreased, while anger can also motivate harmful destructive actions to others or to one-self. Such responses 'in turn can lead to undesirable consequences for the angered person, either from direct retaliation, loss of supportive relation-ships, or social censure' (Novaco, 2000, p. 171). At the same time, as anger is associated with thoughtlessness and lack of focus, it is also seen to restrict or block experiences of empathy, compassion, happiness, and other 'positive' emotions. Furthermore, anger can be physically unhealthy, particularly when experienced chronically or extremely, possibly contributing to heart disease, stroke, and depression (Averill, 2012).

Nussbaum sees anger as primarily negative. Like psychologists, she identifies as constitutive of anger a perception of harms or slights to oneself or close relations, as well as a desire to retaliate. It is the impulse to retaliate that Nussbaum particularly characterises as dangerously irrational within experiences of anger, given the negative consequences it can have for the angry party (2016). At the same time, Nussbaum observes there can be a slight flavour of pleasure in anger, at the thought and desire for retaliation. She worries that this bloodlust can enable anger to be sustained over time despite its irrationality and destructiveness, fuelling an addiction or obsession with revenge, while the more diverse physiological symptoms of anger are otherwise more fleeting, and easier to 'wait out'.

In this context, Nussbaum contends that anger is 'always morally problematic' (2016, p. 5). She describes two desires of angry retaliation, the 'road of payback' and the 'road of status'. The road of payback is the desire to retaliate in kind against perceived wrongdoers. This road is simply irrational in Nussbaum's view, as 'the wrongdoer's suffering does not bring back the person or valued item that was damaged' (2016, p. 5). On the other hand, the road to status is the angry desire to downgrade the status or position of a wrongdoer in relation to oneself. Nussbaum holds that this desire is morally problematic, as it exhibits a narrow obsession with status that is also undesirable and unhelpful, to oneself or others in society. In place of these roads and desires, Nussbaum advocates a transformative response to perceived injury in place of anger that is constructive and oriented toward victims, justice, and well-being, rather than payback.

Nussbaum describes a complicated case to explain the difference, focusing on the example of Angela, who has learned that her friend has been raped. To Nussbaum, the difference between non-anger and anger in this case regards whether Angela wants payback put upon the rapist, rather than to only prevent similar damages in the future: Does Angela want to humiliate or hurt the rapist, or just deter his future raping? The desire for payback is just a continuation of harm and injury in Nussbaum's view. The 'road to status' here invokes 'magical thinking' that the rape has harmed Angela's status in relation to that of the offender, according to Nussbaum. As Nussbaum writes, 'insofar as her emotion is anger ... she does initially wish some sort of bad result for the offender, and she does initially think (magically) that this will set things right' (2016, p. 27). Nussbaum concedes this 'magical thinking' is popular. There is a sense that closure is achieved through punishment in many societies, and people thus tend to take pleasure over punishments around the world. Nussbaum wishes instead for anger to develop here into transformative non-anger, through a recognition of injury that leads to productive resolutions for all, without any focus on payback or status. This non-anger, Nussbaum explains, does not entail non-violence. However, as she further describes, non-anger is a kind of practice involving self-cultivation and personal reflection that can enable a sense of forgiveness (which need not be directed to a particular apologetic – or not apologetic – party), and a general ethic of unconditional love.

That anger is often irrational and therefore can be destructive within relationships is partly backed up by some psychological examinations of everyday, ordinary experiences of anger. As it is understood by ordinary (Western) people, 'anger can occur for no known reason; it is possible to feel anger and not know why' (Russell & Fehr, 1994, p. 188). People report experiencing anger that is not at all well targeted to people or a sense of injury, but relates more to everyday frustrations, where there is no one to blame. Feeling a sense of incapacity and frustration is seen to give rise to anger in babies and children, while 'relatively trivial pervasive situations' can evoke mild or fleeting anger in many people (Berkowitz & Harmon-Jones, 2004, p. 112). Changing temperatures in an environment seems to impact experiences of anger in experimental conditions, while people also experience anger in situations where only themselves are to blame, and in situations where they see their challenges or obstacles as reasonable and justified. For example, one may feel angry at oneself for failing to reserve tickets for an event that they wanted to attend when the tickets were available, while knowing they have only themselves to blame for failing to reserve them in advance. (For some psychologists, such 'self-anger' would actually be shame or guilt, while anger about things without causes would be categorised as sadness; see Lerner & Tiedens, 2006).

Thus, in many cases, factors such as physical pain or even the temperature influence and shape experiences of anger, not just the (perceived) blameworthy acts of others (or oneself). In this context, experiencing irrational anger may lead people to later justify their emotions in terms of external blameworthy parties as a means to categorise their experiences, while 'appraisal components, such as an external agent's judged responsible for the incident, may intensify the anger reaction rather than being necessary for the emotion to occur' (Berkowitz & Harmon-Jones, 2004, p. 115).

In relation, the emotional essence of anger is unclear, as 'anger may be best defined as a combination of uneasiness, discomfort, tenseness, resentment (which is a response to selective stimuli), and frustration' (Stearns, 1972, p. 6). Anger is also commonly conflated with other emotional responses, such as 'envy, jealousy, fury, frustration, annoyance, contempt, and the like' (Averill, 2012, p. 138). At the same time, there is no single widely used definition, or means of distinguishing and precisely identifying anger alongside related experiences, especially across cultures (Russell, 1991). Thus, one's frustration, annoyance, or disappointment can be easily constructed or reframed as anger, and then justified to oneself to rationalise it. After failing to reserve tickets for an event before it sold out, one can blame the event organiser (and their complicated website) for being difficult to work with, although they know that if they had been more careful they would have been able to make a reservation with little difficulty.

Such realities are part of what persuades Nussbaum that anger over minor issues is typically based on a petty sense of status and dignity deprived, and associated with a kind of defensiveness in relation to normal, small challenges that it would probably be more productive to simply try to tolerate. Here she also recalls her own trivial angry experiences, such as being angry over 'large men, usually very out of shape, who grab one's suitcase without asking permission first and try to hoist it into the overhead rack' on an airplane (2016, p. 139). Given that so many causes of anger can be (but perhaps are not genuinely) attributable to petty annoyances, imagined rudeness, and other minor slights, Nussbaum urges looking within oneself first: 'anger must be fought inside oneself' (Nussbaum, 2016, p. 147). She continues:

> Seneca is absolutely right to say that a lot of people's anger ... is the result of mistaken attributions of insult and malice, and that these mistaken attributions, in turn, result from a hypersensitivity often caused by a morbid narcissism ... people in a good psychic condition don't weigh every minor occurrence as a possible slight: they have more important things to occupy their attention.

Boler relatedly argues against what she describes as defensive anger (1999), noting that people become angry sometimes to protect their beliefs and sense of identity. This can happen when people are provided with perspectives and information (for example, in education) that go against their beliefs. Such perspectives may imply, for instance, that one is more privileged than others in society, or has gained from an unequitable social system, in cases of privilege based on race or wealth. As Boler observes (1999, p. 191):

> Defensive anger can be interpreted as a protection of beliefs, a protection of one's precarious sense of identity. To challenge a student's cherished assumptions may be felt as a threat to their very identity. This reaction to anger should be interpreted not so much as a righteous objection to one's honor, but more as a defense of one's investments in the values of the dominant

culture. To respond in defensive anger is to defend one's stake (whether or not one consciously acknowledges that stake). So although this defensive anger may *feel* like Aristotle's Greek man's anger, may *feel* like a response to being shamed, with more nuanced reflection one may come to recognize defensive anger as the protection of precarious identities.

A related problem is the exploitation of people's tendencies towards anger. While the sources of a person's anger are not always clear, even to oneself, at the same time third parties work to enable, rationalise, and help to determine the cause of anger of others, in ways that can benefit those third parties (Ahmed, 2004b). Scapegoating in mainstream media enables people to focus their anger on particular others, rather than social systems. For instance, in a financial crisis, 'bankers' values and behaviour are mocked, blamed, and ridiculed in attempts to understand complex, socio-economic phenomena' (Kelsey, 2017, p. 88). Anger is thus redirected to bankers, rather than to the systems (which are far harder to see and understand) that enable crises that negatively impact masses of ordinary people. People's anger over personal challenges is often reframed by third parties as a means to scapegoat others in society. This is another reason to promote non-anger, rather than anger, in education.

Nussbaum thus encourages 'toning down' and transforming anger through the practice of non-anger. She relatedly claims that 'successful struggles for revolutionary justice' in the cases of British India, US civil rights, and South Africa's end of apartheid were all characterised by leadership (of Gandhi, King, and Mandela, respectively) advocating non-anger. As she writes: 'To the extent that any of them admitted anger as acceptable, it was either our borderline species of "Transition-Anger," a sense of outrage without any wish for ill to befall the offender, or else a brief episode of real anger, but leading quickly to the Transition' (2016, p. 212). In the case of the US civil rights movement, Nussbaum contends that King advocated for the same sense of non-anger that she does: '[King held], as I do, that anger is inherently wedded to a payback mentality ... King speaks of a "strike-back" mentality. That is what [he wants] to get rid of' (2016, p. 221). Mark Jonas similarly applauds apparent non-anger in King and Gandhi, writing: 'We have come to assume that anger and resentment are necessary for justice to be done. This is not the case, however. In the same way that Martin Luther King Jr. and Gandhi were able to rectify injustices without violence, so are individuals able ... without anger and resentment' (2012, p. 46).

In line with these views, Character First Education lessons emphasise that when experiencing hurt or anger, one should acknowledge pain and choose to forgive, not seeking revenge, or dwelling on the past. In one lesson, Corrie ten Boom is praised for practising forgiveness toward

Nazis, despite her experiences in a concentration camp (Character First, 2019e). Another Character First hand-out on self-control praises Abigail Adams for opting to clean the dirty ship *Active* while on board, rather than angrily complaining about being misled about the ship's condition (Character First, 2019f). Such lessons teach students not to focus on, develop or cultivate, or sustain anger, but release or transform it, as quickly as possible. The American Psychological Association (APA) further suggests that people with anger focus on relaxation when encountering anger, cognitive restructuring, using humour, and changing their environment (2019), given the possibly detrimental, self-sabotaging effects of anger. Yet others see anger as less inherently problematic, and more worth acceptance, or even cultivation.

9.2   The Value of Anger

Despite the prevalence of views against anger, some thinkers recognise anger as productive and valuable in some cases. Aristotle held anger as a virtue, when cultivated 'at the right times, about the right things, toward the right people, for the right end and in the right way' (Kristjánsson, 2007, p. 75). In relation, Aristotle observes that the 'inirascible' person, deficient in anger, will appear foolish, willing to accept insults, and slavish to others (Kristjánsson, 2007). Though Aristotle saw an excess of anger as more common and more problematic, there was a positive place for anger in his view. Others also stress social and personal functions of anger which can serve to justify it, as a 'God-given duty' as Lactantius says, to restrain offence and wrongdoing, correct situations, and restore or provide for equity (Averill, 2012).

Audre Lorde writes of the value of anger (1984) in the context of racism and feminist struggle, given that silence in such a case can enable harm, while anger signals recognition of wrongness, and refusal. Lorde (1984) articulates that anger 'is loaded with information and energy' (p. 127). Anger communicates information as it is expressed, and it can be a way of demanding change in a bad situation. Anger can thus be seen as a source of knowledge and of motivation, performing epistemic and mobilising functions within communities (Thompson, 2006). Feminist consciousness-raising is thus one possible method recommended by some for cultivating anger, while feminist and women's self-defence training and related education encourage women (and men) to accept, enable, and harness anger in relation to risks and challenges they face (Tessman, 2005; Leonardo & Porter, 2010).

Nussbaum goes to great lengths to contrast transformative non-anger, which may start with a tiny bit of anger, with inappropriate, irrational, 'stupid' anger. Yet evaluating appropriate levels and types of anger is challenging in reality. Furthermore, the value of tempering and trans-forming anger in relation to extending social justice has been questioned by those who see the positive communicative potential of its expression. Nussbaum compliments Mandela for tempering his angry tendencies, and not focusing on his desire for retaliation against whites in South Africa in his acts and speech. Yet Tessman (2005) argues in contrast that the transformation of anger for the purposes of communication can diminish the potency of anger to generate change. Expressions of felt rage have potential for 'opening up new worlds of sense in which to be creative, instead of being limited to making only backward-looking claims focused on redressing wrongs already committed' (Tessman, 2005, p. 123).

Amia Srinivasan also challenges Nussbaum's assumption that anger must be connected to payback, asking 'Perhaps this was true of the ancients. But is it true for us? The nature of anger – how we experience it, what it calls on us to do – might well shift with historical and political circumstance' (2018, p. 129). Srinivasan goes on: 'I want to suggest that getting angry is a means of affectively registering or *appreciating* the injustice of the world' (p. 132, emphasis in the original). Thus, the com-municative potential of anger is neglected by Nussbaum, as she frames anger as essentially connected to desires for revenge and payback.

At the same time, Nussbaum's view that concern with social status is often petty, and is a morally problematic act of magical thinking, glosses over the direct relationship of social status to issues of justice and injustice in society. Nussbaum does not focus on racism or gender or other forms of patterned social oppression, as much as on inward-looking reflection, in her work. This individual-based orientation enables Nussbaum to see any sense of personal indignation as a personal and individual act of taking things too personally, in a petty way. Yet this also leads Nussbaum to ignore that people experience everyday annoyances and disturbances in a different way than she experiences them, as a privileged member of society. In contrast, Tessman argues:

> [P]eople of color may be subjected to racist insults and degradation daily, and under such conditions, the 'proper' level of anger for people of color (or their friends/political allies) becomes, relative to the anger appropriate to those who do not regularly encounter such anger, extreme. If one believes (correctly) in one's own moral world while others in society – in dominant positions – do not believe in it, one will constantly find oneself 'slighted' (to use Aristotle's term); the frequent or unabating nature of this slighting – or as Lugones points out, the fact that it may be unacceptable to conform to the dominators' require-ment for gaining respectability – are conditions that make the right level of anger a tremendous level, the level of fury or rage.(2005, p. 123)

Boler also questions the view that personal concern about dignity and status is petty, noting that 'Once power relations muddy the water, evaluating a person's perception of feeling slighted becomes exceptional complex. One's sense of "dignity," respect and honor is not an objectively measurable fact. Social status is by no means a fixed given, but rather a shifting relation' (1999, p. 190). Boler is aware, as Nussbaum is, about the problem of defensive anger, and the risks of an obsession with fragile identity positions and desire to maintain a sense of personal security. Yet she still retains a space for righteous moral anger in her account, in light of social injustices that go beyond petty grievances, and require systematic changes.

James Averill (2012, p. 141) similarly observes:

> In most everyday episodes, the transgressions that provoke anger are relatively minor – breaking a promise, ignoring a responsibility, being inconsiderate and the like. This fact tends to obscure the role that anger plays in maintaining the social order. No matter how trifling our everyday promises, responsibilities, and considerations may seem to be, they are the threads from which the fabric of society is woven. If they are too frequently broken without mend, society unravels. In a very real sense, then, the many small mendings that are the everyday experiences of anger, each minor in its own right, help sustain a way of life. Anger can be a tool for social change as well as maintenance.

For Averill, anger plays a significant transitory social role within a cultural context, signalling when social norms and values are in conflict (1982; Parkinson, 1996). In the case of wanting to rectify injustice, being peaceable is not always feasible. In this case, there is a 'short-term social role of getting angry', which is useful precisely because anger is understood as 'involuntary and partly uncontrollable' (Parkinson, 1996, p. 673). Frijda and Mesquita (1994) relatedly observe that anger often has an ultimate function to intimidate another into action (or halting of action), not to harm or punish.

Nussbaum concludes from her assessment of King and other heroes that 'one should not wish to humiliate opponents in any way, or wish them ill, but instead should seek to win their friendship and cooperation', to rectify injustice in society (2016, p. 222). However, such a requirement, that there is no anger, and that there is an approach of friendliness '*above all*', can also be taken as a method of managing and minimising the communication of distressed others, which can be experienced by 'angry' others as a form of silencing. Roxane Gay notes (2016) in this context how in conversations about race, white people often accuse and blame people of colour of being angry, and 'wanting too much or complaining or wasting time or focusing on the wrong things or we are petty or shrill or strident or unbalanced or crazy or overly emotional' (see also Wingfield, 2007).

In contexts of injustice, safety and nonviolence as universal experiences are taken for granted by those expecting pleasant discourses demonstrating concern for civility and friendship. Yet, as Zeus Leonardo and Ronald Porter note, racist violence is experienced in contexts of structural injustice by people of colour, while going unseen by more privileged people in society (2010). As racism is only experienced as an idea and not as a lived reality by white people, they only identify observations about racism provided by people of colour as acts of anger, thereby attributing anger and violence to victims of harm, and blaming the victim (or other related messenger), not recognising racial violence as a painful experience that should not be tolerated.

Nussbaum neglects considering these possibilities deeply in her text, as she takes for granted her position as irrelevant to her views, including (particularly) her race. For example (2016, pp. 39–40, emphases added):

> It might be objected that my proposal sounds all too much like that of the *upper-middle-class (ex)-WASP academic* that I certainly am, schooled from childhood to 'use your words,' and discouraged from strong direct emotional expression. *I simply deny the charge*. First of all, my proposal is not Stoic. ... in any case it seems just wrong to portray lower-class or less educated people as inexpressive or crude .... At the same time, *in my experience* it is people with an overweening sense of their own privilege who seem particularly prone to angry displays. In my gym, I will avoid mildly asking another member if I can work in on a piece of equipment ... to the extent that *I observe that this person is privileged, youngish, and male*. On the road, it is drivers of SUVs who tend, again *in my anecdotal experience*, to behave as if they owned the road. So I think the objector asks a good question, but one to which there is a good reply.

Race and other personal characteristics do not seem relevant in Nussbaum's view to her understanding of anger. However, her own experiences with other people with different identity positions (like those who are 'privileged, youngish, and male') do. Meanwhile, she does not consider experiences and views substantively which diverge from her own on these topics.

In this context, many find such tone policing acts – like those of Nussbaum, admonishing those who are not friendly and polite for being uncivil – as not based in a genuine, moral aim of providing for constructive and friendly dialogical conversation. Rather, they see them as responses to people's own moral discomfort, reflecting a lack of openness to the possibility that they may not fully be understanding the situation of others. Instead of seeing that others face a difficult situation, the focus is on having a comfortable conversation, above all else. As Alison Bailey sees it, 'anger at racial injustices prompts the white woman to make a request for psychological and epistemic comfort' (2018, p. 98). From this view, some want friendship (or perhaps care), while others want justice. William Chafe describes this phenomenon as the 'progressive mystique', wherein 'conflict is inherently bad, disagreement means personal dislike, and consensus offers the only way to preserve a genteel and civilized way of life' (1981).

For disadvantaged minorities, such a demand for constant constructiveness, cooperation, and friendliness functions as a kind of silencing, as they find that when they mention or dare to dwell upon injustices, they are responded to with requests to manage their tone. At the same time, their anger is judged to be the cause of their speech, rather than injustices. This apparent concern enables the listener to not respond to what the angry other says about what angers them, but to respond only to their tone. People can experience this tone policing as maddening, and as a strategy of people who do not understand their distress to reframe it:

> Your anger is a judgement that something is wrong. But in being heard as angry, your speech is read as motivated by anger. Your anger is read as unattributed, as if you are against x because you are angry rather than being angry because you are against x. You become angry at the injustice of being heard as motivated by anger, which makes it harder to separate yourself from the object of anger. ... In becoming angry about that entanglement, you confirm their commitment to your anger as the truth 'behind' your speech.   (Ahmed, 2010, p. 68)

While it is possible for one to just be unreasonably angry and then find an external cause and excuse for it later on, righteous anger can develop as a response to injustices and wrongdoings. In this latter case, admonishments about the importance of friendliness and non-anger can thwart people in expressing and observing injustice, because the very fact that they are upset seems to render their speech invalid. As Ahmed reminds us here, this creates an impossible situation, as this kind of misrecognition can cause further upset, and lead to a further labelling and dismissing of the angry person as just angry, with no good reason.

This uneven, 'quiet' anger management also ripples out beyond interpersonal conversations, and can be seen to take place more broadly within a society. In public dialogue, not everyone is given an equal chance to participate, or a platform to do so. And some people's anger tends to be overlooked, or accepted in the public sphere over that of others, even if it is irrational. Angry white men's sense of 'aggrieved entitlement' flourishes in the US public sphere today, as embodied in Trump and some of his supporters, who are regularly publicly angry, and focus their anger unreasonably upon minorities in society (Kimmel, 2017). Such anger is accepted and even applauded by many people. Bernie Sanders is similarly positively recognised by supporters for his passionate indignation and outraged focus on things he finds intolerable. Meanwhile, mainstream media usually casts women, minorities, and other disadvantaged and unprivileged members of society as angry and against (righteous angry men's) freedom of expression when they voice outrage over problematic views (such as racist views) that are ordinarily disseminated and normalised in the public sphere. Since women and minorities are not so often given the kind of pedestal to articulate their concerns that some are provided with, they are framed as lashing out in an undemocratic way. Women and minorities without sanctioned soapboxes are thus often framed as undemocratic and irrational, for responding negatively to those with soapboxes, rather than being framed as engaging in the public sphere, with the means of communication available to them. As Linda Zerilli notes,

> If you search on Google for 'shouting down,' ... you will find dozens of similar descriptions of uncivil behaviour and the threat to free speech [with] Muslims, gays and lesbians, feminists, racial and ethnic minorities, and other historically disenfranchised groups as the main offenders .... Whether you interpret these protests as uncivil threats to fundamental political freedoms will depend on whether you think everyone is in fact situated equally in the marketplace of ideas .... Uncivil public behaviour is symptomatic of a more general democratic deficit of public space in which grievances can legitimately be raised and meaningfully addressed .... If some citizens are prone to shout, that may well be because those in power are not listening.
>
> (2014, pp. 111–112)

Ben-Porath similarly notes that the 'politics of civility and respectability tends, in particular, to implicate marginalized groups with playing a role in their marginalization, based on their presumed willful failure to adhere by norms of civility' (2017, p. 73).

This situation places disadvantaged 'angry' speakers or would-be speakers in a paradox, because to be read as reasonable and friendly, they have to hide their upset and injury, and convince the listener that their experience is not so bad. Yet to do so is to alienate their view and their feelings from their own sense of self. Bailey describes this sacrifice or burden faced when one wishes to discuss something painful to a community of others who do not seem to want to hear it.

> In a panic, I circle back to restore my audience's comfort. I soften my anger. Sometimes I apologise and repeat my testimony in honey-toned restatements. But, these retreats come at a cost. The terms of exchange

require trading the chance to voice injury and to consider the transformative possibilities of my anger, for the outside chance that restor-
ing my audience's comfort will also restore *my* epistemic credibility.
I almost always lose this wager. And, when I do, I become an accom-
plice in the dominator's anger management project . . . . I lose ground
and my anger is carried forward into the next conversation.

(2018, p. 102)

There are related risks to losing one's anger in cases of harm and repression. Tessman (2005) describes righteous anger as a burdened virtue,
because it can be physically and emotionally unhealthy, and a cause of
suffering for the angry party, even when it may be regarded as morally
praiseworthy. It is therefore unjustly experienced by its bearer in cases of
injustice. On the other hand, such anger can still be better to express than
suppress. Despite observations about the risks of anger, psychologists
continue to allow a place for reasonable anger, due to their concern with
anger suppression and unexpressed anger, which can also be unhealthy
and pathological (APA, 2019). When the appraisal of the situation is
appropriately aligned with the experience and expression of anger,
anger can be highly functional, while its lack can be dysfunctional
(Parrott, 2014). Unexpressed and repressed anger are often seen as more
dangerous to a person than effectively channelled and used anger, leading the APA to recommend healthy expression of anger in many cases,
rather than its suppression. In this context, women suffer more from
depression caused by poor anger management as compared with men,
while women are expected in society to not be angry, and therefore learn
to hide their anger, over the course of life (Averill, 2012).

In other words, lack of anger in the case of harm can be just as pathological as petty or defensive kinds of anger. That not all injustice is met
with anger may indicate to some that anger is a personal choice, such as in
the case of those, like Nussbaum, who uphold the Dalai Lama or Mandela
as models of anger management. However, serious psychological
damage can impair a sense of hurt, injury, and injustice in some cases,
which has been seen among victims of rape and abuse, and concentration
camp survivors, among others (Thompson, 2006). From this perspective,
if Angela in Nussbaum's example smoothly cultivates forgiveness upon
recognising her friend has been raped, this could be a pathological
response representing internalised oppression, rather than a healthy,
productive response to avoid petty anger.

Complications can also arise in healthy expressions of anger in the
context of structural injustice. Lorde (1984) observes how black women
sometimes misdirect their anger toward one another, given internalised
oppression, learned self-hatred, and the fears and risks involved with
properly directed anger, toward powerful, potentially harmful, more

proper targets. Hooks (1995) writes about this same phenomenon that black women 'learned when we were very little that black people could die from feeling rage and expressing it to the wrong white folks . . . Rage was reserved for life at home – for one another' (pp. 13–14). Compassion and empathy for wrongdoers and others can also interrupt anger in dangerous ways (as discussed in Chapter 5), particularly among women and girls, who are systematically discouraged from expressing anger and are expected to be other-oriented, caring more for the happiness and well-being of others than that of themselves (Tessman, 2005; Averill, 2012). Anger can also serve as a cover for pain that is not effectively dealt with. Complicating this picture, when oppression is systematic and intersectional (interlocking), there is no singular agent which precisely deserves all of one's righteous anger, as 'many people are both the agents and the victims of oppression' (Tessman, 2005, p. 122). These various challenges can reinforce each other in a downward spiral, as one has no proper and precise target for being upset, and yet they face wrongdoing and harms, and the exacerbation of experiences of harm when lacking an outlet, or a way of facing (or a face for) the source of problems.

Given that anger is dismissed as irrationality among minorities in society, while it has valuable social functions in cases of injustice, White argues for the need to change expectations related to expressions of anger in the public sphere. As she writes, 'anger is an emotion which can achieve things politically that are important in a democracy. People feel anger . . . when they believe that some damage has occurred to them, or to something or someone dear to them, a damage that is not trivial but significant, done by someone, probably willingly' (2012, p. 8). Relatedly, against Nussbaum, Peters charges that the civil rights movement should be characterised as one of a series of movements in a 'distinctive "culture of anger"' (2012, p. 242). He thus frames anger as productively aligned with non-violent struggle, not as an act of violence or stupidity. While Nussbaum argues that Gandhi's lack of anger enabled revolutionary justice (2016), Peters observes that 'Gandhi once remarked: "I have learned through bitter experience the one supreme lesson to conserve my anger, and as heat conserved is transmitted into energy, even so our anger controlled can be transmitted into a power that can move the world"' (2012, pp. 239–240).

There is thus a danger of Nussbaum whitewashing history, providing examples that are exaggerated in problematic ways to argue her case. This is not only a risk in Nussbaum's work. Fitzgerald describes Buddhism as prescribing non-anger in cases of extreme oppression, as well (1998). Yet, as hooks relays, not all Buddhists are against anger. As discussed in Chapter 3, Thich Nhat Hanh defends anger, encouraging hooks to use anger 'as compost in her garden' (Yancy & hooks, 2015). Other Buddhist texts refer to purification of anger. This is not, in their in-depth descriptions, a renunciation of it (McRae, 2012, 2015). King speaks of 'purifying anger'. Purifying does not indicate 'getting rid of' some-thing, but indicates something more akin to boiling something down, to its essence, to turn it in to something essential. It is thus not clear that revolutionary justice requires anything like dismissing or avoiding anger, from a systematic, historical view. In this context, it seems disingenuous to paint these revolutionary, heroic people as non-angry, when this is not clearly the case, and when the aim is to provide role models for ordinary people in society, who may be normally prone to anger at times, and should not be (implicitly if not explicitly) encouraged to simply suppress or avoid it at the outset.

In sum, anger is more complex than it may initially seem. Even if it has value, in society and in education, its causes and functions are complex, and they require relational and personal reflection to understand and work productively with. From a sociological and political view, there are also ways in which anger is taught and encouraged within society, among some people in some situations, even when it is generally discouraged. In this context, educators can do more to educate for productive, rather than harmful anger.

9.3   Educating Anger

Some argue that educators should teach against anger (White, 2012). It would seem to make things simpler. After all, educators are expected to uphold and encourage 'safe', 'civil' spaces, inside and outside of class-rooms. Some reasons for this include convenience, comfort, and personal preference. Yet this expectation of felt safety and civility can be dismissive toward dissenting and minority views, as it can overlook how some people may not be experiencing apparent convenience, comfort, and safety at school. As Srinivasan observes in relation, 'we think and talk about political anger in the way we do because it serves those whom anger most stands to threaten, and ... this is no mistake at all' (2018, p. 142).

From another view, discouraging anger in education is counterproductive, when it is in some cases unavoidable and is a normal human experience. Anger is not always vain or petty. To banish or forbid anger in this context risks encouraging children and youth to hide their anger and not explore its causes (or lack thereof), not trans-forming, purifying, or constructively utilising it, but supressing it, in possible shame or internalised oppression, despite its possible power and potentially productive effects.

In this context, Boler (1999) advocates a pedagogy of discomfort, wherein the vulnerabilities and fragilities of dignity and equity are explored across parties, without blame, guilt, or attribution, in relation to negative feelings and experiences. Boler recommends moving away from attributions of causes for upset and challenges here, given the complexities of attribution, instead framing discomfort, confusion, uncertainty, and the like as ways of seeing the world. She views such vulnerability and openness to different perspectives, beyond blame, as foundational to calls to action based on mutual understanding (1999). This approach connects to that advocated by Peter Roberts (2016) as a pedagogy of toleration toward distress, in the face of constant appeals for certainty and happiness. It also is aligned with an orientation toward epistemic vulnerability, as discussed in the last chapter.

Kristjánsson, following Aristotle, advocates for a eudemonistic approach to anger, and learning about better and worse dispositions toward anger in the classroom. He writes there is 'no substitute for anger education ... for each student will acquire a certain disposition to anger, in any case, and we had better ensure that it is the proper one if we are concerned for the student's well-being' (2007, p. 78). Because anger is not altogether avoidable and can have functions and value, Kristjánsson recommends that children learn 'to bring emotions within one's own agency', through focused exploration and examination, considering cases in which anger may be more or less helpful or functional (2007, p. 80). Although coming from different theoretical starting points, this view is complementary in its implications with Boler's pedagogy of discomfort. As anger is a part of life, inevitable for reasonable people in a world where wrongdoings (and inconveniences) are not uncommon, so should anger be understood as a normal experience, while reflective anger can be seen as part of education. Anger need not be smothered with endless calls for gratitude, forgiveness, generosity, happiness, and compassion. It may have a proper place in education and society, to be understood and explored.

Peters (2012) relatedly recommends that one should study their culture in the course of education, to understand how anger productively informs protests and countercultures that lead to positive social change. Against thinkers like Nussbaum, he argues that 'we need to convert political anger into mass mobilisations', to empower civil society, in the context of partisan parties using anger to support their own narrower interests (2012, p. 243). Nussbaum uses King, Mandela, and Gandhi as un-angry icons of revolutionary justice. However, this discourse exaggerates their lack of anger, as all three discussed using anger in part, not evading it or 'getting rid of it'. Stitzlein also argues in contrast to anti-anger views that justified anger is 'grounded in hope and strives to provide a positive and hopeful vision to guide change' (2012, p. 146). There can be a positive place for anger in education, and such an education can easily refer to exemplary models, which demonstrate that anger, properly reckoned with, can lead to positive personal and social transformation.

To teach children in this context that the way to goodness and justice is to never be angry is not only unnecessary, but it is also risky, as it may encourage students to feel guilty about their anger, or to more simply recognise it as deviant, or undesirable across contexts. This can lead to young people learning to suppress their anger, which is not a productive or personally beneficial response, from a psychological view. As Gerrod Parrott writes with regard to anger, 'to live life fully inevitably means to experience misfortune, disappointment, betrayal, and loss. To avoid negative emotions under such conditions would require disengagement or denial' (2014, p. 292).

Thus, there is no reason why educators should not explore with students how anger is common, and can be confusing, or lead to (further) harm, without reflection. If the aim is not to thwart and dismiss the distress of those whose views might not initially seem comprehensible or compelling, it is not hard to practice toleration about expressions of anger. On the other hand, an obsession with lack of anger and civility can signal intolerance toward complaints, perceptions, or observations about personal challenges, or even the existence of moral discomfort in relation to the diversity of views and experiences in society.

Given some of the school environments observed in this text – where resilient students are to 'get on with it', while gritty students never complain, and where the classroom may be set up deliberately to challenge students, as if challenges are inherently good or essential for youth (as discussed in Chapters 7 and 8) – admonishments of all forms of anger do not seem entirely compelling, or open toward diverse experiences in the world. Anger should not be discouraged at all costs. Instead it can be educated effectively by those interested in enhancing moral cultivation and social justice. A complicated treatment of anger in education can help students understand how calls for civility can be discriminatory and unequal, with people often tolerating the anger of some people in society, while dismissing that of others, in ways that can perpetuate wrongdoing and social inequity. It can also expose anger's relationship to social and political scapegoating, to help students recognise how their own anger may be exploited for unjust ends. Additionally, students can learn about cultural differences in views about anger, and where views of anger can result in cultural clashes, which can be of particular value given that anger can arise in cross-cultural experiences (Parrott, 2014). That anger is simply undesirable is not a helpful message to teach students in a world where injustice and harm are visible, and when anger is normal, while lack of anger can be unhealthy. A more critical perspective can be cultivated.

9.4 Concluding Thoughts

Anger can be irrational, not clearly attributed to anything reasonable, and it can invite desires for revenge and payback. It can be experienced as physically and emotionally disturbing and unhealthy, and in this sense it can distract from achievement in education, which may require sustained focus, motivation, and a positive attitude. Being constantly angry is, of course, unhealthy, and trying to work through anger in such a case can indeed be a worthwhile project, to enhance one's life and relationships with others in society. Yet stronger claims, such as that anger is always 'stupid' and harmful, go too far. Seen within a social context and in circumstances of inequity and social injustice, intolerance of anger and related pleas for sustained (constant) smiling civility, no matter what, can communicate to others lack of interest or concern with their plights and challenges, sliding into dismissal of diverse experiences and views, and the potential neglect of harms and injustices.

In an educational context, moral assessments of anger as simply unhealthy can also be dismissive and unhelpful. Dismissals of anger and of angry people can similarly result in unintended harms in the classroom to students whose anger is squashed, who may be suffering from harmful experiences that require concrete effective resolutions, or who may face depression if their anger is systematically repressed, which can be an outcome of having anger treated by others as a cause for punishment or personal blame. While anger is a confusing, often complex emotional experience, it can be educated about in a more effective and better informed way, by teachers who understand its potential productivity and its possible harms, and who wish to see students respond to the variety of challenges and injustices they face, rather than always look inward, to continually cultivate a smiling façade.

CHAPTER 10

Sadness, Fear, and Anxiety

Sadness and fear are usually considered as basic emotions. In society and in education, they are normally cast as undesirable, but also as partly unavoidable. Sadness can be seen, like anger, as an umbrella concept. It is said to encompass or often involve a variety of states and dispositions, such as grief, nostalgia, despair, depression, and melancholy. Like anger, these experiences and perceptions related to them are typically regarded as negative. That is, they are often framed as to be avoided or evaded, or worked through or 'gotten over' in educational places, among other contexts in the public sphere. Sadness is often cast as the opposite of happiness, which is broadly encouraged in education, as discussed previously. In this pro-happiness climate, as Peter Roberts writes, 'No national or regional curriculum policy document ever declares that a key goal for the country's education system is to make students unhappy' (2016, p. 102). Fear can be said to underlie courage or be required for courage, as discussed in Chapter 8, or it can be understood as its foil. Fear is also not normally promoted (intentionally) in education, or treated as something that should be cultivated in schools or in society. However, fear is also a basic, to some extent unavoidable emotion, related to truly fearsome things in the world. Fear is also understood to underlie anxiety.

Sadness, fear, and anxiety all are seen as basically disruptive to education, while from a psychological view they are also ordinary states, that cannot be avoided altogether. They can also be complements to vulnerability, and one can be vulnerable to feeling these mixed and negative emotions, although one might desire otherwise, given that they are uncomfortable and often seen as problematic. However, as discussed in Chapter 4, the picture painted of happiness in education sometimes becomes extreme, unthinking, and morally problematic. Meanwhile, unhappy feelings, such as particular sorts of sadness, fear, and anxiety, can be moral and functional, not simply feelings to avoid at all costs. Despite calls to diminish such negative and mixed feelings in education and society, they can be regarded as socially and personally valuable, and psychologically functional in some situations. One should not take for granted the goodness of sadness and fear. However, it can be productive to explore the moral worth, and uses and abuses of sadness, fear, and anxiety. Neither good nor bad in themselves, feelings of sadness, fear, and anxiety can be righteous, functional, and normal, and interrelated with critical understanding, as with the other emotional virtues explored in this text. Yet they can be problematic and pathological in other cases.

10.1 Sadness

Psychologists generally see sadness as an emotional pain, related to crying, chest aching, and a feeling of powerlessness associated with perceptions of loss, such as the death of a loved one, or a sense of failure to achieve important goals (Smith & Lazarus, 1993; Lerner & Tiedens, 2006; Shirai & Suzuki, 2017). Psychologists additionally frame sadness as the most prevalent negative emotion, and as key to depression, as well as to grief and mourning. Psychologists tend to regard sadness and grief critically, contrasting appropriate, functional experiences of them, with less apt, more dysfunctional experiences. That sadness and grief are felt by ordinary people is largely accepted, as people face negative experiences in the world.

Sadness and grief are said to have a positive function, in strengthening social bonds and enabling empathy, sharing, and kindness (Singh-Manoux & Finkenauer, 2001). The states are also valued for their relation to attention and focus, historically and more recently. Parrott notes that in the Middle Ages sadness was considered to have important benefits, with one scholar commending melancholy for its enabling of people 'to be more exact and curious in pondering the very moments of things' (2014, p. 289). However, the more dysfunctional experiences of sadness and grief are also regarded as indicating a negative condition, usually framed as depression.

> The death of a loved one, loss of a job or the ending of a relationship are difficult experiences for a person to endure. It is normal for feelings of sadness or grief to develop in response to such situations . . . .But being sad is not the same as having depression . . . . In grief, painful feelings come in waves, often intermixed with positive memories of the deceased. In major depression, mood and/or interest (pleasure) are decreased for most of two weeks. In grief, self-esteem is usually maintained. In major depression, feelings of worthlessness and self-loathing are common. For some people, the death of a loved one can bring on major depression. Losing a job or being a victim of a physical assault or a major disaster can lead to depression for some people . . . . Despite some overlap between grief and depression, they are different.
> (Parekh, 2017)

These distinctions are somewhat subjective, given that self-esteem and painful feelings and moods are dynamic states that can come and go.

Additionally, given cultural and individual differences in normal expressions and experiences of emotions like sadness, what looks like depression to one person could easily look like a more reasonable form of sustained sadness or grief to another. Cross-culturally, it has also been observed that not all languages and cultures have precise references to sadness, with some associating it linguistically or conceptually with anger, fatigue, or boredom (Russell, 1991).

In this context, an expert (psychologist/psychiatrist) view is required for diagnosis, to evaluate appropriate and functional versus disordered or dysfunctional sadness and grief. However, some question psychological approaches and diagnoses of grief, sadness, and depression, noting how psychologists analysing grief and sadness can profit at the expense of their patients, particularly within health care settings marked by high profit margins for prescription drug companies. In societies like the United States where much of health care and medication are provided privately rather than publicly, over-prescribing of antidepressants for normal experiences is not uncommon. This can have lasting negative consequences, given that antidepressants can change a person's brain and interrelated overall emotional, bodily, and social functioning.

Bereavement is included as a factor for diagnosis of major depression in the fifth edition of the *Diagnostic and Statistical Manual of Mental Disorders*, the main reference point for diagnosing disorders and prescribing treatments (Pies, 2014). Some describe this as the labelling of a normal state of being as disordered to prescribe profit-making medication. In the United States, 23 percent of women aged 40–59 have been treated with antidepressants. Some of these cases are surely unnecessary, with possibly risky prescriptions being given to women facing temporary environmental challenges (Giraldi, 2017). While psychiatrists and psychologists maintain they can distinguish 'uncomplicated bereavement' from major depressive disorder which involves bereavement (Pies, 2014), such statistics encourage reconsideration of what is normal, and whether and how altering the brains (and bodies) of large numbers of people in society to cope with challenges benefits those people, and society at large. On the other hand, it is not the case that psychologists are forcing drugs on unwilling patients.

The psychological literature is more substantive on the topic of sadness than the philosophical literature. In philosophy, sadness is also associated with a sense of loss, and is often discussed in relation to grief. Grief is characterised as a form of sadness and 'as pain over the irrevocable loss of another's personhood' (Kristjánsson, 2018, p. 122). It is thus understood as a response to the death of another, although loss of personhood could also entail loss to disease, or to immense suffering (such as from

Alzheimer's disease), or a loss of a relationship, or quality of relationship with another.

From a virtue ethics perspective, Kristjánsson (2018) suggests more and less morally appropriate mannerisms, experiences, and targets for sadness and grief. As an example, he observes that sadness over losing an object (i.e. a mobile phone) does not qualify as genuine, justified grief (2018, p. 127). In relation, there is an observed normal grieving period, as grief is seen to normally fade over time, or at least become more of a 'background emotion' to everyday life (Nussbaum, 2001, p. 69). As a eudemonistic concept, grief can be useful to acknowledge loss, and to desire and act against unnecessary or unjust loss of life, 'creating a more deserving world' (Kristjánsson, 2018, p. 139).

Jamie Lindemann Nelson discusses the moral character of sadness and grief, despite the impossibility of completely controlling such feelings (2018). As she puts it, 'even if our emotions cannot readily be summoned or dismissed, we can strive to be the kind of people whose emotions can be relied upon to respond in the right ways to present situations, future prospects, and past events' (2018, p. 65). Nelson notes in relation that 'given the importance of emotion in moral judgment and motivation, assessing our own emotional responses seems part of what decency demands and . . . what prudence requires' (2018, p. 66). Nelson articulates as a challenge in evaluating sadness and grief the diversity of individual experiences, however.

A related challenge for evaluating grief or sadness unfolds when one broadens the conception of events of grief and sadness beyond traditional frameworks. Anna Gotlib (2018) emphasises the plurality and complexity of emotions, orientations, and experiences related to sadness or grief. Grief and sadness may also involve despair, anguish, and desolation (Price, 2010). Contrary to some moral philosophers and many psychologists, sadness and grief may not always have a clear target. Instead, they can occur somewhat randomly at times, and they can be vaguely targeted, as with anger, as discussed in the last chapter.

> The emotional objects of sadness, unlike those of regret or love, seem more diffuse, less definite, and the emotion of sadness itself seems not to possess many obvious conceptual boundaries. That is, I can just be generally sad – I can *feel sad*, or *be sad*, with no discernible object, with nothing to point to as a reason for, or justification of, my sadness. So while I can regret particular actions, events, or decisions, and while I can love particular people, or groups of people, or things, or places, this object-directedness does not seem to hold for sadness.
>
> (Gotlib, 2018, p. 5)

While sadness is seen as a basic and universal emotion, whether it is essentially depressing or energising, or motivating or demotivating, is debated by philosophers. Some see it is as motivating, and examine the diverse directions to which it can be pointed.

Another emotion related to sadness is nostalgia. As Gotlib writes, 'the idea of a backward-looking longing, whose objects are sometimes vague and unclear and sometimes painfully sharp, is nearly universally shared' and may unfold as 'a sadness of something certainly lost; of less easily definable losses; of longings for a past that might, or might not, have been' (2018, p. 183). Historically, nostalgia was pathologised as an unhealthy obsession with the past, which can become addictive and is irrational. This nostalgia is often framed as morally and politically suspect. Ahmed (2004a) traces the discourse of deviant melancholy in the case of 'melancholy migrants', ethnic minorities who are said to pose challenges within a postcolonial society (such as Sikhs in the United Kingdom), by holding on to the past of their homeland, a past marked by racism and oppression in colonial experiences, thereby refusing to accept and assimilate (enthusiastically) to present-day conditions and expectations. Ahmed argues that melancholy is characterised as problematic and rejected in this case, when it is not convenient for mainstream members of society to recognise contemporary causes for sadness, such as racism that remains in the present (2004a).

On the other hand, there are instances when dominant parties use nostalgia and related calls for grief and sadness for gain. Nostalgia for a simpler and more basic past is often cultivated by politicians. Trump followed Ronald Reagan in suggesting he would 'Make America Great Again'. The past of the United States (and Britain) is often glorified as simpler and more traditional, with less social problems. Yet this past is marked by government-sanctioned racial oppression and hierarchy, and a lack of rights and protections for women and minorities. In this context, people question whether those wishing to make these societies 'great again' want the societies to become less equitable, and more dominated by white men, as they were in the past.

However, collective grieving can also lead to critical political projects against social injustice. As Butler (2004, pp. 22–23) writes,

> Many people think that grief is privatizing, that it returns us to a solitary situation and is, in that sense, depoliticizing. But I think it furnishes a sense of political community . . . and it does this first of all by bringing to the fore the relational ties that have implications for theorizing fundamental dependency and ethical responsibility. If my fate is not originally or finally separable from yours, then the 'we' is traversed by a relationality that we cannot easily argue against; or, rather, we can argue against it, but we would be denying something fundamental about the social conditions of our very formation.

Similarly, Roberts (2016) highlights despair as essential to the human condition, although it also may not be targeted in an obvious way. Despair and other anguish and suffering are part of the human condition that cannot always be rationalised or moralised away effectively. Yet despair and other suffering can also lead to new kinds of awareness, about one's relations with others, and their place in the world. In other words, reflection on one's experiences with such negative feelings can lead to a kind of enlightenment that can bring with it greater understanding of how to contribute in positive ways to the world around oneself. On the other hand, political and other projects against unhappiness can be movements against authenticity, and away from grappling with the inevitable challenges of life, and of human vulnerability and interdependency. Thus, varieties of sadness, like happiness, can be politicised or depoliticised, and valued or dismissed, for socially just or unjust reasons.

These views echo some work in psychology that also identifies possible cognitive benefits to sadness. As discussed in Chapter 4, people in a sad mood are seen to be more careful and critical in analysing information. This suggests that sadness can have value for understanding complex moral matters in a deep, reflective way. In a sense, sadness can be educational. Additionally, 'viral' mourning events online, featuring an outpouring of many people's grief, are seen in sociological research to contribute to a broadened, more open discourse in the public sphere, revealing community vulnerabilities in ways that enhance a sense of connectedness and interdependency within a community (Papailias, 2016).

Assessments of sadness and grief can be further complicated, by exploring them as interpersonally relational, and significantly educable. While anger is more commonly expressed by boys and men, girls and women are more likely to express being sad or depressed, and more likely to be accepted as sad and depressed. These different tendencies are socialised in relation to disparate social expectations. Research shows that in contrast with girls, 'boys learn to suppress sadness' to avoid teasing by peers (Perry-Parrish & Zeman, 2011, p. 146). Furthermore, boys are more likely to express sadness to girls than to other boys, and less likely to reject or dismiss girls expressing sadness than boys expressing sadness. Thus, 'adolescents' sadness management is evaluated against gender-specific standards' (Perry-Parrish & Zeman, 2011, p. 149). Parents' views follow a similar pattern. They also perceive boys' sadness as more negative and dysfunctional than that of girls. Meanwhile, girls may face more stressors in adolescence than boys, which, in turn, leads to their experiencing more sadness and depression, among other feelings (Girgus & Yang, 2015).

On the other hand, it may be the case that boys' sadness is more often repressed, or transformed into a form of anger in processes of experience and expression, as anger is more common in boys and men (and more commonly accepted). In relation, self-anger is seen in similar circumstances as sadness in some research, suggesting that anger and sadness can be interlinked (Shirai & Suzuki, 2017). In a context such as a school, other social factors, such as class, ethnicity, race, and cultural mannerisms, can also be important parts of evaluations and expectations related to experiences and expressions of sadness (DeCuir-Gunby & Williams-Johnson, 2014).

While in psychology (and some philosophy), sadness and grief can be held as functional in times of loss and upheaval, educational psychologists focused on achievement tend to regard them more generally as negative, and dysfunctional in relation to learning. When academic achievement is the goal, these feelings can be seen as interrupting ideal cognitive function, regardless of their other moral or social value. There is some sensible discourse in schools about grieving, in the context of student suicides, school shootings, and other losses, that relies on psychological understandings of grief and sadness to encourage educators to help students understand, process, and accept important negative feelings in such circumstances (Turunen et al., 2014; Paolini, 2015). However, there are also cases where insights about sadness and grief are not reflected in school practices as they could be.

For instance, there is not always recognition and acceptance in schooling contexts that sadness and grief can be normal and ordinary, apart from extreme traumatic experiences, and that reflecting upon such experiences, which can be vague, fuzzy, and non-targeted, can also be useful, healthy, and educational. As mentioned previously, these feelings can open up students to explore ideas and interpersonal and societal connections in new ways. They can, therefore, ultimately enable and motivate positive experiences and behaviours. However, in many cases, schoolteachers may feel pressured to instead take on the role of coaches for happiness and optimism, sometimes in ways that do not resonate with realistic human experiences (Roberts, 2016). As discussed in Chapter 4, discourses on happiness do not always give space for accepting unhappy experiences as educative and normal.

Schools can do a better job in this context, in allowing students to process and accept their emotions in a less judgemental way, when it comes to sadness and its variants. Students can learn that sad emotions have significant values to themselves and within relationships, while they can also lead to new understandings and awareness. Thus, students should not be discouraged from expressing and experiencing sadness in general. Practically, it does little good to advise a sad or depressed student to stop feeling the way they do, given that some such feelings are not entirely controllable, while moralising about sadness may also possibly lead to students hiding their feelings in harmful ways (Parrott, 2014; Turunen et al., 2014; Paolini, 2015). Students could be instead comforted, by learning and reflecting upon how unpleasant feelings can be dynamic and educational. This is quite different from asking students to deliberately work against feelings of sadness and grief (and related states), which are not always so easily managed and manipulated in real life.

Additionally, in discussions of grief and school violence, tips for educators and parents to manage sadness (and fear) of students sometimes seem to imply that they (educators and parents) are superior at handling emotions than students, as it is expected that adults model emotional maturity and management, and effectively evaluate students' experiences and expressions. Yet adults are not necessarily more emotionally in touch with themselves, or more emotionally adjusted than younger people, including educators in a school setting, who may also need professional mental health care when experiencing tragedy (Turunen et al., 2014). It is true that babies and children must learn to recognise and identify emotions, just as they learn to recognise and identify others things and concepts in relationships with others (e.g. food, furniture, etc.). However, it is an overstatement to suggest that adults are on the whole better at managing emotions than children, given individual differences, among other issues. One study found that teachers had less death acceptance compared to other people in society, and therefore were in greater need of counselling and coaching than the average person in coping with grief and sadness (Reid & Dixon, 1999). In this context, paternalistic discourse that frames teachers as essentially better at emotional management than youth puts teachers in a place to judge, evaluate, and shape the emotional experiences and responses of students in a potentially problematic way, also given cultural differences, gender differences, and other diversity observed when it comes to expectations about emotional virtues, including sadness.

Finally, there has been a relative lack of attention to the place of facilitated mourning and nostalgia in education in support of nationalistic and related political interests. Public mourning can have positive functions as previously mentioned (Fast, 2003). However, such mourning can also be used in the public sphere to pressure people to support potentially problematic causes, through words or actions, such as voting for particular people, or joining the military (Butler, 2004). In relation, there is a danger in some instances that mourning and grief can be used to motivate particular responses, within and beyond schools. Often, educational resources for managing grief encourage people moving into routines quickly after traumatic events in the school or community, as well as mobilising youth involvement to quickly begin to improve things – for example, through participating in emergency drills, or actively engaging in reporting threats to safety (Thornton, 2013). Stitzlein (2019) also recommends hopeful activity and community service in case of despair, as a path to making things better, which will be discussed more in the next section.

Encouraging students to be present in an active state, instead of passive or numb, may be desirable in certain respects, particularly if students seem to be becoming depressed. However, there is a risk of manipulating the situation to motivate behaviours here, of 'doing something' for the sake of 'doing something', so that one does not feel uncomfortable. This desire to do something, to resolve negative or mixed feelings, was discussed earlier, in relation to the cultivation of compassion and altruism (Chapter 5). For instance, older youth might be encouraged to join the military after a national-level tragedy, by well-meaning educators, or others who are simply seeking military recruits. These sorts of responses to sadness and grief should be thought through more carefully in education. Such responses to sadness and grief can fuel action that is moral or immoral, beneficial or harmful, to oneself and others. Applying eudemonistic judgement here is essential, so that sadness, and possibly related fear in such cases, are not exploited to lead people against their own interests, among others, in schools and society. Students can and should also be taught in ways that can enhance their capacities to grapple with sadness, so that they are empowered to work through it with reflective judgement, rather than becoming susceptible to notions of quick fixes and easy outs.

10.2   Fear and Anxiety

In addition to sadness and grief, other emotions stirred up by loss in many cases are fear and anxiety. Fear is normally regarded as a basic affect or instinctive feeling, and a physiological 'response to a more immediate threat'; meanwhile, anxiety 'is a fear reaction to distal or non-present threat, and so is more cognitive in nature' (McNeill et al., 2012, p. 161). Fear is held as a relatively uncommon emotion in education and society, apart from in disaster and emergency situations, while anxiety is more commonplace. Fear and anxiety are both held as negative emotions in education, and anxiety is targeted as a particular challenge, given that experiences of anxiety in education are far more widespread.

Generally speaking, some small amount of anxiety in education and elsewhere in society can be experienced as a good thing. It can motivate people to do their best, aware of the consequences of failure. This can lead to working harder, being more aware and thoughtful, and increasing focus. Yet this kind of anxiety can sometimes go too far. Focus can become paralysis, or develop into a kind of lack of control, becoming obsessive and imbalanced. Both fear and anxiety can lead to tendencies and behaviours of withdrawal, unresponsiveness, freezing up, and submission. Withdrawal and lack of responsiveness are seen to significantly disrupt education, while experiences of freezing up and submission are highly problematic for a person's well-being and autonomy.

Beyond the context of education, one point of debate among scholars is the prevalence of fear, and its significance. From a psychological view, fear has an evolutionary function which is reflected in moments of intensely felt fear and phobia. Fear is part of 'flight or fight' response in dangerous situations, according to this view. Fear and anxiety are functional when approaching dangerous animals, or going sky diving, for example. For this reason, common fears are snakes, heights, natural disasters, and dental treatment. Thinking of or anticipating these things can invoke deep feelings of dread and panic, at the thought of something terrible happening to oneself, such as death or serious harm (McNeill et al., 2012). The fear drives people to protect themselves from or avoid the fearsome things, through physical, cognitive, and emotional experiences. These feelings may also be partly vague and indirect, experienced when the threat is not so close at hand; one might not think about a snake seen at the zoo biting them, specifically, but they may just imagine the snake touching them, as they experience fear.

It is commonly held that there is a normal spectrum of experiences of fear, as fear is related to the extraordinary. Some people are rather fearless, while others are chronically fearful. Pathological anxiety and fear are seen as that which is out of proportion to risks and dangers, and disruptive to social and personal functioning. Measurements of fear and anxiety, most commonly made through the use of self-reports (with observations and bodily monitoring also possible), find that women experience more fear and anxiety than men. Here major factors identified are 'gender role expectations (females allowed greater social latitude to report fear), life events (females have more negative events than males), physiology ... and cognition (females more likely to worry)' (McNeill et al., 2012, p. 165). Additionally, appraisal of situations demanding fear, and how fear is understood and expressed, can be seen to vary cross-culturally (Russell, 1991). However, in general, psychologists see some fear and anxiety as normal. This implies a general view that one should exercise practical reason in relation to experiences of fear and anxiety.

However, fear and anxiety are seen differently by existentialists. For Heidegger and Sartre, fear and anxiety are both essential to being in and experiencing the world in a deep way. While fear relates to the world being inherently threatening to one's sense of reality, and unpredictable, anxiety is provided by a sense of alienation, as one's identity and sense of self get caught up in social and worldly relations, which are experienced as disorienting. Sartre (1943) contends that when one steps back from being in constant motion and preoccupation, they immediately experience anxiety, as things begin to lose their set meanings. Miguel de Unamuno describes anxiety similarly, as part of knowing, and not knowing, in the world (see also Roberts, 2016). As he writes,

> That which lives, that which is absolutely unstable ... is, strictly speaking, unintelligible. Logic tends to reduce everything to identities and genera, to a state where each representation has no more than one single selfsame content ... But nothing is the same for two successive moments of its being. My idea of God is different each time I conceive it ... The mind seeks what is dead, for the living escapes it .... To understand anything it must first be killed, laid out rigid in the mind.
>
> (Unamuno, 1972, p. 100)

For existentialists, cultivating a kind of courage in the face of such anxieties, fears, and deep insecurities can lead to a sense of freedom, from the need for certainty and the rigidity in common views of reality and knowledge, as 'consciousness is radically free, since its structure precludes that it either *contain* or *be acted* on by things' (Crowell, 2015, emphasis in the original). In this context, fear and anxiety are essential parts of the human condition that are frequently denied, ignored, and dismissed, despite their potential productive power for the courageous.

Buddhist texts also recommend a coming to terms with fear as a natural process that can lead to greater freedom from the negative impacts of experiencing fear over time. This approach in Buddhism is not dissimilar from some Christian ideals, which also advocate as part of human nature experiencing and dwelling with fear and anxiety, and finding liberation or freedom in relation to it (Brekke, 1999). Fear is necessary here, and not avoidable. Rather, it should be worked through, lived with, and reckoned with, in an open, vulnerable way.

Attachment theory from psychology also supports a view that anxiety and fear are a major part of life for many people. Yet for proponents of attachment theory, such anxiety and fear are seen not as healthy, but as dysfunctional, as these emotional experiences can disrupt relationships, and social and personal flourishing. Attachment theory observes that the way one learns to relate to others as a young child impacts their sense of self and sense of the fearsome or secure nature of the world at large. This approach is based on studies of the 'Strange Situation', an experiment to examine how babies respond to their mothers leaving the room, and coming back shortly after (Ainsworth & Bell, 1970). Researchers found that some babies would cry when their mothers left the room, and would stop crying when they returned. Other babies did not show a major response to either event, appearing to turn away from their caregivers in the first place. Another group was distressed before their mothers left the room, and clingy and inconsolable upon their return. Attachment theorists claim that babies who indicate clinginess, and those who appear to turn away, have been educated, in a sense, to be anxious about their relationship with their caregiver, and that this suggests that their caregivers may not be (sufficiently) consistently caring. The babies' patterns of anxiety, shaped by their experiences with caregivers, are said to influence their behaviour in later stages of life, and possibly throughout the lifespan, as their anxiety can become chronic, leading to emotional and cognitive challenges, and ongoing relationship problems.

As attachment theorists observe, chronically anxious people focus on risks and challenges to a dysfunctional degree. They expect the worst to happen, and see themselves as helpless and alone in the world (Tsachi & Doron, 2015). Their anxiety is sustained over time, across situations, because they seek out relationships which follow interpersonal patterns that can cause them anxiety, as the experiences seem more logical and consistent with past experience. In their search for security, they associate their norm of anxiety as a usual situation, thereby stabilising and securing their experience of anxiety. Meanwhile, they see other experiences, of relationships that foster a sense of security – which others would see as less anxious and more secure – paradoxically as more vulnerable and risky. Thus, a person whose mother was neglectful of their needs may be more attracted to and accepting of others in their lives, such as teachers and relationship partners, who similarly seem to neglect their needs, or who act randomly rather than consistently toward them.

As attachment theorists focus on the impact of early childhood experiences to well-being throughout the lifespan, they have particularly considered how such patterns may be brought into, alleviated, or worsened in education. Those who develop high levels of anxiety in early childhood may initially appear whiny and clingy to teachers. This can lead to teachers lowering their expectations about their maturity, which can unfortunately enable their behaviour and help cultivate a clingy relationship pattern (Watson & Ecken, 2019). At the same time, the pattern can be difficult to break through intervention. In line with care ethics views, psychologists concerned about sustainably reducing attachment anxiety encourage the providing of care in consistent ways, to try to break down negative patterns. They also advocate that concerned teachers in this context think through their own assumptions and patterns, as many people are seen in this orientation to employ different attachment styles that tend to 'follow' them in their lives and relationships in unconscious ways.

However, this schema can appear unnecessarily complicated for a person not well versed in this perspective. Take the following extract:

> As teachers, we have often been warned that if we are too helpful we encourage laziness or create dependency. On the other hand, the research in attachment theory has demonstrated just the opposite: If we are able to meet children's needs with reasonable consistency, they will become secure in their necessarily dependent relationship with us and will gradually grow more independent and self-sufficient. However, as most teachers have experienced, when we help some students, they seem to want more and more help, which would seem to confirm the notion that providing help encourages dependence and even laziness. Again, the research in attachment theory casts this behaviour in a new light. Children with a history of anxious attachment often try to get our help, not because they need it, but because they need to test our availability. If we respond by lowering our expectations and providing these students with too much help, we inadvertently convey our lack of confidence that they can succeed on their own . . . . But gradually, with insecurely attached children, as we demonstrate in a wide variety of ways that we are trustworthy, these acts of kindness will increase children's feelings of security in their relationship with us, allowing them to take more risks, develop more confidence in themselves, and grow in independence – not dependence.   (Watson & Ecken, 2019, pp. 88–90)

There are many other challenges to attachment theory. One set of concerns surrounds whether and how such patterns may be similar or different across cultures, and whether or not they would have the same meanings around the world (Burman, 1994). Others contend that attachment theory wrongly frames children as 'blank slates', with no influences apart from nurturing on their development (Pinker, 2002). At the same time, as with some proponents of care theory, attachment theorists tend to conclude that mothers should be physically and emotionally attached throughout early childhood to their babies, a psychologically and politically problematic assumption, resulting in some cases in mothers feeling pressured to be completely selfless and focused on nurturing others throughout their children's early lives (Duschinsky, Greco, & Solomon, 2015). As Erica Burman also notes, 'links between early experience and later development have been spectacularly difficult to establish', while attachment discourse unreasonably implicates 'neglectful' mothers as responsible for social problems, such as drug use and other socially inappropriate youth activity, letting governments off the hook for failing to provide stable resources to children and families (1994, p. 91).

Nonetheless, attachment theory highlights one basic insight: Fear and anxiety can be educated through relationships. Other research on fear and anxiety indicates other ways the emotions are taught deliberately in society, specifically to manipulate and harm some people for others' gain. Right-wing discourse across countries encourages people to feel fear, by expressing doomsday scenarios, manipulating people to follow particular priorities. Politicians and news media make losing one's job, dangerous foreigners and strangers, losing national autonomy, losing cultural traditions, and climate change seem like ever-present threats, demanding immediate responses through voting behaviours and other actions (Wodak, 2015). People thereby legitimise questionable and problematic causes, such as cutting welfare, engaging in hostile military action, and increasing invasive state security apparatus, which may be harmful and oppressive, through cultivating a political climate of fear. 'Group-based fear' of criminals and fear of foreigners is also known to attract people to causes that are discriminatory and oppressive, against human rights values (Porat et al., 2018). Catarina Kinnvall notes in this context the phenomena of 'elite fear', as a fear of losing power in society can be contained through actions that 'enhance the subject's own capacities, and generally re-align power relations and render innocuous the prospects that were feared' (2013).

Such fears also impact students, teachers, and others in schools. Donald Rogers (1972, pp. 391–393) observes how fear is encouraged in schools, and shapes classrooms as places of fear:

> As the pressure for concrete, statistical evidence of progress mounts, the tension within the school system increases. School board members worry … School administrators, the superintendent, and the principals worry …. Teachers worry …. As a result, the children are the dubious benefactors of all this anxiety …. The principle [sic] may crack down on disorderly lines on the playground, or on noise in the school hallways, or on activity-filled classrooms, once rated as creative but now frowned on as simply messy. In the classrooms, teachers are a bit less patient with repetitive questions, or shout … to keep the class in order …. the Indian philosopher Jiddu Krishnamurti has come to these conclusions: 'If children are to be free from fear … the educator himself must have no fear. But that is the difficulty: to find teachers who are not themselves the prey of some kind of fear …. Like goodness, fear is contagious. If the educator himself is secretly afraid, he will pass that fear on to his students, although its contamination may not be immediately seen'.

Educators should teach against irrational or chronic fear, which can be distracting and unhelpful, if not debilitating and disabling. Yet unfortunately, in many cases teachers can be seen to exacerbate rather than ameliorate student fear and anxiety through their actions. While no one recommends this approach, this can happen when teachers ignore fear and anxiety, or dismiss, mock, or belittle expressions and experiences of it. It can also happen when teachers experience fear themselves, and feel powerless or trapped rather than able to work through and make sense of it. These processes and practices do not help students to respond effectively to their feelings of fear, but can make the emotional and personal experiences of students worse.

In other cases, teachers may encourage students to be afraid, by alerting them to dangers. Of course, there may be dangers students need to learn about, such as deadly snakes (if they are in Australia), or tsunamis (if they live near the ocean). Such things can be taught about in more or less effective ways. Students can learn about ways to take the risks seriously, while not becoming obsessed with them.

In the United States, many educators and psychologists have focused on how to manage fear and related student anxiety in relation to the possibility of school shootings. Methods to prevent shootings have been brought into schools there, such as increased discipline and security practices, and profiling of possible shooters (Borum et al., 2010). Meanwhile, students (and teachers) may be taught what to do in the case of a shooting, with techniques including shooting drills. Yet critics observe these interventions often do more harm than good, as they can be seen to reveal vulnerabilities to attack, and thus exacerbate fear by increasing thoughts about possible risks (Burns & Crawford, 1999; Borum et al., 2010; Jonson, 2017).

These techniques also distract attention from political possibilities to intervene more effectively in regard to school shootings, such as through banning the public sale of assault rifles in that country. As one student expresses it, children may feel like they are political pawns in this case, with their rational fear being denied, or even fuelled by schooling practices that seem to reflect that school shootings are the only status quo possible, while all opportunities for increasing security in schools and society are not adequately considered (Shelanski, 2019).

Fear and anxiety can also be used by teachers as motivational tools, in ways that are dishonest, manipulative, and harmful. For instance, a teacher might say that students are bound to fail in life if they do not do their homework, or succeed in examinations. Such tactics may be used to gain classroom control by teachers, who may not realise how they can negatively contribute to fear and anxiety. Teachers should be mindful about such cases, as they also consider how they can more effectively interact with other public discourses of fear which can be discussed in more or less helpful and balanced ways in the classroom. For instance, fear of strangers and fear of immigrants and foreigners are often cultivated in subtle ways in classrooms that aim to be oriented toward student safety, yet most risks to children come from people who are well known to them, such as other students, family, and family friends (Jackson, 2019a).

When considering the politics of fear, it may be difficult for teachers to control or influence students, compared to other parties. Media is a powerful source of fear, as it sensationalises events, constructs and disseminates dark visions of villains, and provides a captivating view that anyone can be a victim of apparently ever-present, random evil (Jackson, 2014a). However, teachers can at least take a critical orientation toward this politics, rather than unwittingly add to it. For example, teachers can teach students to understand how the media and politicians cultivate fear for their own reasons (such as to sell newspapers or get website page clicks), and explore how such fear is constructed, as part of media literacy (Jackson, 2014a).

Fear of future environmental damages may be spread by the media and in education in relation to the need for sustainable development, to motivate students and others to be good environmental actors. While some want to harness this fear to manipulate students and other people – for good ends, such as purchasing ecologically friendly products – such manipulative tactics are not ideal from the perspective of youth emotional development in schools. Instead, in this case, 'understanding the moral driving forces behind future-oriented projects' can enable 'an educational discussion less prone to incite immediate action and more geared toward the careful study of human behaviors and power geographies' (Dahlbeck, 2013, p. 168). In such contexts, teachers should be cautious about fear as a possible indoctrinatory influence that can lead students to be irrational and other-centred in possibly dysfunctional and harmful ways. It may be necessary to act (relatively) quickly in light of what is known about climate change and environmental destruction, but this does not mean that fear should be fuelled and enabled to the detriment of clear-headed thinking about solutions. As with sadness, fear can be used and abused in education and the public sphere, and teachers can do better than to echo such public manipulation of emotional virtues.

In relation to these challenges, one can also teach and inspire students to cultivate courage or hope. Teaching for courage was discussed in Chapter 8, in relation to accepting and even cultivating some kinds of vulnerability, in a limited rather than overzealous way. As Palmer notes (1997), fear is natural among teachers and among students, based on desires for connection, fear of the loss of self, and fear of conflict. In this context, Palmer recommends seeing and grappling with one's fear in the first instance, rather than trying to hide it in order to be 'manly', which can allow fear to run amok. As also discussed in Chapter 8, Vogler (2018) similarly encourages small, everyday lessons in courage in her classroom as fundamental to learning, such as using collaborative techniques to help students become less fearful about expressing themselves, or making mistakes in the course of class discussions.

Others advocate for hope in place of fear. Stitzlein (2019) notes that fear is natural and quite reasonable for some people in society, in light of

202 *Sadness, Fear, and Anxiety*

racism and other forms of oppression (see also Leonardo & Porter, 2010). As an antidote, Stitzlein frames hope as similar to Stengel's courage in solidarity (also examined in Chapter 8). Stitzlein (2019) argues that through recognising shared fate, young people can develop hope in place of fear through engaging in service learning, which teaches students they can make a difference in the lives of others (and can be looked after by others, in turn), and engage in collaborative projects that help develop trust across students, school stakeholders, and other community members. Stitzlein argues that teachers as well can develop hope where it has been lost, by engaging in community activities that build networks of mutual support, recognition, trust, and hope. Stitzlein concludes, "'Are there reasons to hope?' Yes, we are those very reasons. We have the ability to create, engage, and sustain hope through our habits' (2019). However, as mentioned previously, there also can be a tendency to 'do something' which is not necessarily beneficial, if fear is treated firstly as intolerable, without a critical view of better and worse responses. Despite the challenges of teaching for inclusive and courageous hope in place of fear, with a sense of vulnerability, this approach has potential as part of moral education, however, in contrast to many other responses to fear and anxiety in education.

10.3 Concluding Thoughts

This chapter has considered two basic emotions held as negative in education and society, and other related states: sadness, grief, and melancholy; and fear and anxiety. These feelings are often held as negative, as they are experienced as uncomfortable by people. They are rarely framed as educationally valuable, because they are seen to distract from educationally motivating, 'academic' feelings, of focus, contentment, curiosity, and drive. Nonetheless, there are ways these feelings can be positively framed and understood. Sadness and grief can serve to communicate and recognise value, and motivate just action that is compassionate, and deeply aware of the interconnectedness and interdependency of people in society. Fear and anxiety can also be motivational, to help avoid dangers at personal and community levels, and to encourage just action to ensure safety in the future despite vulnerability. On the other hand, these emotions can also be used and abused in personally and socially harmful ways; there are ways they are taught about and taught to people in life, sometimes intentionally and sometimes unintentionally, that teachers should be aware of, as they respond to these feelings as part of students' experiences. These feelings should be reflected upon in education rather than dismissed, mocked, or discouraged. They should also be discussed as experiences that can be evaluated by individuals and communities, as they can motivate action and behaviour in beneficial or harmful ways.

Sadness, fear, and anxiety are part of life. Thus, they should also be a part of education. In this context, teachers should also understand how their own feelings of sadness and fear, and expectations about these feelings in others – what the feelings look like, and who should have them – can impact their classroom relations, and shape students' views and experiences of these feelings in turn. Finally, these feelings should be recognised as sophisticated and complicated in human experience, even while they are often understood as 'basic'. In relation, they should be explored in their complexity, to help students recognise and respond to these feelings and their triggers, rather than enable students to overlook these feelings, or be manipulated by others in relation to them.

CHAPTER 11

Conclusion

In this text, the role of emotions in education and society has been examined from various perspectives, particularly from psychological, philosophical, and other theoretical and political views. To develop more in-depth understanding about moral development and emotions in social life, a number of emotional virtues have also been explored at length. These include basic emotions, like happiness, sadness, and fear; emotional virtues often idealised, such as gratitude and compassion; and more complex emotional and cognitive-based dispositions prized in contemporary education and society, like resilience, grit, and mindfulness. A complicated account has been given, based on an interdisciplinary orientation toward emotional virtues and educating emotions in society. As seen here, the means and ends of educating emotional virtues are not simple and straightforward, given diversity in experiences, identities, and norms around emotional expectations. While educational implications have been discussed across chapters, thus far such considerations have been specific to particular emotional domains and contexts. This conclusion elaborates further on a more global perspective on educating emotional virtues in schools and society.

11.1 Must We Educate Emotional Virtues?

Positive, functional, and pleasant feelings and emotional experiences are valued across societies, as part of good living. How to manage and cultivate emotions properly has always been examined by people around the world, because emotions are central to human experience. Due to the difference emotion makes in human life, many models have been developed over time to make sense of how emotions operate, and how one can in turn operate upon their own emotions, and those of others. These models, socially constructed, have informed practices to help people manage their emotions and cultivate more positive and pleasant emotional experiences. With transformations in knowledge and culture, these models have shifted and changed.

While some models have prevailed over others in different times and places, no single model has gained widespread acceptance and consensus across fields. This is because emotions are not only very complex and diverse in their experiences and expressions, but because they are also related to moral and religious deeply held beliefs.

Throughout history and across cultures, some people have been attracted to models of emotions that highlight their mysterious essence, their irreplaceability, and a sense of freedom, enlightenment, or divine that can be found in acceptance, or awareness, of one's emotional state. Diverse orientations toward accepting one's emotions can be found, for example, in existentialism, transcendental religious views, and in Daoism, Buddhism, and Stoicism. Meanwhile, other people have felt certain that being a good person and a good member of a community requires something quite different: managing and controlling one's emotions, and directing them precisely toward the good, against the bad. Virtue ethics and care ethics both highlight the cultivation of positive emotional experiences, something also endorsed in popular psychological approaches, such as positive psychology. For other thinkers, following deontological, consequentialist, and Confucian views, one should not work toward good based on emotional moods and related desires, but develop a more rational approach to good living.

Given the diversity of views merely hinted at in the last few sentences and explored across this text, it is not likely that one single model of the role of emotions in life is going to prevail in the future. This is due, in part, to the fact that these matters are not ones where transparent, broadly accepted empirical data can light the way. Instead, these matters relate to understandings of goodness, God, and flourishing. Even as more knowledge about emotions in relation to cognition and human biological and physical processes develops, this knowledge does not clarify what is good or bad, right or wrong.

Yet this does not mean that people can or should do nothing, when it comes to their emotions or those of others. Models for understanding emotions have led to diverse methods and techniques to enhance emotions in relation to personal and social life. Such methods include engaging in personal reflection, psychotherapy, meditation, and even yoga and other physical exercise. More broadly, part of learning to be a human involves entering into the cultural and social norms of a family and a community. Emotional experiences and expressions are deeply embedded in these practices, and in community norms. Because emotions are held to be of vital importance to well-being in society, they have become part of education, particularly for developing character, and for social and emotional learning. Because of the importance of emotions in human social life, other industries have also emerged to support emotional cultivation, alongside other organisations which aim to impact people's emotions for other reasons, such as to create desires or fears.

Emotional virtues education often has noble goals, to enhance personal and social life for all, and lead to more flourishing communities, inside and outside schools. It may aim to develop more 'affective equality', recognising as morally and politically problematic apparent emotional experience gaps that correlate with other signs of advantage and disadvantage in society. Nobody wants to feel bad, and yet across societies young people (among others) grapple with anxiety, depression, fear, anger, unhappiness, and other forms of negative emotional vulnerability. An obvious solution here is to help people learn how to cultivate more positive emotional experiences, when they are able to do so.

Yet given the diversity of views about emotions and experiences with emotions within a society, it should not be surprising to find that there is not a clear 'one-size-fits-all' approach to educating emotional virtues. Some argue otherwise, charging that 'we' know what to do, to cultivate positive and pro-social emotional experiences that lead to personal and social flourishing, and that 'we' should therefore teach these practices and skills (or intelligences) to others. Yet proponents of particular variants of social and emotional learning and related character education, as seen here, tend to leave some people out of the moral picture. Goleman describes it as deviant and as a 'moral failing' that some cannot develop emotional intelligence (EI) as he conceives it, as they lack requisite emotional awareness. For Goleman, this appears to be a deficiency. Yet other thinkers observe that emotions are much less easy to sense and control than Goleman posits. Emotions can be misidentified, as the combination of sensations, feelings, and evaluations accompanying emotions can be complex and dynamic. Emotions can also be experienced for seemingly no reason, or in unpredictable ways. Meanwhile, dangers and risks can accompany the socially-informed desire and attempt to always control and manage one's emotions, in rigid ways.

Likewise, virtue ethicists hold assumptions about how emotions can operate in relation to morality that are far from universally experienced or held. That people are far from such perfect ideals may be known and recognised by virtue ethicists, but this may be obscured in classroom lessons and teacher expressions in the complex real world. Additionally, some remain suspicious of virtues education that holds personal reflection and meditation above social action, particularly in contexts of social injustice, and where young people (among others) face real external social harms that demand active reactions, rather than passive, individual emotional self-cultivation.

A central problem of this text is that what works for one person may not work for another, when it comes to educating emotional virtues. Worse, what works for one student in a classroom may be negatively experienced by another. An educator aiming to cultivate or promote happiness, non-anger, gratitude, or compassion may help some students develop positively, while other students experience mixed feelings and reactions to such education, unable to set aside challenging emotional dispositions, that then may be reframed through emotional virtues education as deviant 'bad signs'. This means that educators face a serious challenge in educating emotional virtues in classroom settings in an equitable way. In this context, there is a real risk to teaching emotional virtues in a hasty and partially informed way, without cognisance about (normal and common) deviations from common expectations, and related challenges. Furthermore, as no singular view on emotions in life can claim a monopoly in relation to human experience and values, relying on a single approach to emotional virtues can be a partial act, even in the best of cases.

As explored across this text, there is also a risk that some emotional virtues education can exacerbate rather than ameliorate apparent affective inequality, as political attitudes and cultural and other forms of bias in society structure informal (if not formal) aspects of planned approaches to social and emotional learning, in ways that can reinforce problematic status quos. As expectations about emotional experiences and expressions vary in societies by gender, race, class, and more, diverse students thus face challenges to cultivating a full range of emotional experiences in the classroom.

When it comes to happiness, women and minorities indicate feeling social pressure to conform to expectations of others to demonstrate happiness, and never show anger, or even dissatisfaction, in everyday life and the public sphere. However, some (e.g. privileged, white) men's anger continues to be applauded broadly in society, as can be observed in the discourse of men political leaders today. These trends and experiences also educate and influence youth, while the cultural norms they reflect inevitably enter classroom spaces, like others. However, this does not necessarily mean that boys and men fare better than girls and women, on the whole. As also seen here, boys and men face immense pressure to not show sadness, likely transforming their possible sadness into a more socially acceptable anger in many cases. The value of boys and men cultivating and expressing care and compassion, gratitude, and other mixed negative emotions, of fear, anxiety, and vulnerability is also neglected in many societies, which can negatively impact boys and men's capacities to benefit from emotional virtues education focused on these experiences.

On the other hand, calls and expectations for girls and women to be caring, compassionate, and have gratitude are mixed blessings. While these emotions may help people (girls and women) to be other-centred, they can be experienced as a double-edged sword, as burdened virtues that disable them from ensuring their own well-being over time, in relation to that of others they care for. Similarly, courage can be expected of people in self-sacrificing situations, wherein it is burdensome as a virtue, even if its cultivation can at the same time be seen as warranted to resolve cases of harm and injustice. Indeed, when taken to an extreme, the promotion of any emotional virtue can risk alienating people who experience various commonplace and more distinctive kinds of difficulty with emotional self-awareness and self-cultivation, and effective emotional expression. Practices of encouraging gratitude, which many see as harmless, can be experienced as threatening and unproductive for some. While this may not be the majority experience, it should not be overlooked as unlikely, as discussed here. Furthermore, people normally have mixed feelings, and complex situations require that people consider many different feelings and values, rather than focusing on only one preferred value or ranking. Thus, the dogmatic treatment of any emotional virtue in the classroom, or any single strategy for emotional regulation, as 'always good' is not helpful.

When it comes to emerging emotional virtues such as resilience, mindfulness, and grit, evidence shows how they can be used and abused. They can be cultivated by teachers deliberately so that students 'get on with it' and do not make their teaching difficult by indicating challenges, internal or external, that could be distracting. Such emotional virtues or emotion-like dispositions can also be held on a pedestal, to defend choices that are actually bad for students, and are likely to be widely negatively perceived as such. One example of this is the case of the Ontario policymaker, who wanted to increase class sizes apparently to cultivate student resilience, effectively suggesting that there is a good reason to make young people's lives harder through schooling – the reason being the apparently vital benefits of their developing resilience and grit, no matter what.

Finally, evidence that good things actually happen – to students themselves, or others around them – specifically due to cultivating positive emotional experiences, or specifically due to particular educational interventions for emotional virtues, is lacking. There is little compelling evidence that increasing happiness, compassion, and gratitude through educational interventions leads to students feeling or being better, more moral, or doing more for others. Self-reported changes, even of personal emotional experiences, are much less impressive for any given emotional virtue than one would expect, based on the strong claims made in this domain, with few people effectively indicating positive changes in personal experience or pro-social behaviour, based on emotional virtues education or related interventions. Where positive changes observed are significant, it is not clear that they are long term, suggesting that much 'effective' emotional virtues education is akin to a simple kind of training, as disciplining to resolve short-term classroom challenges.

It is possible in many cases that students learn that gratitude or happiness or resilience is 'good' in the views of their educators, and act on that knowledge, but the related internal development processes (or lack thereof) are unclear here. The students could just be learning moral education as content knowledge, as Buber observed: 'I have made the fatal mistake of *giving instruction* in ethics, and what I said is accepted as current coin of knowledge; nothing of it is transformed into character-building substance' (1947, p. 124, emphasis in original). Overall, evidence of the benefits of much emotional virtues education is particularly lacking in relation to the bold claims made by their proponents about their efficacy.

Worse, in some cases it is clear that interventions have significant negative backfire effects. Some students experience stigmatisation, and vivid and anxious awareness that they do not feel the way they should according to teachers and others' 'feeling rules', enabling a sense of alienation, exclusion, deficiency, and even hopelessness. In the case of grit, some gritty students are seen to experience more negative stress than less gritty students, suggesting that grit discourse and related education can encourage young people to suppress and repress negative experiences, but not to rid themselves of these challenging experiences – or to effectively face their possible direct, external causes. It should be unsurprising that when challenges experienced are related to things or events outside a person, 'cowboying up' is not going to resolve painful or harmful emotional responses to those challenges. In this case, the cultivation of grit can be seen to lead to more negative experiences, rather than less negative experiences, down the line, as it can serve as a means of ignoring real obstacles faced. These problematic possibilities must also be considered alongside the potential benefits, in identifying the value of various practices and programs for emotional virtues education.

The major problem here, in a nutshell, is that changing feelings has become the exclusive goal, dismissing the value of possibly changing situations. Prevalent emotional virtues discourse discourages reactions to negative experiences in the world, before personal reflection, which is to be sustained and ongoing. Popular and mainstream discourses about the benefits of resilience and grit (and happiness, gratitude, and non-anger) generally encourage first and foremost a looking away from negative situations and possibilities, which is often a major component of cognitive behavioural therapy. Being virtuous, any virtue ethicist will observe, is not to be dogmatic or 'do nothing', when one experiences or observes challenges and problems in the world around them. However, a message nonetheless reverberates across the majority of social and emotional learning and character education strategies, which often invoke virtue ethics, that one's feelings are the main locus of one's moral responsibility, that they should aim to control, above and before anything else. Meanwhile, messages about the importance of acting against negative environmental and relational conditions are in the hazy background in most approaches, effectively replacing more active civic education curricula with apolitical, and arguably often amoral, techniques. Thus, 'pedagogies of emotional control' are effectively employed, as narrow strategies for emotional regulation are embraced, while 'pedagogies of autonomy' (Maxwell & Reichenbach, 2007), for acting possibly against and in any case in relation with diverse others, in reflective and flexible ways, remain underexplored, and undervalued.

11.2   What Can Be Done?

This text does not mean to blame hard-working researchers and educators, whose ideas and practices have been critically evaluated and scrutinised in these pages. Most who aim to educate emotional virtues have good intentions, and reasonable justifications for the practices they encourage. That is, emotional virtues education can be seen to work, sometimes, and from certain perspectives. As discussed here, when a supportive environment is in place, within a cultural community where contextually relevant practices and values are relied upon, and when all stakeholders are on the same page, such an education can work to enhance student well-being. Otherwise, it can be seen to work in a more instrumental way, as pedagogies of control. That is, it can work to 'get rid of' 'negative emotions' in education that visibly distract from classroom goals, largely unrelated to student overall development, or cultivating a sustainable environment for flourishing. Yet from a broader view, such approaches often fail to cultivate students as good social actors, as they do not encourage interacting with the world, and working to change it for the better, beyond oneself and their school.

To restate it, the main problem here boils down to a challenge faced in moral education more generally, which has been mentioned in some previous chapters as the 'chicken-and-egg' problem. Should we (educators, politicians, researchers) emphasise in educational contexts the need for and value of changing the political-economic and social system, which is as a totality unwieldy, hardly decipherable, and nearly immeasurable? Or should we aim to change people, namely children as individuals, who are widely seen to be more responsive, flexible, and manageable? This question hinges on a broader quandary, about whether schooling should be a practice of social conservation and preservation, or a process of social reflection and societal transformation.

The response to these questions is obvious: Education should do both. It should prepare the next generation to live in the world of the present effectively, while it should also prepare them in part for a future, inevitably dynamic, which is the world young people will inherit. In this context, it is not wrong to cultivate emotions in line with status quo understandings and expectations, as young people must learn to be in a community and society, and function well within it. However, the problem is when this is done as the only form of moral and civic education, in narrow-minded and rigid ways, and as the main means of reaction to a status quo that is not infrequently harmful, unjust, and otherwise problematic.

Looking at curricula around the world from a broad view, civic and citizenship education is being replaced in many societies with education of emotional virtues or related character education, with this being justified as what is desired (within societies, and by parents and teachers), and as what 'works' (Jackson, 2019a). Yet such curricula only work in a limited and partial way, as explored here. It 'works' primarily to discipline and pacify young people, to make them manageable and attentive for the time being, with (mostly immediately observable) benefits, for themselves and for others around them. It also 'works', in that once students learn about emotional control and its apparent benefits, they can speak about emotional control and its apparent benefits, like they can learn to communicate, and thereby demonstrate proficiency with, aspects of maths, science, and grammar. Yet moral and political questions have been evaded here in favour of the instrumental, and in favour of a false sense of certainty.

Social and emotional learning, virtues education, and related character education approaches thus appear to 'work' particularly for educators and educational leaders, who are held as accountable in society for demonstrating visible learning of students, and for maintaining discipline and a sense of safety and security in classrooms. These are, to be fair, increasingly difficult, nearly impossible jobs in many places. These are difficult jobs, because intangible skills – soft skills, twenty-first-century skills, and the like – have become as valuable if not more valuable than tangible ones, in schools and in society. Meanwhile, societies around the world are experienced as less and less secure, and as more unsafe and precarious for many people, making it increasingly difficult to take for granted that schools and classrooms are or ever can be generally 'safe' places for all students. With climate change and other social challenges appearing ever present today, caring teachers and those with a sense of moral duty toward their students may feel lost in doing this work, with no foundational knowledge that can be safely relied upon, in light of the urgency of young people's needs for well-being, and for assistance with understanding their role in the world.

Thus, a quick but ultimately problematic solution has been implemented to tackle these unwieldy problems – work on young people's feelings and emotional grammar, with clear-cut instructions and assessable curricula – but this precludes deep consideration of larger important questions, about whether and how civic education for enhanced social participation and organisation, and for changing society, can also 'work'. How could education to enhance social justice and moral understanding in relation to societal matters work, and how should it work? What specifically is left out of the picture when the end of civic and moral education is (a particular narrow vision of) demonstrated personal well-being? These questions do not have easy answers, and answers that come to mind may not be conceded across diverse members of a society. Yet if there is agreement that young people should learn to act against harm and injustice in the world, emotional self-cultivation cannot be the only strategy.

In line with a more critical understanding of psychological research findings, virtue ethics, and other relevant moral and political philosophies, students should not be discouraged from thinking about and taking action, in relation to negative, harmful experiences they face and observe in society. Furthermore, young people should be encouraged to also critically reflect on dogmatic approaches to emotional virtues, which blame people for their lack of emotional self-control, but do not query social injustices and harmful social structures seen at the same time. Young people should learn to act, not just feel, in education. And they should be encouraged to think about larger matters of justice and taking moral action in relation to their feelings. Social and emotional learning and character education as study of the self, devoid of relations and an external world, cannot be the total means, or effectively dictate the ends, of moral education. Being a good person in society is not just about having and expressing good feelings. Indeed, most would say that this really misses the point. Instead, studying good action, not just good feelings, is important if schools are to cultivate good moral and political beings and actors.

Teachers and other types of educators must develop and ensure a better balance between moral and other social education, as a means to develop young people with good character and good behaviour. Here, good behaviour does not just mean sitting still and being obedient, but it also involves critically questioning and observing harm and injustice, and taking actions in relation to them. In this context, teachers should also recognise that students will have bad days and bad experiences that may require more active responses than cognitive reframing. There may also be many cases where emotional virtues education can go wrong, and incidentally send unhelpful messages to learners, against educators' best intentions. The previous chapters gave various examples of these possible risks and challenges. While these risks and challenges need not signal the demise of social and emotional learning approaches, they signal that educating emotional virtues is not a perfectly controlled practice in the real world. As the real world is complex, diverse, and far from ideal, so too is emotional virtues education. In this domain teachers and educators should proceed with caution rather than zealotry, to enable positive experiences and possibilities for young people coming from across society.

If a student expresses anger, anxiety, or sadness in class, they can be encouraged to focus on ways to alleviate their negative or upsetting experiences of these feelings. Yet they should not be framed as lone individuals by the teacher, in this quest. Their anger, anxiety, or sadness is not simply related to their inner state, so it can be disingenuous to encourage students to take accountability for their feelings in a simplistic way. Teachers can remind all students in such cases that they can take responsibility for one another's experiences, to some extent, as they all play roles in a community context. Teachers can also encourage students to recognise their feelings not as simply good or bad, to cultivate or to diminish. They can teach a complex grammar of emotions that also recognises diverse views about emotions in social life.

That is, students can be encouraged to understand more deeply what emotions are: that emotions are fluid and dynamic; that they can sometimes be difficult to define or distinguish from related mental and emotional states; that they can be loosely or directly related to understandings, beliefs, and perceptions about the world; that sometimes it can help to 'work on' them and try to relieve them through focus and reflection, while at other times they are benefited more by acceptance, by oneself and others, or 'waiting them out'. Here, an important implication is that it is not productive to frame emotions as always following a precise formula, as always having reasons or being reasonable, as always being the same thing, and as always malleable to direct positive (moral) impact, through the immediate use of cognitive training. Finally, part of understanding emotions as social and relational is that students learn that they can help those around them by appreciating that emotions are experienced in diverse and complex ways across communities. This also implies that students learn to be careful in judging and applying feelings rules to themselves or others in a harsh way, and can instead develop a more reflective disposition toward emotional experiences and expressions among others, as in their own case.

One might ask here what teachers are to encourage young people to do exactly, beyond working on their understanding of emotions, in societies increasingly marked by widespread ideological and partisan controversy, and declining levels of confidence in political and social leaders. In the real world, teachers do not want to be seen as partisan or indoctrinatory, but often are idealised as (impossibly) politically neutral. Thus, the inward-looking focus in moral and civic education also 'works' for educators, because it serves to free them from potential risks of unfair accusations, about using their role to politically brainwash, or otherwise spread inappropriately ideological messages to students (Jackson, 2019a). This challenge, although real, is quite paradoxical upon further reflection. As noted here, pedagogies of control are often unthinkingly employed in education, as simply useful for manipulating 'academic' emotions (Maxwell & Reichenbach, 2007), while the major challenges of enacting a pedagogy for student autonomy in this context have hardly been explored.

This is an important issue that cannot be fully addressed here. However, there is low-hanging fruit in this case, and clear possibilities to begin to reach toward. At least, teachers can encourage students to understand emotional virtues as requiring (sometimes or often) action, not just an even temperament. Exploring moral decision making, beyond virtue ethics or positive psychology orientations, can be easily done in a nonpartisan way in schools, to indicate as an enduring challenge knowing what to *do*, as well as what to feel, in politically charged environments (including classrooms and playgrounds), when one encounters injustices and other ills. This means that teaching emotional virtues should not remain superficial and idealistic, but it should concede grey and fuzzy areas, uncomfortable and maybe even impossible choices, and the burdens that can often accompany aiming to cultivate and realise emotional virtues.

As discussed in previous chapters, educators can also explore as part of moral and civic education heroism as found within collective social movements, and not just in a few actions and words of (impossibly) saintly individuals. While common practices of education for emulation of heroic individuals often serve to obscure significant aspects of their lives, such as their ties to others around them, this can be easily remedied through engaging students in a more reflective, deeper examination of heroes' lives and communities, which may require going beyond the textbook or model lesson plan. Thus, educators can explore with students what it means to be a good and just person within interpersonal relationships, in communities, and within societies, and various means of effectively organising and sustainably identifying with collective others. Students can also learn to appreciate that the right thing for people as individual or collective actors to do is not usually given by school curricula, or any other 'rules for life', in this context; practical judgement is also needed, to consider what virtues and principles are relevant, and what unique situations demand.

None of this requires educators to push students to the front lines of particular political battles. On the other hand, it does require that students and teachers grapple with political and moral complexity in classrooms, where lessons do not have clear right and wrong answers, when it comes to what people as individuals and communities should do. Yet this is what teaching students to understand the real world demands. Meanwhile, encouraging students to look only at themselves in understanding the solutions to all the world's predicaments hardly helps students to grow as moral persons, as individuals, or as members of society. As seen here, it may not even help many of them at all, beyond providing a short-term means of ensuring a well-disciplined classroom that can keep on studying and 'getting on with it'.

Furthermore, in neglecting societal causes of challenges faced, such emotional virtues education, which looks inward only or primarily, and places responsibility for emotions on students as individuals, can implicitly promote individualism and self-centeredness, in not focusing attention to society engagement and interconnection. The focus on cultivation of oneself apart from others provides no clear paths for aiding others and contributing to society, through social actions and relations. A more balanced approach can empower students to develop themselves in connection with others, not losing sight of how ultimately goodness cannot be understood or pursued meaningfully in the human world without relations.

*****

The perspective in this book may seem pessimistic at times. Yet emotional virtues education is often justified in relation to observing that large numbers of young people are suffering from structural disadvantage and patterned forms of negative vulnerability which make happiness and optimism an abnormal state for them, without interventions. Life is challenging at many times even for fortunate people. Many regard suffering as an essential part of life, regardless of their view of the merits of suffering, or lack thereof. For the majority of people, young and old alike, hardships are often if not always present, while serious risks and harms remain unfortunately close at hand. Imagining Rousseau's Emile, it is lovely to think about how to educate the emotions of children living in a world of safety and security, with unbounded joy and safely caring relations, who can easily learn to benefit others, in recognition of and with gratitude for all of the benefits they have received. However, I am also interested in thinking about how to improve life and education for ordinary people in the world of today.

Thinking of young people preparing for standardised tests around the world, thereby crafting keys meant to ensure their future financial and physical security, why should they not learn to feel joy and gratitude, caring for others and creating a more hopeful and courageous world through their acts? Who would deny that many of them might be able to use a bit of grit, as the stakes seem ever higher in this fast-paced and challenging time?

In this context, young people can and should also be given tools to redesign the imperfect, and often highly problematic environments they find themselves in, rather than just bend themselves emotionally (and otherwise) in relation to them. Young people can learn to protect what is good in the world, while collaboratively reconceptualising and reorganising their societies, so that cruel and crass competitive testing regimes (among other things) do not continue to dictate to them and others what counts as good (i.e. grit), while they also serve to sort young people en masse in the world into either positions of political and material hardship and continuous suffering, or less tragic and hopeless forms of precariousness.

Things in the world need to change, and young people's initial dispositions and responses to the world are not particularly urgent among them. It is not the duty of young people to smile and persevere in dysfunctional and unjust societies. They can and should feel more, and learn and be empowered to do more. Learning the right feeling rules, as seen in virtue ethics, positive psychology, and related views of emotions, is not only insufficient in this context. It risks distracting attention from more essential factors in personal and social flourishing. Emotional virtues education can complement an education to cultivate effective moral and political participation in society, but it cannot replace it. Students need to learn how to engage, not only how to disengage, with the challenges of life.

Beyond the cultivation of emotional virtues, young people need to learn how to operate in relations with others in a positive and effective way, in a world marked by injustice and risks of harm, recognising that any real virtue is not just an inside emotional issue, but must also be an outward disposition toward reasoned moral action. A broader and deeper view of the complex grammar of emotional virtues in society can benefit educators and students to be not only good achieving educators and students in the classroom, but also effective social actors, who can contribute meaningfully to a more equitable and just world.

References

Abeles, V. (2015). *Beyond Measure: Rescuing an Overscheduled, Overtested, Underestimated Generation*. New York: Simon & Schuster.

Abiola, T. & Udofia, O. (2011). Psychometric assessment of the Wagnild and Young's resilience scale in Kano, Nigeria. *BMC Research Notes*, 4, 509.

Adorno, T. (1941). On popular music. *Studies in Philosophy and Social Science*. New York: Institute of Social Research, IX, pp. 17–48.

Ahmed, S. (2010). *The Promise of Happiness* . Durham: Duke University Press.

Ahmed, S. (2004a). *The Cultural Politics of Emotion*. Edinburgh: Edinburgh University Press.

Ahmed, S. (2004b). Affective economies. *Social Text*, 79(2), 117–39.

Ainsworth, M. D. & Bell, S. M. (1970). Attachment, exploration, and separation: illustrated by the behaviour of one-year-olds in a strange situation. *Child Development*, 41, 49–67.

Aldao, A. (2013). The future of emotional regulation research capturing context. *Perspectives on Psychological Science*, 8(2), 155–72.

Alexander, H. (2013). Caring and agency: Noddings on happiness in education. *Educational Philosophy and Theory*, 45(5), 488–93.

Alexandrova, A. (2016). The science of well-being. In G. Fleter, ed., *The Routledge Handbook of Philosophy of Well-Being*. London: Routledge, pp. 389–401.

Algoe, S. B. (2012). Find, remind, and bind: the functions of gratitude in everyday relationships. *Social and Personality Psychology Compass*, 6, 455–69.

Allen, S. (2018). Do men have a gratitude problem? *Greater Good Magazine*, August 15.

Allen, V., Maccann, C., Matthews, G., & Roberts, R. D. (2014). Emotional intelligence in education: from pop to emerging science. In R. Pekrun & L. Linnenbrink-Garcia, eds., *International Handbook of Emotions in Education*. London: Routledge, pp. 162–82.

Alloy, L. B. & Abramson, L. Y. (1988). Depressive realism: four theoretical perspectives. In L. B. Alloy, ed., *Cognitive Processes in Depression*. New York: Guilford Press, pp. 223–65.

American Psychological Association (APA). (2019). Anger. *APA Online*.

Angle, S. C. & Slote, M., eds. (2013). *Virtue Ethics and Confucianism*. New York: Routledge.

Appiah, K. A. (2008). *Experiments in Ethics*. Cambridge: Harvard University Press.

Appiah, K. A. (1994). Identity, authenticity, survival: multicultural societies and social reproduction. In A. Gutmann, ed., *Multiculturalism: Exploring the Politics of Recognition*. Princeton: Princeton University Press, pp. 149–64.

Applebaum, B. (2017). Comforting discomfort as complicity: white fragility and the pursuit of invulnerability. *Hypatia: A Journal of Feminist Philosophy*, 32(4), 862–75.

Applebaum, B. (2016). Needing not to know: ignorance, innocence, denials, and discourse. In E. Duarte, ed., *Philosophy of Education 2015*. Urbana: Philosophy of Education Society, pp. 448–56.

Applebaum, B. (1998). Is caring inherently good? In S. Tozer, ed., *Philosophy of Education 1998*. Urbana: Philosophy of Education Society, pp. 415–22.

Aristotle. (1984). *The Complete Works of Aristotle: The Revised Oxford Translation*, ed. J. Barnes. Princeton: Princeton University Press.

Arthur, J., ed. (2019). *Virtues in the Public Sphere*. Abingdon: Routledge.

Arthur, J., Harrison, T., Carr, D., Kristjánsson, K. & Davison, I. (2014). *Knightly Virtues: Enhancing Virtue Literacy through Stories*. Birmingham: Jubilee Centre.

Arthur, J., Kristjánsson, K., Gulliford, L., & Morgan, B. (2015). *An Attitude for Gratitude: How Gratitude is Understood, Experienced and Valued by the British Public*. Birmingham: Jubilee Centre.

Arthur, J., Walker, D. I. & Thoma, S. (2018). *Soldier of Character: Research Report*. Birmingham: Jubilee Centre.

Averill, J. R. (2012). Anger. In V. S. Ramachandran, ed., *Encyclopedia of Human Behavior*, 2nd ed. London: Elsevier, pp. 37–144.

Azevedo, R., Taub, M., Mudrick, N., Farnsworth, J., & Martin, S. A. (2016). Interdisciplinary research methods used to investigate emotions with advanced learning technologies. In M. Zembylas & P. A. Schutz, eds., *Methodological Advances in Research on Emotion and Education*. Cham: Springer, pp. 231–44.

Bailey, A. (2018). On anger, silence, and epistemic injustice. *Royal Institute of Philosophy Supplement*, 84, 93–115.

Banks, J. A. (2008). *An Introduction to Multicultural Education*. Boston: Pearson.

Baron-Cohen, S. (2003). *The Essential Difference: Males, Females, and the Truth about Autism*. New York: Basic.

Bartky, S. (1990). On psychological oppression. In S. L. Bartky, ed., *Femininity and Domination: Studies in the Phenomenology of Oppression*. New York: Routledge, pp. 22–32.

Bartlett, M. Y. & DeSteno, D. (2006). Gratitude and prosocial behaviour: helping when it costs. *Psychological Science*, 17(4), 319–25.

Batson, C. D. (1991). *The Altruism Question: Toward a Social-Psychological Answer*. Hillsdale: Erlbaum.

Bazzano, A. N., Anderson, C. E., Hylton, C., & Gustat, J. (2018). Effect of mindfulness and yoga on quality of life for elementary school students and teachers: results of a randomized controlled school-based study. *Psychological Research and Behavior Management*, 11, 81–9.

Beltman, S., Mansfield, C., & Price, A. (2011). Thriving, not just surviving: a review of research on teacher resilience. *Educational Research Review*, 6(3), 185–207.

Ben-Porath, S. (2017). *Free Speech on Campus*. Philadelphia: University of Pennsylvania Press.

Ben-Porath, S. (2008). Care ethics and dependence – rethinking jus post bellum. *Hypatia: A Journal of Feminist Philosophy*, 23(2), 61–71.

Bentall, R. P. (1992). A proposal to classify happiness as a psychiatric disorder. *Journal of Medical Ethics*, 18, 94–8.

Bentham, J. (1789/2005). *An Introduction to the Principles of Morals and Legislation*. Boston: Adamant Media Corporation.

Berges, S. (2015). *A Feminist Perspective on Virtue Ethics*. New York: Palgrave Macmillan.

Berila, B. (2016). *Integrating Mindfulness into Anti-Oppression Pedagogy: Social Justice in Higher Education*. London: Routledge.

Berkowitz, L. & Harmon-Jones, E. (2004). Toward an understanding of the determinants of anger. *Emotion*, 4(2), 107–30.

Berland, L. (2011). *Cruel Optimism*. Durham: Duke University Press.

Biesta, G. J. J. (2017). *The Rediscovery of Teaching*. London: Routledge.

Biesta, G. J. J. (2007). Why 'what works' won't work: evidence-based practice and the democratic deficit in educational research. *Educational Theory*, 57 (1), 1–22.

Bluhm, R. (2017). Gender and empathy. In H. L. Maibom, ed., *The Routledge Handbook of Philosophy of Empathy*. New York: Routledge, pp. 377–87.

Blum, L. A. (1980). *Friendship, Altruism, and Morality*. London: Routledge.

Boler, M. (2004). All speech is not free: the ethics of 'affirmative action pedagogy'. *Counterpoints*, 240, 3–13.

Boler, M. (1999). *Feeling Power: Emotions and Education*. New York: Routledge.

Boler, M. & Zembylas, M. (2016). Interview with Megan Boler: from 'feminist politics of emotions' to the 'affective turn'. In M. Zembylas & P. A. Schutz, eds., *Methodological Advances in Research on Emotion and Education*. Cham: Springer, pp. 17–30.

Borum, R., Cornell, D. G., Modzeleski, W., & Jimerson, S. R. (2010). What can be done about school shootings? A review of the evidence. *Educational Researcher*, 39(1), 27–37.

Brackett, M. A. & Rivers, S. E. (2014). Transforming students' lives with social and emotional learning. In R. Pekrun & L. Linnenbrink-Garcia, eds., *International Handbook of Emotions in Education*. London: Routledge, pp. 1368–88.

Brekke, T. (1999). The role of fear in Indian religious thought with special reference to Buddhism. *Journal of Indian Philosophy*, 27, 439–67.

Brewer, R. & Murphy, J. (2016). People with autism can read emotions, feel empathy. *Scientific American*, July 13.

Bronfenbrenner, U. (1979) *The Ecology of Human Development: Experiments by Nature and Design*. Cambridge: Harvard University Press.

Brown, B. (2014). *Daring Greatly: How the Courage to be Vulnerable Transforms the Way We Live, Love, Parent, and Lead*. New York: Penguin.

Brownell, C. A. & Kopps, C. B. (2007). *Socioemotional Development in the Toddler Years: Transitions and Transformations*. New York: Guilford Press.

Buber, M. (1947). *Between Man and Man*. London: Routledge.

Burman, E. (1994). *Deconstructing Developmental Psychology*. London: Routledge.

Burns, R. G. & Crawford, C. (1999). School shootings, the media, and public fear: ingredients for a moral panic. *Crime Law and Social Change*, 32(2), 147–68.

Bush, M. (2011). Mindfulness in higher education. *Contemporary Buddhism*, 12 (1), 183–97.

Butler, J. (2004). *Precarious Life: The Powers of Mourning and Violence*. New York: Verso.

Butler, J. (1990). *Gender trouble*. London: Routledge.

Bywater, T. & Sharples, J. (2012). Effective evidence-based interventions for emotional well-being: lessons for policy and practice. *Research Papers in Education*, 27(4), 409–22.

Cacioppo, J. T., Tassinary, L. G., & Bernston, G. G. (2007). Psychophysiological science: interdisciplinary approaches to classic questions about the mind. In J. Cacioppo, L. G. Tassinary, & G. G. Bernston, eds., *The Handbook of Psychophysiology*. Cambridge: Cambridge University Press, pp. 1–18.

Cadwalladr, C. (2018). 'I made Steve Bannon's psychological warfare tool': meet the data war whistleblower. *The Guardian*, March 18.

Callan, E. (1997). *Creating Citizens*. Oxford: Oxford University Press.

Card, C. (1990). Caring and evil. *Hypatia: A Journal of Feminist Philosophy*, 5(1), 101–08.

Card, C. (1988). Gratitude and obligation. *American Philosophical Quarterly*, 25, 115–27.

Carr, D. (2015). Is gratitude a moral virtue? *Philosophical Studies*, 172, 1475–84.

Carr, D., Arthur, J., & Kristjánsson, K. (2017). Varieties of virtue ethics: introduction. In D. Carr, J. Arthur, & K. Kristjánsson, eds., *Varieties of Virtue Ethics*. London: Palgrave MacMillan, pp. 1–14.

Carr, D., Morgan, B., & Gulliford, L. (2015). Learning and teaching virtuous gratitude. *Oxford Review of Education*, 41, 766–81.

Carr, D. & Steutel, J. (1999). The virtue approach to moral education: pointers, problems and prospects. In D. Carr & J. Steutel, eds., *Virtue Ethics and Moral Education*. London: Routledge, pp. 241–55.

Cassidy, S. (2015). Resilience building in students: the role of academic self-efficacy. *Frontiers in Psychology*, 6, 1781.

Chafe, W. H. (1981). *Civilities and Civil Rights: Greensboro, North Caroline and the Black Struggle for Freedom*. Oxford: Oxford University Press.

Challen, A., Noden, P., West, A., & Machin, S. (2010). *UK Resilience Programme Evaluation: Final Report*. London: Department of Education.

Character First. (2019a). *Family Connection*. Oklahoma City: Character First.

Character First. (2019b). *Gratefulness Story*. Oklahoma City: Character First.

Character First. (2019c). *Courage Story*. Oklahoma City: Character First.

Character First. (2019d). *Glory of Freedom*. Oklahoma City: Character First.

Character First. (2019e). *Self-Control Story*. Oklahoma City: Character First.

Character First. (2019f). *Forgiveness Story*. Oklahoma City: Character First.

Character First. (1997). *Gratefulness*. Oklahoma City: Character First.

Chatel, A. (2015). The 6 biggest yoga scandals, from Bikram Choudry to Lululemon. *Bustle*, April 2.

Chen, J. & Caicedo, C. (2018). *Understanding Quality Guanxi in China – A Study on Vigor Group*. Master Thesis. Gavle: University of Gavle.

Chi, Z. & Hong, S.-J. (2017). *Guanxi* culture: how it affects the business model of Chinese firms. In E. Paulet & C. Rowley, eds., *The China Business Model: Originality and Limits*. Cambridge: Elsevier, pp. 19–40.

Chouliaraki, L. (2010). Post-humanitarianism: humanitarian communication beyond a politics of pity. *International Journal of Cultural Studies*, 13(2), 107–26.

Cialdini, R. B., Brown, S. L., Lewis, B. P., Luce, C., & Neuberg, S. L. (1997). Reinterpreting the empathy-altruism relationship: when one into one equals oneness. *Journal of Personality and Social Psychology*, 73, 481–94.

Cieslik, M. (2016). *The Happiness Riddle and the Quest for a Good Life*. London: Palgrave Macmillan.

Cigman, R. (2012). We need to talk about well-being. *Research Papers in Education*, 27(4), 449–62.

Clark, A. E., Fleche, S., Layard, R., Powdthavee, N., & Ward, G. (2018). *The Origins of Happiness: The Science of Well-being over the Life Course*. Princeton: Princeton University Press.

Colby, A. & Kohlberg, L. (1987). *The Measurement of Moral Judgment, Vol. 1. Theoretical Foundations and Research Validation: Vol. 2. Standard Issue Scoring Manual*. New York: Cambridge University Press.

Cole, A. (2016). All of us are vulnerable, but some are more vulnerable than others: the political ambiguity of vulnerability studies, an ambivalent critique. *Critical Horizons: A Journal of Philosophy and Social Theory*, 2, 260–77.

Conoley, C. W., Conoley, J. C., Spaventa-Vancil, K. Z., & Lee, A. N. (2014). Positive psychology in schools: good ideas are never enough. In M. J. Furlong, R. Gilman, & E. S. Huebner, eds., *Handbook of Positive Psychology in Schools*, 2nd ed. New York: Routledge, pp. 497–506.

Cook, N. (2012). 'I'm here to help': development workers, the politics of benevolence and critical literacy. In V. de I. Andreotti & L. M. T. M. de Souza, eds., *Postcolonial Perspectives on Global Citizenship Education*. New York: Routledge.

Corbett, B. (1995). Moral obligations to distant others. *Webster Education*.

Coyne, J. C. & Tennen, H. (2010). Positive psychology in cancer care: bad science, exaggerated claims, and unproven medicine. *Annals of Behavioral Medicine*, 39(1), 16–26.

Crittenden, P. (1999). Justice, care, and other virtues: A critique of Kohlberg's theory of moral development. In D. Carr & J. Steutel, eds., *Virtue Ethics and Moral Education*. London: Routledge, pp. 169–83.

Crowell, S. (2015). Existentialism. In E. N. Zalta, ed., *The Stanford Encyclopedia of Philosophy*. plato.stanford.edu

Crown Prosecution Service (CPS). (2019). *Violence against Women and Girls Report, 2018–2019*. London: Crown Prosecution Service.

Cua, A. S. (1998). *Moral Vision and Tradition: Essays in Chinese Ethics*. Washington: The Catholic University of America Press.

Cudd, A. (2006). *Analyzing Oppression*. New York: Oxford University Press.

Curzer, H. J. (2017). Against idealization in virtue ethics. In D. Carr, J. Arthur and K. Kristjánsson, eds., *Varieties of Virtue Ethics*. London: Palgrave Macmillan, pp. 53–72.

D'Alessandro, A. H. (2015). Lawrence Kohlberg's legacy: radicalizing the educational mainstream. In B. Zizek, D. Garz, & E. Nowak, eds., *Kohlberg Revisited. Moral Development and Citizenship Education*. Rotterdam: Sense Publishers, pp. 27–49.

Dahlbeck, J. (2013). Hope and fear in education for sustainable development. *Critical Studies in Education*, 2, 154–69.

Davies, B. (1987). Marriage and the construction of reality revisited: an educational exercise in rewriting social theory to include women's experience. *Educational Philosophy and Theory*, 19(1), 12–22.

Davis, M. (1996). *Empathy: A Social Psychological Approach*. Boulder: Westview Press.

De Beauvoir, S. (1949/1984). *The Second Sex*. Trans. H. M. Pashley. Harmondsworth: Penguin.

Decety, J. & Yoder, K. J. (2016). Empathy and motivation for justice: cognitive empathy and concern, but not emotional empathy, predict sensitivity to injustice for others. *Social Neuroscience*, 11(1), 1–14.

Deci E. L. & Ryan, R. M. (1985). *Intrinsic Motivation and Self-Determination in Human Behaviour*. New York: Plenum.

Decuir-Gunby, J. T. & Williams-Johnson, M. R. (2014). The influence of culture on emotions: implications for education. In R. Pekrun & L. Linnenbrink-Garcia, eds., *International Handbook of Emotions in Education*. London: Routledge, pp. 539–58.

Demetriou, H. (2018). *Empathy, Emotion and Education*. London: Palgrave Macmillan.

Denham, A. E. (2017). Empathy and moral motivation. In H. Maibom, ed., *The Routledge Handbook of Philosophy of Empathy*. New York: Routledge, pp. 227–41.

Derntl, B., Finkelmeyer, A., Eickhoff, S., Kellermann, T., Falkenberg, D. I., Schneider, F., & Habel, U. (2010). Multidimensional assessment of empathetic abilities: neural correlates and gender differences. *Psychoneuroendocrinology*, 35(1), 67–82.

Doris, J. M. (2005). *Lack of Character: Personality and Moral Behavior*. Cambridge: Cambridge University Press.

Draaisma, M. (2019). Larger high school class sizes will make Ontario students more resilient, education minister says. CBC News, March 20.

Dreyfus, G. (2011). Is mindfulness present-centred and non-judgmental? A discussion of the cognitive dimensions of mindfulness. *Contemporary Buddhism*, 12(1), 41–54.

Dubs, H. H. (1951). The development of altruism in Confucianism. *Philosophy East and West*, 1(1), 48–55.

Duckworth, A. (2016). *Grit: The Power of Passion and Perseverance*. New York: Scribner.

Durkheim, E. (1951). *Suicide, a Study in Sociology*. New York: Free Press.

Duschinsky, R., Greco, M., & Solomon, J. (2015). The politics of attachment: lines of flight with Bowlby, Deleuze and Guattari. *Theory, Culture and Society*, 32 (7–8), 173–95.

Dweck, C. S. (2007). *Mindset: The New Psychology of Success*. London: Ballantine Books.

Eberhardt, J. L. (2019). *Biased: Uncovering the Hidden Prejudice that Shapes What We See, Think, and Do*. New York: Penguin Random House.

Ecclestone, K. (2012). From emotional and psychological well-being to character education: challenging policy discourses of behavioural science and 'vulnerability'. *Research Papers in Education*, 27(4), 463–80.

Ecclestone, K. & Goodley, D. (2016). Political and educational springboard or straitjacket? Theorising post/human subjects in an age of vulnerability. *Discourse: Studies in the Cultural Politics of Education*, 37(2), 175-88.

Education Bureau. (2017). *A Resource Handbook for Schools: Detecting, Supporting, and Making Referral for Students with Suicidal Behaviours*. Hong Kong: Education Bureau.

Ehrenreich, B. (2009). *Bright-Sided: How Positive Thinking is Undermining America*. New York: Holt & Company.

Eisenberg, N. & Strayer, J. (1987). *Empathy and Its Development*. Cambridge: Cambridge University Press.

Elias, M. J. & Moceri, D. C. (2014). Developing social and emotional aspects of learning: the American experience. *Research Papers in Education*, 27:4, 423–34.

Emmons, R. & McCullough, M. (2003). Counting blessings versus burdens: an experimental investigation of gratitude and subjective well-being in daily life. *Personality & Social Psychology*, 88, 377–89.

Emmons, R. & Mishra, A. (2011). Why gratitude enhances well-being: what we know, what we need to know. In K. M. Sheldon, T. B. Kashdan, & M. F. Steger, eds., *Designing Positive Psychology: Taking Stock and Moving Forward*. Oxford: Oxford University Press, pp. 248–62.

Engers, J. & Teichler, U. (1997). A victim of their own success? Employment and working conditions of academic staff in comparative perspective. *Higher Education*, 34, 347–72.

Epley, K. (2015). Care ethics and Confucianism: caring through *li*. *Hypatia: A Journal of Feminist Philosophy*, 30(4), 881–96.

Ergas, O. (2019). Mindfulness *in*, as, and *of* education: three roles of mindfulness in education. *Journal of Philosophy of Education*, published online first.

Fanon, F. (1961). *The Wretched of the Earth*. Paris: Maspero.

Fast, J. D. (2003). After Columbine: how people mourn sudden death. *Social Work*, 48(4), 484–91.

Fineman, M. A. (2008). The vulnerable subject: anchoring equality in the human condition. *Yale Journal of Law & Feminism*, 20(1), 1-23.

Fitzgerald, P. (1998). Gratitude and justice. *Ethics*, 109, 119–53.

Foot, P. (1967). The problem of abortion and the doctrine of the double effect, *Oxford Review*, 5, 1–6.

Foucault, M. (1984). *The Foucault Reader*. New York: Random House.

Foucault, M. (1979). *Discipline and Punish*. New York: Vintage.

Fowers, B. (1991). His and her marriage: a multivariate study of gender and marital satisfaction . *Sex Roles*, 4(3–4), 209–21.

Fox, N. A., Schmidt, L. A., Henderson, H. A., & Marshall, P. J. (2007). Developmental psychophysiology: conceptual and methodological issues. In J. Cacioppo, L. G. Tassinary, & G. G. Bernston, eds., *The Handbook of Psychophysiology*. Cambridge: Cambridge University Press, pp. 453–81.

Frankl, V. E. (1973) *The Doctor and the Soul*. New York: Vintage Books.

Frederickson, B. (2009). *Positivity: Discover the Upward Spiral that Will Change Your Life*. New York: Random House.

Frederickson, B. (2004). Gratitude, like other positive emotions, broadens and builds. In R. A. Emmons & M. E. McCullough, eds., *The Psychology of Gratitude*. Oxford: Oxford University Press, pp. 145–66.

Freiberg, H. (1993). A school that fosters resilience in inner-city youth. *The Journal of Negro Education*, 62(3), 364–76.

Frenzel, A. C. (2014). Teacher emotions. In R. Pekrun & L. Linnenbrink-Garcia, eds., *International Handbook of Emotions in Education*. London: Routledge, pp. 494–519.

Freund, H. (2019). Gratitude on the dark side of life: what can we learn from clients in psychotherapy? Paper at the International Conference: The Shadow Side of Gratitude, Erfurt, Germany.

Frey, B. S. (2008). *Happiness: A Revolution in Economics*. Cambridge: MIT Press.

Friborg, O., Hjembdal, O., Rosenvinge, J. H., & Martinussen, M. (2003). A new rating scale for adult resilience: what are the central protective resources behind healthy adjustment? *International Journal of Methods in Psychiatric Research*, 12(2), 65–76.

Friedland, N. (2005). Introduction–The 'elusive' concept of social resilience In N. Friedland, A. Arian, A. Kirschnbaum, A. Karin, & N. Fleischer, eds., *The Concept of Social Resilience*. Haifa: The Technion Samuel Neaman Institute, pp. 7–10.

Frijda, N. H. & Mesquita, B. (1994). The social role of emotions. In S. Kitayama & H. R. Markus, eds., *Emotion and Culture: Empirical Studies of Mutual Influence*. Washington: American Psychological Association, pp. 51–87.

Froh, J. J., Bono, G., Fan, J., Emmons, R. A., Henderson, K., Harris, C., Leggio, H., & Wood, A. M. (2014). Nice thinking! An educational intervention that teaches children to think gratefully. *School Psychology Review*, 42, 132–52.

Froh, J., Sefick, W., & Emmons, R. (2008). Counting blessings in early adolescents: an experimental study of gratitude and subjective well-being. *Journal of School Psychology*, 46, 213–33.

Fuda, P. & Badham, R. (2011). Fire, snowball, mask, movie: how leaders spark and sustain change. *Harvard Business Review* 89(11), 145–8.

Furedi, F. (2004). *Therapy Culture: Cultivating Vulnerability in an Uncertain Age.* London: Routledge.

Gallwey, S. K. & Wilgus, G. (2014). Equitable partnerships for mutual learning or perpetuator of north-south power imbalances? Ireland-South Africa school links. *Compare: A Journal of Comparative and International Education*, 44 (4), 522–44.

Gay, R. (2016). Who gets to be angry? *The New York Times*, June 10.

Gibbons, A. (2013). Like a stone: a happy death and the search for knowledge. *Educational Philosophy and Theory*, 45(11), 1092–103.

Gill, C. (2018). Stoicism today: an alternative approach to cultivating the virtues. In T. Harrison & D. I. Walker, eds., *The Theory and Practice of Virtue Education.* London: Routledge, pp. 44–55.

Gillham, J. E., Hamilton, J., Freres, D. R. Patton, K., & Gallop, R. (2006). Preventing depression among early adolescents in the primary care setting: a randomized controlled study of the Penn Resiliency Program. *Journal of Abnormal Child Psychology*, 34(2), 203–19.

Gilligan, C. (1982). *In a Different Voice.* Cambridge: Harvard University Press.

Gilligan, R. (2001). *Promoting Resilience: A Resource Guide on Working with Children in the Care System.* London: British Agencies for Adoption and Fostering.

Gilman, R., Huebner, E. S., & M. J. Furlong. (2014). Toward a science and practice of positive psychology in schools: a conceptual framework. In M. J. Furlong, R. Gilman, & E. S. Huebner, eds., *Handbook of Positive Psychology in Schools.* New York: Routledge, pp. 1–11.

Gilson, E. (2014). *The Ethics of Vulnerability: A Feminist Analysis of Social Life and Practice.* New York: Routledge.

Giner-Sorolla, R. (2012). *Judging Passions: Moral Emotions in Persons and Groups.* New York: Psychology Press.

Giraldi, T. (2017). *Unhappiness, Sadness and 'Depression': Antidepressants and the Mental Disorder Epidemic.* London: Palgrave Macmillan.

Girgus, J. & Yang, K. (2015). Gender and depression. *Current Opinion in Psychology*, 4, 53–60.

Godrej, F. (2016). The neoliberal yogi and the politics of yoga. *Political Theory*, 45 (6), 772–800.

Godwin, R. (2017). 'He said he could do what he wanted': the scandal that rocked Bikram yoga. *The Guardian*, February 18.

Goerlich, K. S. (2018). The multifaceted nature of alexithymia – A neuroscientific perspective. *Frontiers in Psychology*, 9(1614), 1–7.

Goleman, D., ed. (1997). *Healing Emotions: Conversations with the Dalai Lama on Mindfulness, Emotions, and Health.* Boston: Shambhala

Goleman, D. (1995). *Emotional Intelligence: Why It Can Matter More than IQ*. New York: Bantam.

Gorski, P. S. (2017). Recovered goods: Durkheimean Sociology as virtue ethics. In D. Carr, J. Arthur, & K. Kristjánsson, eds., *Varieties of Virtue Ethics*. London: Palgrave MacMillan, pp.181–98.

Gotlib, A., ed., (2018). *The Moral Psychology of Sadness*. London: Rowman and Littlefield.

Graham, S. & Taylor, A. Z. (2014). An attributional approach to emotional life in the classroom. In R. Pekrun & L. Linnenbrink-Garcia, eds., *International Handbook of Emotions in Education*. London: Routledge, pp. 96–119.

Grant, K. L. (2015). A list of yoga scandals involving gurus, teachers, students, sex and other inappropriate behaviour. *Yoga Lunchbox*, January 17.

Greco, S., Holmes, M., & McKenzie, J. (2015). Friendship and happiness from a sociological perspective. In M. Demir, ed., *Friendship and Happiness: Across Life-Span and Cultures*. London: Springer, pp. 19–28.

Greenberg, M. T. & Harris, A. R. (2011). Nurturing mindfulness in children and youth: current state of research. *Child Development Perspectives*, 6(2), 161–66.

Greene, J. (2013). *Moral Tribes: Emotion, Reason, and the Gap between Us and Them*. New York: Penguin.

Greene, J. (2007). The secret joke of Kant's soul. In W. Sinnott-Armstrong, ed., *Moral Psychology, Volume 3: The Neuroscience of Morality*. Cambridge: MIT Press, pp. 35–79.

Greene, J., Nystrom, L., Engell, A., Darlez, J., & Cohen, J. (2004). The neural bases of cognitive conflict and control in moral judgment. *Neuron*, 44, 389–400.

Grubb, W. L. & McDaniel, M. A. (2007). The fakability of bar-on's emotional quotient inventory short form: catch me if you can. *Human Performance*, 20, 43–59.

Guha, M. & Carson, J. (2014) Positive psychology, utilitarianism and the pursuit of happiness. *Journal of Mental Health*, 23(4), 159–61.

Gulliford, L. (2018). *Can I Tell You About Gratitude?* London: Jessica Kingsley Publishers.

Gulliford, L. & Morgan, B. (2019). Ingratiation: gratitude's vicious cousin. Paper at the International Conference: The Shadow Side of Gratitude, Erfurt, Germany.

Gulliford, L., Morgan, B., & Kristjánsson, K. (2013). Recent work on the concept of gratitude in philosophy and psychology. *Journal of Value Inquiry*, 47, 285–317.

Hahn, T. N. (1999). *The Heart of the Buddha's Teaching*. New York: Broadway Books.

Hall, D. L. & Ames, R. T. (1995). *Anticipating China: Thinking through the Narratives of Chinese and Western Culture*. Albany: State University of New York Press.

Hand, M. (2018). *A Theory of Moral Education*. London: Routledge.

Hand, M. (2011). Patriotism in schools. *Impact: Philosophical Perspectives on Education Policy*, 19, 1–40.

Harpham, E. J. (2004). Gratitude in the history of ideas. In R. A. Emmons & M. E. McCullough, eds., *The Psychology of Gratitude*. Oxford: Oxford University Press, pp. 19–36.

Harrington, A. & Dunne, J. D. (2015). When mindfulness is therapy: ethical qualms, historical perspectives. *American Psychologist*, 70(7), 621–31.

Harrison, T., Arthur, J., & Burn, E. (2016). *Character Education Evaluation Handbook for Schools*. Birmingham: Jubilee Centre.

Harrison, T. & Walker, D. I. (2018). *The Theory and Practice of Virtue Education*. London: Routledge.

Hattie, J. A. C. (2008). *Visible Learning: A Synthesis of Over 800 Meta-Analyses Relating to Achievement*. Oxon: Routledge.

Hawkins, J. (2017). *Feelings and Emotion-Based Learning: A New Theory*. New York: Springer.

Haybron, D. (2011). Happiness. In E. N. Zalta, ed., *The Stanford Encyclopedia of Philosophy*. https://plato.stanford.edu/cite.html

Haybron, D. M. (2008). *The Pursuit of Unhappiness: The Elusive Psychology of Well-Being*. New York: Oxford University Press.

Heidegger, M. (1962). *Being and Time*. Oxford: Blackwell.

Held, V. (2005). *The Ethics of Care*. Oxford: Oxford University Press.

Herr, R. S. (2003). Is Confucianism compatible with care ethics? A critique. *Philosophy East and West*, 53(4), 471–89.

Ho, S. M. Y., Duan, W., & Tang, S. C. M. (2014). The psychology of virtue and happiness in Western and Asian thought. In N. Snow & F. V. Trivigno, eds., *The Philosophy and Psychology of Character and Happiness*. London: Routledge, pp. 215–39.

Hochanadel, A. & Finamore, D. (2015). Fixed and growth mindset in education and how grit helps students persist in the face of adversity. *Journal of International Education Research*, 11(1), 47–50.

Hochschild, A. (1983). *The Managed Heart: Commercialisation of Human Feeling*. Berkeley: University of California Press.

Hoffman, M. (2000). *Empathy and Moral Development*. Cambridge: Cambridge University Press.

Hollan, D. (2017). Empathy across cultures. In H. L. Maibom, ed., *The Routledge Handbook of Philosophy of Empathy*. New York: Routledge, pp. 341–52.

Hong Kong Committee on Prevention of Student Suicides (2016). *Final Report*. Hong Kong: Education Bureau.

hooks, b. (1995). *Killing Rage: Ending Racism*. New York: Holt.

hooks, b. (1989). *Talking Back: Thinking Feminist, Thinking Black*. Cambridge: South End Press.

Hori, M. & Kamo, Y. (2018). Gender differences in happiness: the effects of marriage, social roles, and social support in East Asia. *Applied Research in Quality of Life*, 13(4), 839–57.

Houston, B. (1990). Caring and exploitation. *Hypatia: A Journal of Feminist Philosophy*, 5(1), 115–9.

Hoy, W. K. (2003). An analysis of enabling and mindful school structures: some theoretical, research and practical considerations. *Journal of Educational Administration*, 41(1), 87–109.

Hughes, P. M. & Warmke, B. (2017). Forgiveness. In E. N. Zalta, ed., *The Stanford Encyclopedia of Philosophy*. https://plato.stanford.edu/cite.html

Hung, R. (2014). To be *as* not to be: in search of an alternative humanism in light of early Daoism and deconstruction. *Journal of Philosophy of Education*, 49(3), 418–34.

van den Hurk, P. A., Wingens, T., Giommi, F., Barendregt, H. P., Speckens, A. E., & van Schie, H. T. (2011). On the relationship between the practice of mindfulness meditation and personality: an exploratory analysis of the mediating role of mindfulness skills. *Mindfulness*, 2(3), 194–200.

Hursthouse, R. (1999). *On Virtue Ethics*. Oxford: Oxford University Press.

Hyland, T. (2015). On the contemporary applications of mindfulness: some implications for education. *Journal of Philosophy of Education*, 49(2), 170–86.

Hyland, T. (2009). Mindfulness and the therapeutic function of education. *Journal of Philosophy of Education*, 43(1), 119–31.

Hytten, K. & Warren, J. (2003). Engaging whiteness: how racial power gets reified in education, *Qualitative Studies in Education*, 16(1), 65–89.

Ilyes, I. (2017). Empathy in Hume and Smith. In H. L. Maibom, ed., *The Routledge Handbook of Philosophy of Empathy*. New York: Routledge, pp. 98–109.

Immordino-Yang, M. H. & Christodoulou, J. A. (2014). Neuroscientific contributions to understanding and measuring emotions in educational contexts. In R. Pekrun & L. Linnenbrink-Garcia, eds., *International Handbook of Emotions in Education*. London: Routledge, pp. 607–24.

Jackson, L. (2019a). *Questioning Allegiance: Resituating Civic Education*. London: Routledge.

Jackson, L. (2019b). The smiling philosopher: emotional labor, gender, and harassment in conference spaces. *Educational Philosophy and Theory*, 51(7), 684–92.

Jackson, L. (2019c). Relations of blood? Racialization of civic identity in twenty-first century Hong Kong. *Discourse: Studies in the Cultural Politics of Education*, 40(6), 761–72.

Jackson, L. (2019d). Must children sit still? The dark biopolitics of mindfulness and yoga in education. *Educational Philosophy and Theory*, 52(2), 120–5.

Jackson, L. (2019e). Gratitude as a moral virtue and its implications for civic and social justice education. Paper at the International Conference: The Shadow Side of Gratitude, Erfurt, Germany.

Jackson, L. (2018a). Care and Justice. In P. Smeyers, ed., *International Handbook of Philosophy of Education*. Cham: Springer, pp. 951–64.

Jackson, L. (2018b). Reconsidering vulnerability in higher education. *Tertiary Education and Management*, 24(3), 232–41.

Jackson, L. (2017a). Leaning out of higher education: a structural, postcolonial perspective, *Policy Futures in Education*, 15(3), 295–308.

Jackson, L. (2017b). Altruism, non-relational care, and global citizenship education. In M. Moses, ed., *Philosophy of Education 2014*. Urbana: Philosophy of Education Society, pp. 409–15.

Jackson, L. (2017c). Questioning gratitude in an unequal world with reference to the work of Toni Morrison, *Concentric: Literary and Cultural Studies*, 43(1), 227–43.

Jackson, L. (2016). Why should I be grateful? The morality of gratitude in contexts marked by injustice. *Journal of Moral Education*, 45(3), 276–90.

Jackson, L. (2014a). *Muslims and Islam in US Education: Reconsidering Multiculturalism*. New York: Routledge.

Jackson, L. (2014b). 'Won't somebody think of the children?' Emotions, child poverty, and post-humanitarian possibilities for social justice education. *Educational Philosophy and Theory*, 46(9), 1069–108.

Jackson, L. (2013). They don't not want babies: globalizing philosophy of education and the social imaginary of international development. In C. Mayo, ed., *Philosophy of Education 2013*. Urbana: Philosophy of Education Society, pp. 353–61.

Jackson, L. (2007). The individualist? The autonomy of reason in Kant's philosophy and educational views. *Studies in Philosophy of Education*, 26, 335–44.

Jackson, L. & Muñoz-García, A. L. (2019). Reaction is not enough: decreasing gendered harassment in academic contexts in Chile, Hong Kong, and the United States. *Educational Theory*, 69(1), 17–34.

Jackson, L. & Peters, M. A., eds. (2019). *Feminist Theory in Diverse Productive Practices: An Educational Philosophy and Theory Gender and Sexualities Reader, Vol. VI*. London: Routledge.

Jacobs, J. (2017). Aristotelian ethical virtues: naturalism without measure. In D. Carr, J. Arthur, & K. Kristjánsson, eds., *Varieties of Virtue Ethics*. London: Palgrave Macmillan, pp. 125–42.

Jacobs, S. E. & Gross, J. J. (2014). Emotion regulation in education: conceptual foundations, current applications, and future directions. In R. Pekrun & L. Linnenbrink-Garcia, eds., *International Handbook of Emotions in Education*. London: Routledge, pp. 183–202.

James, W. (1982). *The Varieties of Religious Experience*. London: Fount.

Janov, A. (1991). *The New Primal Scream: Primal Therapy Twenty Years On*. Wilmington: Enterprise.

Jennings, J. R. & Gianaros, P. J. (2007). Methodology. In J. Cacioppo, L. G. Tassinary, and G. G. Bernston, eds., *The Handbook of Psychophysiology*. Cambridge: Cambridge University Press, pp. 812–33.

Johansson, J. & Svensson, F. (2018). Objections to virtue ethics. In N. Snow, ed., *The Oxford Handbook of Virtue*. Oxford: Oxford University Press, pp. 491–507.

Johnson, G. M. (1997). Resilient at-risk students in the inner city. *Revue des Sciences de L'Education de McGill*, 32(1), 35–50.

Jonas, M. (2012). Gratitude, resentment, and citizenship education. *Studies in Philosophy and Education*, 31, 29–46.

Jonson, C. L. (2017). Preventing school shootings: the effectiveness of safety measures. *Victims & Offenders*, 12(6), 956–73.

Jubilee Centre. (n.d.). *Character Education: Teacher's Guide*. Birmingham: Jubilee Centre.

Jubilee Centre. (2017). *A Framework for Character Education in Schools.* Birmingham: Jubilee Centre.

Jubilee Centre. (2014). *The Knightly Virtues.* Birmingham: Jubilee Centre.

Kanevsky, L, Corke, M., & Frangkiser, L. (2008). The academic resilience and psychosocial characteristics of inner-city English learners in a museum-based school program. *Education and Urban Society,* 40(4), 452–75.

Kang, S.-Y. (2006). Identity-centered multicultural care theory: white, black, and Korean caring, *Educational Foundations* 20(3–4).

Kant, I., (1981). *Lectures on Ethics,* L. Infield, trans. Cambridge: Hackett.

Kant, I. (1784/1970). Answer to the question: 'What is enlightenment?' In H. S. Reiss, ed., H. N. Nisbet, trans., *Kant: Political Writings.* Cambridge: Cambridge University Press.

Kant, I. (1797/1996). *The Metaphysics of Morals, in Practical Philosophy,* M. J. Gregor, trans. Cambridge: Cambridge University Press.

Kashdan, T. B., Mishra, A., Breen, W. E., & Froh, J. J. (2009). Gender differences in gratitude: examining appraisals, narratives, the willingness to express emotions, and changes in psychological needs. *Journal of Personality,* 77(3), 691–730.

Kavar, L. F. (2010). *Stumbling into Life's Lessons: Reflections on the Spiritual Journey.* Bloomington: iUniverse.

Kelsey, D. (2017). *Media and Affective Mythologies: Discourse, Archetypes and Ideology in Contemporary Politics.* London: Palgrave Macmillan.

Kennedy, J. F. (1956). *Profiles in Courage: Decisive Moments in the Lives of Celebrated Americans.* New York: Harper & Row.

Kennett, J. (2017). Empathy and psychopathology. In H. L. Maibom, ed., *The Routledge Handbook of Philosophy of Empathy.* New York: Routledge, pp. 364–76.

Kesebir, P. & Diener, E. (2014). A virtuous cycle: the relationship between happiness and virtue. In N. Snow & F. V. Trivigno, eds., *The Philosophy and Psychology of Character and Happiness.* London: Routledge, pp. 287–306.

Kimmel, M. (2017). *Angry White Men: American Masculinity at the End of an Era.* New York: Nation Books.

Kinnvall, C. (2013). Trauma and the politics of fear: Europe at the crossroads. In N. Demertzis, ed., *Emotions in Politics: The Affect Dimension in Political Tension.* London: Palgrave Macmillan, pp. 167–85.

Kohlberg, L. (1981). *The Psychology of Moral Development.* New York: Harper & Row.

Kohlberg, L., Levine, C., & Hewer, A. (1983). *Moral Stages: A Current Formulation and a Response to Critics.* London: Karger.

Konarzewski, K. (1992). Empathy and protest: two roots of heroic altruism. In P. M. Oliner, S. P. Oliner, L. Baron, L. A. Blum, D. L. Krebs, & M. Z. Smolenska, eds., *Embracing the Other: Philosophical, Psychological, and Historical Perspectives on Altruism.* New York: New York University Press.

Konstan, D. (2012). Epicurean happiness. A pig's life? *Journal of Ancient Philosophy,* 6(1), 1–22.

Konstan, D. (2001). *Pity Transformed.* London: Duckworth.

Koole, S. L., van Dillen, L. F., & Sheppes, G. (2011). The self-regulation of emotion. In K. D. Vohs & R. F. Baumeister, eds., *Handbook of Self-Regulation: Research, Theory, and Applications*. New York: Guilford Press, pp. 22–40.

Kranzler, A., Hoffman, L. J., Parks, A. C., & Gilham, J. E. (2014). Innovative models of dissemination for school-based interventions that promote youth resilience and well-being. In M. J. Furlong, R. Gilman, & E. S. Huebner, eds., *Handbook of Positive Psychology in Schools*. London: Routledge, pp. 381–98.

Kraut, R. (2018). Aristotle's ethics. In E. N. Zalta, ed., *The Stanford Encyclopedia of Philosophy*. https://plato.stanford.edu/cite.html

Kristjánsson, K. (2018). *Virtuous Emotions*. Oxford: Oxford University Press.

Kristjánsson, K. (2013a). Ten myths about character, virtue and virtue education – Plus three well-founded misgivings. *British Journal of Educational Studies*, 61(3), 269–87.

Kristjánsson, K. (2013b). *Virtues and Vices in Positive Psychology: A Philosophical Critique*. Cambridge: Cambridge University Press.

Kristjánsson, K. (2007). *Aristotle, Emotions, and Education*. London: Routledge.

Kristjánsson, K., Gulliford, L., Arthur, J., & Moller, F. (2017). *Gratitude and Related Character Virtues*. Birmingham: Jubilee Centre.

Kukar, P. (2016). 'The very unrecognizability of the other': Edith Stein, Judith Butler, and the pedagogical challenge of empathy, *Philosophical Inquiry in Education*, 24(1), 1–14.

Kupperman, J. J. (1995). The emotions of altruism, east and west. In J. Marks & R. T. Ames, eds., *Emotions in Asian Thought: A Dialogue in Comparative Philosophy*. New York: State University of New York, pp. 123–30.

Lambert, N. M., Graham, S. M., & Fincham, F. D. (2009). A prototype analysis of gratitude: varieties of gratitude experiences. *Personality and Social Psychology Bulletin*, 35, 1193–207.

Layard, R. & Clark, D. M. (2015). *Thrive: The Power of Psychological Therapy*. London: Penguin.

Lazarus, R. S. (1991). *Emotion and Adaptation*. Oxford: Oxford University Press.

Leighton, J. (2011). *The Battle for Compassion: Ethics in an Apathetic Universe*. Oxford: Blackwell.

Leithart, P. J. (2014). *Gratitude: An Intellectual History*. Baylor University Press.

Leonardo, Z. & Porter, R. K. (2010). Pedagogy of fear: toward a Fanonian theory of 'safety' in race dialogue. *Race, Ethnicity and Education*, 13(2), 139–57.

Lerner, J. S. & Tiedens, L. Z. (2006). Portrait of the angry decision maker: how appraisal tendencies shape anger's influence on cognition. *Journal of Behavioral Decision Making*, 19, 115–37.

Levinson, M. (2014). *No Citizen Left Behind*. Cambridge: Harvard University Press.

Levinson, M. & Fay, J., eds. (2019). *Democratic Discord in Schools: Cases and Commentaries in Educational Ethics*. Cambridge: Harvard University Press.

Levinson, M. & Fay, J., eds. (2016). *Dilemmas of Educational Ethics: Cases and Commentaries*. Cambridge: Harvard University Press.

Li, C. (1994). The Confucian concept of Jen and feminist ethics of care: a comparative study. *Hypatia: A Journal of Feminist Philosophy*, 9(1), 70–89.

Liberman, K. (2008). The reflexivity of the authenticity of hatha yoga. In B. Diken & C. B. Lausten, eds., *Yoga in the Modern World: Contemporary Perspectives*. New York: Routledge, pp. 100–16

Linnenbrink-Garcia, L., Wormington, S. V., & Ranellucci, J. (2016). Measuring affect in educational contexts: a circumplex approach. In M. Zembylas & P. A. Schutz, eds., *Methodological Advances in Research on Emotion and Education*. Cham: Springer, pp. 165–78.

Liu, Y. (2004). *The Unity of Rule and Virtue: A Critique of a Supposed Parallel Between Confucian Ethics and Virtue Ethics*. London: Marshall Cavendish.

Lorde, A. (1984). *Sister Outsider*. Trumansburg: Crossing Press.

Lu, L. (2001). Understanding happiness: a look into the Chinese folk psychology. *Journal of Happiness Studies*, 2, 407–32.

Lugones, M. C. & Spelman, E. V. (1983). Have we got a theory for you! Feminist theory, cultural imperialism, and the demand for 'the woman's voice'. *Women's Studies International Forum*, 6(6).

Luo, S. (2007). Relation, virtue, and relational virtue: three concepts of caring. *Hypatia: A Journal of Feminist Philosophy*, 22(3), 92–110.

MacIntyre, A. (1989). *After Virtue*. Notre Dame: University of Notre Dame Press.

MacKenzie, M. (2018). Buddhism and the virtues. In N. Snow, ed., *The Oxford Handbook of Virtue*. Oxford: Oxford University Press, pp. 153–71.

MacLeod, J. (2009). *Ain't No Makin' It: Aspirations and Attainment in a Low-Income Neighborhood*. London: Routledge.

Maki, W. J. (2018). The cadence of nature for educating: uncovering a path to knowing in a comparative study of Daoism and lost gospels. *Educational Philosophy and Theory*, 51(2), 1216–26.

Maki, W. J. (2016). Dewey's link with Daoism: ideals of nature, cultivation practices, and applications in lessons. *Educational Philosophy and Theory*, 48(2), 150–64.

Manela, T. (2019). The virtue of gratitude and its associated vices. In R. Roberts & D. Telech, eds., *The Moral Psychology of Gratitude*. London: Rowman and Littlefield.

Manela, T. (2016). Gratitude and appreciation. *American Philosophical Quarterly*, 53(3), 281–94.

Manela, T. (2015). Gratitude. In E. N. Zalta, ed., *The Stanford Encyclopedia of Philosophy*. https://plato.stanford.edu/cite.html

Manne, K. (2017). *Down Girl: The Logic of Misogyny*. Oxford: Oxford University Press.

Marcuse, H. (2002). *One Dimensional Man: Studies in the Ideology of Advanced Industrial Society*. London: Routledge.

Matsuoka, M. (2017). Embracing vulnerability: a reflection on my academic journey as a Japanese early career feminist academic abroad. In R. Thwaites & A. Pressland, eds., *Being an Early Career Feminist Academic: Global Perspectives, Experiences, and Challenges*. London: Palgrave Macmillan.

Maxwell, B. & Reichenbach, R. (2007). Educating moral emotion: a praxiological analysis. *Studies in Philosophy and Education*, 26, 147–63.

Maxwell, B. & Reichenbach, R. (2005). Imitation, imagination and re-appraisal: educating the moral emotions. *Journal of Moral Education*, 34(3), 291–307.

May, J. (2017). Empathy and intersubjectivity. In H. L. Maibom, ed., *The Routledge Handbook of Philosophy of Empathy*. New York: Routledge, pp. 169–79.

Mayo, C. (2016). Anger and pedagogy. *Philosophical Inquiry in Education*, 24(1), 86–90.

Mayo, C. (2014). *LGBTQ Youth and Education: Policies and Practices*. New York: Teachers College.

McAleer, S. (2012). Propositional gratitude. *American Philosophical Quarterly*, 49, 55–66.

McCartney, P. (2017). Politics beyond the yoga mat: yoga fundamentalism and the 'Vedic way of life'. *Global Ethnographic*, 4, 1–18.

McConnell, T. (2019). Inapt gratitude. Paper at the International Conference: The Shadow Side of Gratitude, Erfurt, Germany.

McConnell, T. (1993). *Gratitude*. Philadelphia: Temple University.

McCullough, M. E., Kilpatrick, S. D., Emmons, R. A., & Larson, D. B. (2001). Is gratitude a moral affect? *Psychological Bulletin*, 127, 249–66.

McGee, E. O. & Stovall, D. (2015). Reimagining critical race theory in education: mental health, healing, and the pathway to liberatory praxis. *Educational Theory*, 65(5), 491–511.

McGee, K. (2014). Ethics for yogis. *Mantra*, 4, 12.

McMahon, D. M. (2006). *Happiness: A History*. New York: Atlantic Monthly Press, 12.

McNeill, D. W., Vargovich, A. M., Ries, B. J., & Turk, C. L. (2012). Anxiety and fear. In V. S. Ramachandran, ed., *Encyclopedia of Human Behavior*. Elsevier, pp. 161–68.

McRae, E. (2017). Empathy, compassion, and 'exchanging self and other' in Indo-Tibetan Buddhism. In H. L. Maibom. ed., *The Routledge Handbook of Philosophy of Empathy*. New York: Routledge, pp. 123–34.

McRae, E. (2015). Anger and the oppressed: Indo-Tibetan Buddhist perspectives. In M. Cherry & O. Flanagan, eds., *The Moral Psychology of Anger*. London: Rowman and Littlefield, pp. 105–21.

McRae, E. (2012). A passionate Buddhist life, *Journal of Religious Ethics*, 99–121.

Meiklejohn, J., Phillips, C., Freedman, L. M., Griffin, M. L., Biegel, G., Roach, A., Frank, J., Burke, C., Pinger, L., Soloway, G., Isberg, R., Sibinga, E., Grossman, A., & Saltzman, A. (2012). Integrating mindfulness training into K-12 education: fostering the resilience of teachers and students. *Mindfulness*, 3(4), 291–307.

Merry, M. S. (2013). *Equality, Citizenship, and Segregation: A Defense of Separation*. New York: Palgrave Macmillan.

Merseyside Youth Association. (2019). *Resiliency Framework*. https://resilience framework.co.uk.

Meyer, H. F. & Land, R. (2003). Threshold concepts and troublesome knowledge: linkages to ways of thinking and practicing within the disciplines. In C. Rust, ed., *Improving Student Learning – Ten Years On*. Oxford: OCSLD, pp. 412–24.

Mill, J. S. (1861/1952). *Utilitarianism*. Indianapolis: Bobbs-Merrill.

Miller, C. B. (2014). The real challenge to virtue ethics from psychology. In N. Snow & F. V. Trivigno, eds., *The Philosophy and Psychology of Character and Happiness*. London: Routledge, pp. 15–34.

Miller, D. N., Nickerson, A. B., & Jimerson, S. R. Positive psychological interventions in U.S. schools: a public health approach to internalizing and externalizing problems. In M. J. Furlong, R. Gilman, and E. S. Huebner, eds., *Handbook of Positive Psychology in Schools*. New York: Routledge, pp. 478–93.

Monroe, K. R. (1996). *The Heart of Altruism: Perception of a Common Humanity*. Princeton: Princeton University Press.

Montessori Academy. (2017). *Montessori and Mindfulness*. https://montessoriacademy.com.au/montessori-and-mindfulness/.

Morgan, B., Gulliford, L., & Carr, D. (2015). Educating gratitude: some conceptual and moral misgivings. *Journal of Moral Education*, 44, 97–111.

Morgan, B., Gulliford, L., & Kristjánsson, K. (2014). Gratitude in the UK: a new prototype analysis and cross-cultural comparison. *The Journal of Positive Psychology*, 9, 249–66.

Morris, S. G. (2012). The science of happiness: a cross-cultural perspective. In H. Selin & G. Davey, eds., *Happiness Across Cultures: Views of Happiness and Quality of Life in Non-Western Cultures*. Dordrecht: Springer, pp. 435–50.

Mulryan, S. (2011). *Confront Death: Cultivating Courage for Cross-Cultural Understanding*. PhD Diss. University of Illinois at Urbana-Champaign.

Munro, B. & Pooley, J. A. (2009). Differences in resilience and university adjustment between school leaver and mature entry university students. *The Australian Community Psychologist*, 21(1), 50–61.

Munro, D. J. (2002). Reciprocal altruism and the biological basis of ethics in neo-Confucianism. *Dao: A Journal of Comparative Philosophy*, 1(2), 131–41.

Nagel, T. (1979). *Mortal Questions*. Cambridge: Cambridge University Press.

Nagel, T. (1970). *The Possibility of Altruism*. Princeton: Princeton University Press.

Navarrete, C. D, McDonald, M. M., Mott, M. L., & Asher, B. (2012). Virtual morality: emotion and action in a simulated three-dimensional 'trolley problem'. *Emotion*. 12(2), 364–70.

Nelson, J. L. (2018). Sadness, sense, and sensibility. In A. Gotlib, ed., *The Moral Psychology of Sadness*. London: Rowman and Littlefield, pp. 53–68.

Nesterova, Y. & Jackson, L. (2016). Transforming service learning for global citizenship education: moving from affective-moral to social-political, *Revista Espanola de Educacion Comparada (REEC, Spanish Journal of Comparative Education)*, 28, 73–90.

Ng, O. C. (2018). Confucian exegesis, hermeneutic theory, and comparative thought. In M. D. Gu, ed., *Why Traditional Chinese Philosophy Still Matters: The Relevance of Ancient Wisdom for a Global Age*. New York: Routledge, pp. 118–32.

Nietzsche, F. (1997). *Daybreak: Thoughts on the Prejudices of Morality*. Cambridge: Cambridge University Press.

Noddings, N. (2003). *Happiness and Education*. Cambridge: Cambridge University Press.

Noddings, N. (2002). *Starting at Home: Caring and Social Policy*. Berkeley: University of California Press.

Noddings, N. (1999). Two concepts of caring. In R. Curren, ed., *Philosophy of Education 1999*. Urbana: Philosophy of Education Society, pp. 36–9.

Noddings, N. (1993). *Educating for Intelligent Belief or Unbelief*. New York: Teachers College Press.

Noddings, N. (1984). *Caring: A Feminine Approach to Ethics and Moral Education*. Berkeley: University of California Press. Reprinted as *Caring: A Relational Approach to Ethics and Moral Education* in 2003.

Norwood, R. (2008). *Women Who Love Too Much: When You Keep Wishing and Hoping He'll Change*. New York: Pocket Books (Simon & Schuster).

Novaco, R. W. (2016). Anger. In G. Fink, ed., *Stress: Concepts. Cognition, Emotion, and Behavior: Handbook of Stress Series, Vol. 1*. London: Academic Press, pp. 285–92.

Novaco, R. W. (2000). Anger. In American Psychological Association, ed., *Encyclopedia of Psychology, Vol. 1*. New York: APA, pp. 170–4,

Nussbaum, M. C. (2016). *Anger and Forgiveness: Resentment, Generosity, Justice*. Oxford: Oxford University Press.

Nussbaum, M. C. (2013). *Political Emotions*. Cambridge: Harvard University Press.

Nussbaum, M. C. (2012). Who is the happy warrior? Philosophy, happiness research, and public policy. *International Review of Economics* 59, 335.

Nussbaum, M. C. (2001). *Upheavals of Thought: The Intelligence of Emotions*. Cambridge: Cambridge University Press.

Nussbaum, M. C. (1999). Virtue ethics: a misleading category? *The Journal of Ethics*, 3(3), 163–201.

Nussbaum, M. C. (1995). Emotions and women's capabilities. In M. C. Nussbaum & J. Glover, eds., *Women, Culture, and Development: A Study of Human Capabilities*. Oxford: Clarendon Press, pp. 360–78.

Nussbaum, M. C. (1994). Patriotism and cosmopolitanism. *Boston Review*, Fall.

O'Keefe, T. (2019). Epicurus. In J. Fieser & B. Dowden, eds., *The Internet Encyclopedia of Philosophy*. Internet Encyclopedia of Philosophy.

Okin, S. M. (1989). Reason and feeling in thinking about justice. *Ethics*, 99(2), 229–49.

Palmer, P. J. (1997). *The Courage to Teach: Exploring the Inner Landscape of a Teacher's Life*. San Francisco: John Wiley & Sons.

Panaite, V. & Bylsma,M. (2012). Alexithymia. In V. S. Ramachandran, ed., *Encyclopedia of Human Behavior*. London: Elsevier, pp. 92–9.

Paolini, A. (2015). School shootings and student mental health: role of the school counselor in mitigating violence. *Vistas Online*, Article 90. counseling .org

Papailias, P. (2016). Witnessing in the age of the database: viral memorials, affective publics, and the assemblage of mourning. *Memory Studies*, 9(4), 437–54.

Parekh, R. (2017). What is depression? *American Psychological Association*.

Parkinson, B. (1996). Emotions are social. *British Journal of Psychology*, 87, 663–83.

Parrott, W. G. (2014). *The Positive Side of Negative Emotions*. New York: Guilford Press.

Parrott, W. G. (1993). Beyond hedonism: motives for inhibiting good moods and for maintaining bad moods. In D. M. Wegner & J. W. Pennebaker, eds., *Handbook of Mental Control*. Englewood Cliffs: Prentice Hall, pp. 278–308.

Pekrun, R. (2016). Using self-report to assess emotions in education. In M. Zembylas & P. A. Schutz, eds., *Methodological Advances in Research on Emotion and Education*. Cham: Springer, pp. 43–54.

Pekrun, R. & Buhner, M. (2014). Self-report measures of academic emotions. In R. Pekrun & L. Linnenbrink-Garcia, eds., *International Handbook of Emotions in Education*. London: Routledge, pp. 561–79.

Pekrun, R. & Linnenbrink-Garcia, L. (2014). Conclusions and future directions. In R. Pekrun & L. Linnenbrink-Garcia, eds., *International Handbook of Emotions in Education*. London: Routledge, pp. 659–76.

Pekrun, R. & Perry, R. (2014). Control-value theory of achievement emotions. In R. Pekrun & L. Linnenbrink-Garcia, eds., *International Handbook of Emotions in Education*. London: Routledge, pp. 120–41.

Penn Resiliency Program. (2019). *Penn Resilience Program and Perma Workshops*. Trustees of the University of Pennsylvania.

Perry-Parrish, C. & Zeman, J. (2011). Relations among sadness regulation, peer acceptance, and social functioning in early adolescence: the role of gender. *Social Development* 20(1), 135–53.

Peters, M. A. (2012). Looking forward in anger. *Educational Philosophy and Theory*, 44(3), 238–44.

Peterson, A. (2017). *Compassion and Education: Cultivating Compassionate Children, Schools and Communities*. London: Springer Nature.

Peterson, H. (2013). Outrageous remarks by Lululemon founder Chip Wilson. *Business Insider*, December 10.

Pett, S. (2012). The contribution of religious education the well-being of students. *Research Papers in Education*, 27(4), 435–48.

Pettit, P. (1997). The consequentialist perspective. In M. W. Baron, P. Pettit, & M. A. Slote, eds., *Three Methods of Ethics*. Blackwell: Oxford, pp. 163–69.

Pies, R. (2014). The bereavement exclusion and *DSM-5*: an update and commentary. *Innovations in Clinical Neuroscience*, 11(7–8), 19–22.

Pinker, S. (2002). *The Blank Slate: The Modern Denial of Human Nature*. London: Allen Lane.

Pinsent, A (2017). 'Till we have faces': second-person relatedness as the object, end and crucial circumstance of perfect of 'infused' virtues. In D. Carr, J. Arthur, & K. Kristjánsson, eds., *Varieties of Virtue Ethics*. London: Palgrave MacMillan, pp. 267–79.

Porat, R., Tamir, M., Wohl, M. J. A., & Halperin, E. (2018). Motivated emotion and the rally around the flag effect: liberals are motivated to feel collective angst (like conservatives) when faced with existential threat. *Cognition and Emotion*, 1–12.

Posner, M. I., Rueda, M. R., & Kanske, P. (2007). Probing the mechanisms of attention. In J. Cacioppo, L. G. Tassinary, & G. G. Bernston, eds., *The Handbook of Psychophysiology*. Cambridge: Cambridge University Press, pp. 410–32.

Powell, K. (2013). Higher education: on the lookout for true grit. *Nature*, 504, 471–3.

Power, F. C., Higgins, A., & Kohlberg, L. (1989). *Lawrence Kohlberg's Approach to Moral Education*. New York: Columbia University Press.

Price, C. (2010). The rationality of grief. *Inquiry*, 53(1), 20–40.

Priest, G. W. (2017). Sexual abuse in yoga – the secret we can't ignore. *Healthista*, December 18.

Prinz, J. J. (2007). *The Emotional Construction of Morals*. Oxford: Oxford University Press.

Purser, R. & Loy, D. (2013) Beyond McMindfulness. *Huffington Post*, 1 July.

Pury, C. L. S. & Starkey, C. B. (2010). Is courage an accolade or a process? A fundamental question for courage research. In C. L. S. Pury & S. J. Lopez, eds., *The Psychology of Courage: Modern Research on an Ancient Virtue*. Washington: American Psychological Association, pp. 67–88.

Putman, D. (2010). Philosophical roots of the concept of courage. In C. L. S. Pury & S. J. Lopez, eds., *The Psychology of Courage: Modern Research on an Ancient Virtue*. Washington: American Psychological Association, pp. 9–22.

Rawls, J. (2000) *Justice as Fairness: A Restatement*. Cambridge: Harvard University Press.

Rawls, J. (1993). *Political Liberalism*. New York: Columbia University Press.

Reid, J. K. & Dixon, W. A. (1999). Teacher attitudes on coping with grief in the public school classroom. *Psychology in the Schools*, 36(3), 219–29.

Reisenzein, R., Junge, M., Studtmann, M., & Huber, O. (2014). Observational approaches to the measurement of emotions. In R. Pekrun & L. Linnenbrink-Garcia, eds., *International Handbook of Emotions in Education*. London: Routledge, pp. 580–606.

Riegle-Crumb, C. & Humphries, M. (2012). Exploring bias in math teachers' perceptions of students' ability by gender and race/ethnicity. *Gender & Society*, 26(2), 290–322.

Rippon, G. (2019). *The Gendered Brain: The New Neuroscience that Shatters the Myth of the Female Brain*. New York: Random House.

Roberts, P. (2016). *Happiness, Hope, and Despair: Rethinking the Role of Education*. New York: Peter Lang.

Roberts, P. (2013). Acceptance, resistance and educational transformation: a Taoist reading of *The First Man*. *Educational Philosophy and Theory*, 45(11), 1175–89.

Roberts, R. C. (2017). Varieties of virtue ethics. In D. Carr, J. Arthur & K. Kristjánsson, eds., *Varieties of Virtue Ethics*. London: Palgrave MacMillan, pp. 17–34.

Roberts, R. C. (2013). *Emotions in the Moral Life*. Cambridge: Cambridge University Press.

Roberts, R. C. (2003). *Emotions: An Essay in Aid of Moral Psychology*. Cambridge: Cambridge University Press.

Roberts, R. C. (1989). Aristotle on virtues and emotions. *Philosophical Studies*, 56, 293–306.

Roberts, Y. (2009). *Grit: The Skills for Success and How They Are Grown*. London: The Young Foundation.

Robertson, D. (2014). Stoic mindfulness and resilience training (SMRT) 2014. *Stoicism Today*.

Rogers, D. J. (1972). How to teach fear. *The Elementary School Journal*, 72(8), 391–95.

Rogerson, L. (2015). *Give Thanks – Give Back: Gratitude and Service in School and the Community: Programme Report*. Birmingham: Jubilee Centre.

Rousseau, J. J. (1762/1979). *Emile, or On Education*, trans. A. Bloom. New York: Basic.

Russell, J. A. (1991). Culture and the categorization of emotions. *Psychological Bulletin*, 110(3), 429–50.

Russell, J. A. & Fehr, B. (1994). Fuzzy concepts in a fuzzy hierarchy: varieties of anger. *Journal of Personality and Social Psychology*, 67(2), 186–205.

Sandel, M. (1981). *Liberalism and the Limits of Justice*. Cambridge: Cambridge University Press.

Sarkissian, H. (2014). Is self-regulation a burden or a virtue? A comparative perspective. In N. Snow & F. V. Trivigno, eds., *The Philosophy and Psychology of Character and Happiness*. London: Routledge, pp. 181–96.

Sartre, J.-P., (1943/1992). *Being and Nothingness*, trans. Hazel Barnes. New York: Washington Square Press.

School Speciality. (2018). *Premier Esteem Primary Planner*. Greenville: School Speciality.

Schutz, P. A., DeCuir-Gunby, J. T., & Williams-Johnson, M. R. (2016). Using multiple and mixed methods to investigate emotions in educational contexts. In M. Zembylas & P. A. Schutz, eds., *Methodological Advances in Research on Emotion and Education*. Cham: Springer, pp. 217–30.

Schwimmer, M. & McDonough, K. (2018). Mindfulness and 'educational new ageism'. In K. Hytten, ed., *Oxford Research Encyclopedia of Philosophy of Education*. Oxford: Oxford University Press.

Seligman, M. E. P. (2011). *Flourish: A Visionary New Understanding of Happiness and Well-being*. New York: Free Press.

Seligman, M. E. P. (2007). *What You Can Change . . . And What You Can't*. New York: Random House.

Seligman, M. E. P. (2002). *Authentic Happiness: Using the New Positive Psychology to Realize Your Potential for Lasting Fulfilment.* New York: Random House.

Serwacki, M. L. & Cook-Cottone, C. (2012). Yoga in the schools: a systematic review of the literature. *International Journal of Yoga Therapy,* 22, 101–10.

Shelanski, N. (2019). Opinion: we are the children of gun violence, fear, racism and hate. Will you love us more than your guns? *The Colorado Sun,* August 5.

Sherman, N. (1999). Character development and Aristotelian virtue. In D. Carr & J. Steutel, eds., *Virtue Ethics and Moral Education.* London: Routledge, pp. 35–48.

Shirai, M. & Suzuki, N. (2017). Is sadness only one emotion? Psychological and physiological responses to sadness induced by two different situations: 'Loss of someone' and 'failure to achieve a goal'. *Frontiers in Psychology,* 8, 288.

Shuman, V. & Scherer, K. R. (2014). Concepts and structures of emotions. In R. Pekrun & L. Linnenbrink-Garcia, eds., *International Handbook of Emotions in Education.* London: Routledge, pp. 13–35.

Sim, M. (2017). Confucian and Daoist virtue ethics. In D. Carr, J. Arthur, & K. Kristjánsson, eds., *Varieties of Virtue Ethics.* London: Palgrave Macmillan, pp. 105–22.

Simmel, G. (1950). *Faithfulness and Gratitude.* In K. Wolff, ed., *The Sociology of George Simmel.* New York: Free Press, pp. 377–95.

Singer, P. (2019). *The Life You Can Save: How to Do Your Part to End World Poverty.* 10th anniversary edition. New York: Random House.

Singer, P. (1993). *Practical Ethics.* Cambridge: Cambridge University Press.

Singer, P. (1972). Famine, affluence, and morality. *Philosophy and Public Affairs,* 1 (1), 229–43.

Singh-Manoux, A. & Finkenauer, C. (2001). Cultural variations in social sharing of emotions: an intercultural perspective. *Journal of Cross-Cultural Psychology,* 32(6), 647–61.

Skinner, E., Pitzer, J., & Brule, H. (2014). The role of emotion in engagement, coping, and the development of motivational resilience. In R. Pekrun & L. Linnenbrink-Garcia, eds., *International Handbook of Emotions in Education.* London: Routledge, pp. 331–47.

Slegers, R. (2010). *Courageous Vulnerability: Ethics and Knowledge in Proast, Bergson, Marcel, and James.* London: Brill.

Slote, M. (2007). *The Ethics of Care and Empathy,* London: Routledge.

Slote, M. (1999). Caring versus the philosophers. In R. Curren, ed., *Philosophy of Education 1999.* Urbana: Philosophy of Education Society, pp. 25–35.

Smilansky, S. (1997). Should I be grateful to you for not harming me? *Philosophy and Phenomenological Research,* 57, 585–97.

Smith, A. (1759/1969). *The Theory of the Moral Sentiments.* Indianapolis: Liberty Classics.

Smith, C. A. & Lazarus, R. S. (1993). Appraisal components, core relational themes, and the emotions. *Cognition and Emotion,* 7(3/4), 233–69.

Snow, N. (2010). *Virtue as Social Intelligence: An Empirically Grounded Theory.* London: Routledge.

Spelman, E. (1989). Anger and insubordination. In A. Garry & M. Pearsall, eds., *Women, Knowledge, and Reality: Explorations in Feminist Philosophy.* Winchester: Unwin Hyman, pp. 263–73.

Sreenivasan, G. (2020). *Emotion and Virtue.* Princeton: Princeton University Press.

Srinivasan, A. (2018). The aptness of anger. *The Journal of Political Philosophy*, 26 (2), 123–44.

SRI International (2018). *Promoting Grit, Tenacity, and Perseverance: Critical Factors for Success in the 21st Century.* Menlo Park: SRI International.

Stearns, F. R. (1972). *Anger: Psychology, Physiology, Pathology.* Thomas.

Steele, C. M. (1997). A threat in the air: how stereotypes shape intellectual identity and performance. *American Psychologist*, 52, 475–88.

Stengel, B. (2018). Practicing courage in a communal key. *Educational Theory*, 68 (2), 213–33.

Stewart, F. (2001). Book review, *Women and Human Development: The Capabilities Approach*, by Martha Nussbaum. *Journal of International Development*, 13(8): 1191–2.

Stitzlein, S. M. (2019). *Learning How to Hope: Reviving Democracy in America.* Oxford: Oxford University Press.

Stitzlein, S. M. (2018). Teaching for hope in the era of grit. *Teachers College Record*, 120, 1–28.

Stitzlein, S. M. (2012). *Teaching for Dissent: Citizenship Education and Political Activism.* London: Paradigm.

Stokas, A. G. (2015). A genealogy of grit: education in the new gilded age. *Educational Theory*, 65(5), 513–28.

Stueber, K. (2019). Empathy. In E. N. Zalta, ed., *The Stanford Encyclopedia of Philosophy.* https://plato.stanford.edu/cite.html

Sullivan, G. B. (2014). Collective pride, happiness, and celebratory emotions: aggregative, network, and cultural models. In C. Von Scheve & M. Salmela, eds., *Collective Emotions: Perspectives from Psychology, Philosophy, and Sociology.* Oxford: Oxford University Press, pp. 266–80.

Suissa, J. (2016). Improvisation, resilience and character education: how to seem politically progressive without actually being so. Paper at the International Network of Philosophy of Education Society Conference, Calabria, Italy.

Suissa, J. (2015). Character education and the disappearance of the political. *Ethics and education*, 10(1), 105–17.

Suleri, S. (1992). Woman skin deep: feminism and the postcolonial condition. *Critical Inquiry*, 18(4), 756–69.

Superson, A. (2012). Feminist moral psychology. In E. N. Zalta, ed., *The Stanford Encyclopedia of Philosophy.* https://plato.stanford.edu/cite.html

Ta, V. P. & Ickes, W. (2017) Empathic accuracy. In H. L. Maibom, ed., *The Routledge Handbook of Philosophy of Empathy.* New York: Routledge, pp. 364–376.

Tamboukou, M. (2000). The paradox of being a woman teacher. *Gender and Education*, 12(4), 463–78.

Tamir, M. (2011). The maturing field of emotion regulation. *Emotion Review*, 3 (1), 3–7.

Tamir, M. & Mauss, I. B. (2011). Social cognitive factors in emotion regulation: implications for well-being. In I. Nyklicek, A. Vingerhoets, & M. Zeelenberg, eds., *Emotion Regulation and Well-Being*. Dordrecht: Springer, pp. 31–47.

Taylor, C. (1992). *Multiculturalism and the Politics of Recognition*. Princeton: Princeton University Press.

Taylor, C. (1985). *Philosophy and the Human Sciences: Philosophical Papers 2*. Cambridge: Cambridge University Press.

Taylor, G. J. & Taylor-Allan, H. L. (2007). Applying emotional intelligence in treating individuals with severe psychiatric disorder: a psychotherapeutic model for educating people to be emotionally intelligent. In R. Bar-On, G. Maree, & M. J. Elias, eds., *Educating People to be Emotionally Intelligent*. Westport: Praeger, pp. 211–24.

Tessman, L. (2005). *Burdened Virtues: Virtue Ethics for Liberatory Struggles*. Oxford: Oxford University Press.

Thaler, R. H. & Sunstein, C. R. (2008). *Nudge: Improving Decisions about Health, Wealth, and Happiness*. New Haven: Yale University Press.

Thayer-Bacon, B. J. (2019). Care and peace building. In K. Hytten, ed., *The Oxford Research Encyclopaedia of Philosophy of Education*. Oxford: Oxford University Press.

Thompson, S. (2006). Anger and the struggle for justice. In S. Clarke, P. Hoggett, & S. Thompson, eds., *Emotion, Politics and Society*. New York: Palgrave Macmillan, pp. 123–44.

Thornton, S. (2013). Teaching through tragedy: help students cope with national and global tragedies, and be prepared to deal with a crisis in a school. *National Geographic Magazine*, November 20.

Tian, L., Li, Z., Chen, H, Han, M., Wang, D., Huang, S., & Zheng, X. (2014). Applications of positive psychology to schools in China. In M. J. Furlong, R. Gilman, & E. S. Huebner, eds., *Handbook of Positive Psychology in Schools*. New York: Routledge, pp. 433–49.

Tronto, J. (1993). *Moral Boundaries: A Political Argument for an Ethic of Care*. New York: Routledge.

Tsachi, E.-D. & Doron, G. (2015). Psychopathology and attachment. In J. A. Simpson & W. S. Rholes, eds., *Attachment Theory and Research: New Directions and Emerging Themes*. New York: Guilford Press, pp. 346–73.

Turner, J. C. & Trucano, M. (2014). Measuring situated emotion. In R. Pekrun & L. Linnenbrink-Garcia, eds., *International Handbook of Emotions in Education*. London: Routledge, 643–58.

Turunen, T., Haravuori, H., Pihlajamaki, J. J., Marttunen, M., & Punamaki, R. (2014). Framework of the outreach after a school shooting and the students' perceptions of the provided support. *European Journal of Psychotraumatology*, 5.

Tye, B. & O'Brien, L. (2002). Why are experienced teachers leaving the profession? *Phi Delta Kappan*, 84(1), 24.

Unamuno, M. de (1972). *The Tragic Sense of Life in Men and Nations*, trans. A. Kerrigan. Princeton: Princeton University Press.

Van Norden, B. (2007). *Virtue Ethics and Consequentialism in Early Chinese Philosophy*. New York: Cambridge University Press.

Veenhoven, R. (2008). Sociological theories of subjective well-being. In M. Eid & R. Larsen, eds., *The Science of Subjective Well-Being: A Tribute to Ed Diener*. New York: Guilford Publications, pp. 44–61.

Vogler, C. (2018). Courage in the classroom. In T. Harrison & D. I. Walker, eds., *The Theory and Practice of Virtue Education*. London: Routledge, pp. 210–9.

Walker, A. D. M. (1988). Political obligation and the argument from gratitude. *Philosophy & Public Affairs*, 17(3): 191–211.

Walzer, M. (1985). *Thick and Thin: Moral argument at Home and Abroad*. Notre Dame: University of Notre Dame Press.

Wang, D. & Hagins, M. (2016). Perceived benefits of yoga among urban school students: a qualitative analysis. *Evidence-based Complementary and Alternative Medicine*, 1–7.

Wang, M. (2013). *Guanxi, Renqing, and Mianzi in Chinese Social Relations and Exchange Rules – A Comparison between Chinese and western societies (A case study on China and Australia)*. Master thesis. Aalborg: Aalborg University.

Wang, M. C., Haertel, G. D., & Walberg, H. J. (1994). Educational resilience in inner cities. In M. C. Wang & E. W. Gordon, eds., *Educational Resilience in Inner-city America: Challenges and Prospects*. Hillsdale: Erlbaum, pp. 45–72.

Warren, J. & Hytten, K. (2004). The faces of whiteness: pitfalls and the critical democrat. *Communication Education*, 53, 320–30.

Watkins, P. C. (2019). Pathologies of gratitude. Paper at the International Conference: The Shadow Side of Gratitude, Erfurt, Germany.

Watkins, P. C. (2014). *Gratitude and the Good Life: Toward a Psychology of Appreciation*. Dordrecht: Springer.

Watkins, P. C. (2004). Gratitude and subjective well-being. In R. Emmons & M. McCullough, eds., *The Psychology of Gratitude*. Oxford: Oxford University Press, pp. 167–92.

Watson, M. & Ecken, L. (2019). *Learning to Trust: Attachment Theory and Classroom Management*. Oxford: Oxford University Press.

Weber, M. (2010/1959). *The Protestant Work Ethic and the Spirit of Capitalism*. Oxford: Oxford University Press.

Wei, X. (2007). Caring: Confucianism, feminism, and Christian ethics. *Contemporary Chinese Thought*, 39(2), 32–48.

White, J. (2011). *Exploring Well-Being in Schools: A Guide to Making Children's Lives More Fulfilling*. New York: Routledge.

White, J. (1990). *Education and the Good Life: Beyond the National Curriculum*. London: Kogan Page.

White, P. (2012). Making political anger possible: a task for civic education. *Journal of Philosophy of Education*, 46(1), 1–13.

Williams, D. R. & Wyatt, R. (2015). Racial bias in health care and health: challenges and opportunities. *Journal of the American Medical Association*, 314(6), 555–6.

Williams, J. M. G. & Kabat-Zinn, J. (2011). Mindfulness: diverse perspectives on its meaning, origins, and multiple applications at the intersection of science and dharma. *Contemporary Buddhism*, 12(1), 1–18.

Williams, K. (2008). Troubling the concept of the 'academic profession' in 21st century higher education. *Higher Education*, 56, 533–44.

Wilson-Strydom, M. (2017) Disrupting structural inequalities of higher education opportunity: 'grit', resilience and capabilities at a South African university. *Journal of Human Development and Capabilities*, 18(3), 384–98.

Wingfield, A. H. (2007). The modern mammy and the angry black man: African American professionals' experiences with gendered racism in the workplace. *Race, Gender & Class*, 14(1–2), 196–212.

Wodak, R. (2015). *The Politics of Fear: What Right-Wing Populist Discourses Mean*. London: Sage.

Wong, B. S. K. (2017). Lone student on Hong Kong suicide prevention committee blasts report. *South China Morning Post*, October 29.

Wong, D. B. (2013). On learning what happiness is. *Philosophical Topics*, 41(1), 81–101.

Wong, Y. & Tsai, J. (2007). Cultural models of shame and guilt. In J. L. Tracy, R. W. Robins, & J. P. Tangney, eds., *The Self-Conscious Emotions: Theory and Research*. New York: Guilford Press, pp. 209–23.

Wood, A. M., Emmons, R. A., Algoe, S. B., Froh, J. J., Lambert, N. M., & Watkins, P. (2016). A dark side of gratitude? Distinguishing between beneficial gratitude and its harmful imposters for the positive clinical psychology of gratitude and well-being. In A. M. Wood & J. Johnson, eds., *Wiley Handbook of Positive Clinical Psychology*. Chichester: Wiley, pp. 137–51.

Yancy, G. & hooks, b. (2015). bell hooks: Buddhism, the beats, and loving blackness. *New York Times*, December 10.

Yeager, D. S., Hanselman, P., Walton, G. M., et al. (2019). A national experiment reveals where a growth mindset improves achievement. *Nature*, 573, 364–69.

You, Z., Rud, A. G., & Hu, Y. (2018). *The Philosophy of Chinese Moral Education: A History*. New York: Palgrave Macmillan

Young, I. (1988). Five faces of oppression. *Philosophical Forum*, 19(4): 270–90.

Zeidner, M. (2014). Anxiety in education. In R. Pekrun & L. Linnenbrink-Garcia, eds., *International Handbook of Emotions in Education*. London: Routledge, pp. 265–88.

Zembylas, M. (2014). Theorizing 'difficult knowledge' in the aftermath of the 'affective turn': implications for curriculum and pedagogy in handling traumatic representation. *Curriculum Inquiry*, 44(3), 390–412.

Zembylas, M. (2008). Trauma, justice, and the politics of emotion: the violence of sentimentality in education. *Discourse*, 29(1), 1–17.

Zembylas, M. & Schutz, P. A., eds. (2016). *Methodological Advances in Research on Emotion and Education*. Cham: Springer.

Zerilli, L. M. G. (2014). Against civility: a feminist perspective. In A. Sarat, ed., *Civility, Legality, and Justice in America*. Cambridge: Cambridge University Press, pp. 107–31.

Index

STUDIES IN EMOTION AND SOCIAL INTERACTION

Ingram Content Group UK Ltd.
Milton Keynes UK
UKHW022044120723
425038UK00014B/129

9 781108 711609

THE 1995 ENLARGEMENT OF THE EUROPEAN UNION

For Alex

The 1995 Enlargement of the European Union

Edited by
JOHN REDMOND
University of Birmingham

Ashgate

Aldershot • Brookfield USA • Singapore • Sydney

Published by
Ashgate Publishing Limited
Gower House
Croft Road
Aldershot
Hants GU11 3HR
England

Ashgate Publishing Company
Old Post Road
Brookfield
Vermont 05036
USA

British Library Cataloguing in Publication Data
The 1995 enlargement of the European Union
  1.European Union - Membership 2.Europe - Economic
  integration
  I.Redmond, John, 1953-
  337.1'42'09049

Library of Congress Cataloging-in-Publication Data
Redmond, John, 1953-
    The 1995 enlargement of the European Union / John Redmond.
      p. cm.
    Includes index.
    ISBN 1-85521-823-2 (hb)
    1. European Union. 2. European Free Trade Association countries.
  3. Europe--Economic integration. I. Title.
  HC241.2.R424 1997
  341.242'2--dc21   96-29590
  ISBN 1 85521 823 2   CIP

Printed and bound by Athenaeum Press, Ltd.,
Gateshead, Tyne & Wear.

Contents

List of Tables

List of Abbreviations

CAP	Common Agricultural Policy
CCP	Common Commercial Policy
CDU	(German) Christian Democrat Union
CEEC	Central and East European country
CFP	Common Fisheries Policy
CFSP	Common Foreign and Security Policy
COMECON	Council for Mutual Economic Assistance
COREPER	Committee of Permanent Representatives
CP	Common Position
CSCE	Conference on Security and Cooperation in Europe
CSU	(Bavarian) Christian Social Union
DCP	Draft Common Procedure
DG	Directorate General
EC	European Communities
ECSC	European Coal and Steel Community
ECJ	European Court of Justice
ECU	European Currency Unit
EDF	European Development Fund
EEA	European Economic Area
EEC	European Economic Community
EFTA	European Free Trade Association
EIB	European Investment Bank
EMS	European Monetary System
EMU	Economic and Monetary Union
EP	European Parliament
ERM	Exchange Rate Mechanism
ESA	EFTA Surveillance Authority
EU	European Union
EURATOM	European Atomic Community
FCMA	Friendship, Cooperation and Mutual Assistance (Treaty)

FDI	Foreign Direct Investment
FPO	Austrian Freedom Party
FTA	Free Trade Agreement
GATT	General Agreement on Tariffs and Trade
GDP	Gross Domestic Product
GFU	(Norway's) Gas Negotiating Committee
GISELA	Groupe Interservice d'Elargissement
HLSG	High Level Steering Group
IGC	Intergovernmental Conference
JHA	Justice and Home Affairs
LFA	Less Favoured Area
LO	Norwegian and Swedish labour organisations
LRF	Finnish Agricultural Producers' Organisation
MEP	Member of the European Parliament
MTK	Finnish agricultural producers organisation
NACC	North Atlantic Cooperation Council
NATO	North Atlantic Treaty Organisation
OECD	Organisation for Economic Cooperation and Development
OEEC	Organisation for European Economic Cooperation
OVP	Austrian People's Party
SALT	Strategic Arms Limitation Treaty
SEA	Single European Act
SEM	Single European Market
SME	(Norwegian) Social Democrats against the EU
SPÖ	(Austrian) Social Democratic Party
TAC	Total Allowable Catch
TEN	Trans-European Network
TEU	Treaty of European Union
UK	United Kingdom
US	United States
USSR	Union of Soviet Socialist Republics
WEU	Western European Union